THE COMPLETE GUIDE TO

MEMORY MASTERY

DEVELOP A SUPER MEMORY AND DISCOVER THE SECRETS OF MIND POWER

HARRY LORAYNE

MJF BOOKS
New York

Published by MJF Books
Fine Communications
589 Eighth Avenue, 6th Floor
New York, NY 10018

The Complete Guide to Memory Mastery
LC Control Number: 2018939078
ISBN 978-1-60671-410-2

Compilation copyright © 2002 by Harry Lorayne

Originally published as:
How to Develop a Super Power Memory
Copyright © 1963 by Harry Lorayne
and
Secrets of Mind Power
Copyright © 1961 by Harry Lorayne

This edition is published by MJF Books in arrangement
with Frederick Fell Publishers, Inc.

Printed in the United States of America.

MJF Books and the MJF colophon are trademarks of Fine Creative Media, Inc.

BG   10   9   8   7   6   5

CONTENTS

HOW TO DEVELOP A
SUPER MEMORY

To Renee,
whose love, assistance, devotion, urging,
confidence and faithfulness,
I need no trained memory to remember.

CONTENTS

Page

Foreword

Chapter

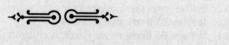

Foreword

MARK TWAIN is reported to have said that "everyone talks about the weather, but no one does anything about it." Similarly, everyone talks or brags about their bad memory, but few people ever do anything about it. Let's face it, there isn't much you can do about the weather, but there's a great deal that you can do about your bad memory.

Many people have told me that they would "give a million dollars" if they could acquire a memory like mine. Well, don't misunderstand me, I wouldn't turn down your offer of a million dollars; but, actually the price of this book is all you need to spend.

This isn't true in its strictest sense; you'll also have to spend just a little bit of your time, and just a little effort to get the brain working. Once you've started on my system, you may be surprised as to how simple and obvious it really is.

If you purchased this book expecting a theoretical harangue of technical terms, you are doomed to disappointment. I have tried to write and explain the system as if I were sitting in your living room and explaining it to you there.

Although naturally, quite a bit of research was necessary, I've discarded most of the technical ideas and thoughts because I found them difficult to understand and to apply myself. I am an entertainer and a memory expert, not a psychiatrist or a doctor, and I didn't think it necessary to go into an explanation of the workings of the human brain, and just how the memory actually works in terms of cells, curves, impressions, etc.

So you will find that all the ways and methods in the book are those that I use myself and therefore feel qualified to teach to you.

Psychologists and educators have said that we use only a small percentage of our brain power — I think the system here will enable you to use just a little more than average. So, if like your operations, you have been bragging about your poor memory, I think that after you've read this book, you'll still brag about your memory, but to the other extreme. Now, you'll be able to boast of possessing a wonderfully retentive and accurate memory!

CHAPTER ONE
How Keen Is Your Observation?

Which light is on top of the traffic light? Is it the Red or the Green? Your first thought, probably is that this is an easy question to answer. However, put yourself in this position — you are on one of the current quiz shows that pays a lot of money for correct answers. You must answer this question correctly to win the top prize. Now then, which light is on top, the Red or the Green?

If you have been able to picture yourself in the above position, you are probably hesitating now, because you're not really sure which light is on top, are you? If you are sure, then you're one of the minority who has observed what most people only see." There is a world of difference between seeing and observing; proven, of course, by the fact that most of the people to whom I put the above question, either give the wrong answer or are not sure. This, even though they see the traffic lights countless times every day!

By the way, Red is always on top of the traffic light. Green is always on the bottom. If there is a third color, it is usually Yellow, for caution, and that one is always in the center. If you were sure that Red was the correct answer, let me see if I can't puncture your pride a bit with another observation test.

Don't look at your wrist watch! Don't look at your wrist watch, and answer this question: Is the number six on your watch dial, the Arabic #6, or is it the Roman Numeral VI? Think this over for a moment, before you look at your watch. Decide on your answer as if it were really important that you answer correctly. You're on that quiz show again, and there's a lot of money at stake.

All right, have you decided on your answer? Now, look at your watch and see if you were right. Were you? Or were you wrong in either case, because your watch doesn't have a six at all!? The small dial that ticks off the seconds usually occupies that space on most modern watches.

Did you answer this question correctly? Whether you did or did not, you had to look at your watch to check. Can you tell now, the exact time on your watch? Probably not, and you just looked at it a second ago! Again, you saw, but you didn't observe.

Try this on your friends. Although people see their watches innumerable times every day, few of them can tell you about the numeral six.

Here's another one to try on your friends, but you'd better see if you can answer it first. If you are a cigarette smoker, you have seen a blue tax stamp on your pack of cigarettes each time you take it out to remove a cigarette. On this tax stamp is the picture of a man, and his name is printed under the picture.

For the top prize on our imaginary quiz show, name this man! I guess you'll have to leave the quiz show with only the consolation prize. I say this so definitely because only about two or three of the many people I've tested, have answered this one correctly. The man pictured on the revenue stamp is De Witt Clinton! Check it.

I don't want to be sneaky, but if you've just looked at the stamp and at the picture of De Witt Clinton, you must have seen what Clinton was doing with his left hand. You also saw, or probably saw, four letters, two on the upper left and two on the upper right of the stamp. I say that you saw these things, I don't think you observed them. If you did, you should be able to tell yourself right now, what De Witt Clinton is doing with his left hand, and also name the four letters.

Had to look again, didn't you? Now you've observed that his left hand is at Clinton's temple, as if he were thinking, and the letters are, U.S.I.R. for United States Internal Revenue.

Don't feel too badly if you couldn't answer any of these questions; as I said before, most people can't. You may recall a motion picture a few years ago which starred Ronald Colman, Celeste Holm and Art Linkletter. The picture was "Champagne for Caesar," and it was about a man who couldn't be stumped with any question on a quiz show. The finale of the film was the last question of the quiz, which was worth some millions of dollars. To earn these millions, Ronald Colman was asked to give his own social security number. Of course, he didn't know it. This was amusing and interesting, to me, anyway, since it struck home. It proves, doesn't it, that people see but do not observe? Incidentally, do you know your social security number?

Although the systems and methods contained in this book make you observe automatically, you will find some interesting observation exercises in a later chapter. The system will also make you use your imagination with more facility than ever before.

I've taken the time and space to talk about observation because it is one of the things important to training your memory. The other, and more important thing, is association. We cannot possibly remember anything that we do not observe. After something is observed, either by sight or hearing, it must, in order to be remembered, be associated in our minds with, or to, something we already know or remember.

Since you will observe automatically when using my system, it is association with which we will mostly concern ourselves.

Association, as pertaining to memory, simply means the connecting or tying up of two (or more) things to each other. Anything you manage to remember, or have managed to remember, is only due to the fact that you have subconsciously associated it to something else. "Every Good Boy Does Fine." Does that sentence mean anything to you? If it does, then you must have studied music as a youngster. Almost every child that studies music is taught to remember the lines of the music staff or treble clef, by remembering, "Every Good Boy Does Fine."

I've already stressed the importance of association, and I want to prove to you that you have used definite conscious associations many times before, without even realizing it. The letters, E, C, B, D and F don't mean a thing. They are just letters, and difficult to remember. The sentence, "Every Good Boy Does Fine" does have meaning, and is something you know and understand. The new thing, the thing you had to commit to memory was associated with something you already knew.

The spaces of the music staff were committed to memory with the same system; the initial system. If you remembered the word, "face," you remembered that the spaces on the staff are, F, A, C, and E. Again you associated something new and meaningless to something you already knew and to something that had meaning to you.

It is probably many years since you learned the jinglet, thirty days hath September, April, June and November, all the rest have thirty-one, etc.," but how many times have you relied on it when it was necessary to know the number of days in a particular month?

If you were ever taught to remember the nonsense word, "vibgyor," or the nonsense name, "Roy B. Giv," then you still remember the colors of the spectrum: Red, Orange, Yellow, Blue, Green, Indigo and Violet. This again is the association and initial system. I am sure that many times you have seen or heard something which made you snap your fingers, and say, "Oh, that reminds me. . . ." You were made to remember something by the thing you saw or heard, which usually had no obvious connection to the thing you remembered. However, in your mind, the two things were associated in some way. This was a subconscious association. Right now, I am pointing out a few examples of conscious associations at work; and they certainly do work. People who have forgotten many things that they learned in their early grades, still remember the spaces and lines of the treble clef. If you have read this chapter so far, concentrating as you read, you should know them by now, even if you've never studied music.

One of the best examples I know, is the one which was a great help to me in my early grade spelling classes. We were being taught that the word, "believe" was spelled with the e following the i. In order to help us to commit this to memory, we were told to remember a short sentence, "Never believe a lie."

This is a perfect instance of a conscious association. I know for a fact that many adults still have trouble spelling, "believe." They are never quite sure if the i is first, or if it is the e. The spelling of the word, "believe" was the new thing to remember. The word, "lie" is a word we all already knew how to spell. None of the students that heard that little sentence, ever again misspelled the word, "believe." Do you have trouble spelling the word, "piece?" If you do, just remember the phrase, "piece of pie." This phrase will always tell you how to spell, "piece."

Can you draw anything that resembles the map of England, from memory? How about China, Japan or Czechoslovakia? You probably can't draw any of these. If I had mentioned Italy, ninety percent of you would have immediately seen a picture of a boot in your mind's eye. Is that right? If you did, and if you draw a boot, you will have the approximate outline of the map of Italy.

Why did this picture appear in your mind's eye? Only because, at one time or another; perhaps many years ago, you either heard or noticed that the map of Italy resembled a boot. The shape of Italy, of course, was the new thing to remember; the boot was the something we already knew and remembered.

You can see that simple conscious associations helped you memorize abstract information like the above examples very easily. The initial system that I mentioned earlier, can be used to help you memorize many things. For example, if you wanted to remember the names of the Dionne quintuplets, you could try to remember the word, "macey." This would help you to recall that the girls' names are Marie, Annette, Cecile, Emilie and Yvonne.You can see that simple conscious associations helped you memorize abstract information like the above examples very easily. The initial system that I mentioned earlier, can be used to help you memorize many things. For example, if you wanted to remember the names of the Dionne quintuplets, you could try to remember the word, "macey." This would help you to recall that the girls' names are Marie, Annette, Cecile, Emilie and Yvonne.

There's only one thing wrong with this idea in its present stage. There is nothing to make you remember that the word, "macey" is connected with the Dionne quintuplets, or vice versa.

If you remembered the word, fine, then you would probably know the names of the quints; but, how do you remember the word? I'll show you how to do this in future chapters.

The systems and methods in this book will show you how the principles and ideas of simple conscious associations can be applied to remembering anything. Yes, that's right — remembering anything, including names and faces, items, objects, facts, figures, speeches, etc. In other words, the Systems and Methods you will learn in this book, can be applied to anything and everything in every day social or business life.

CHAPTER TWO
Habit is Memory

I feel assured that there is no such thing as ultimate forgetting; traces once impressed upon the memory are indestructible.
                                                      —*Thomas De Quincey*

An accurate and retentive memory is the basis of all business success. In the last analysis, all our knowledge is based on our memories. Plato said it this way, "All knowledge is but remembrance." Cicero said of memory, "It is the treasury and guardian of all things." One strong example should suffice for the time being — you could not be reading this book right now, if you didn't remember the sounds of the twenty-six letters of our alphabet.

This may seem a bit far fetched to you, but it is true, nevertheless. Actually, if you were to lose your memory completely, you would have to start learning everything from scratch, just like a new born baby. You wouldn't remember how to dress, or shave, or apply your makeup, or how to drive your car, or whether to use a knife or fork, etc. You see, all the things we attribute to habit, should be attributed to memory. Habit is memory.

Mnemonics, which is a large part of a trained memory, is not a new or strange thing. As a matter of fact, the word, "mnemonic" is derived from the name of the Greek Goddess, Mnemosyne; and, memory systems were used as far back as early Greek civilization. The strange thing is that trained memory systems are not known and used by many more people. Most of those who have learned the secret of mnemonics in memory, have been amazed, not only at their own tremendous ability to remember, but also at the kudos they received from their families and friends.

Some of them decided it was too good a thing to teach to anyone else. Why not be the only man at the office who could remember every style number and price; why not be the only one who could get up at a party, and demonstrate something that everyone marveled at?

I, on the other hand, feel that trained memories should be brought to the foreground, and to this end—this book is dedicated. Although some of you may know me as an entertainer, it is not my purpose, of course, to teach you a memory act. I have no desire to put you on the stage. I do want to teach you the wonderful practical uses of a trained memory. There are many memory stunts taught in this book; these are fine for showing your friends how bright you are. More important, they are excellent memory exercises, and the ideas used in all the stunts can be applied practically.

The question that people ask me most often, is, "Isn't it confusing to remember too much?"

My answer to that is, "No!" There is no limit to the capacity of the memory. Lucius Scipio was able to remember the names of all the people of Rome; Cyrus was able to call every soldier in his army by name; while Seneca could memorize and repeat two thousand words, after hearing them once.

I believe that the more you remember, the more you can remember. The memory, in many ways, is like a muscle. A muscle must be exercised and developed in order to give proper service and use; so must the memory. The difference is that a muscle can be overtrained or become muscle-bound while the memory cannot. You can be taught to have a trained memory just as you can be taught anything else. As a matter of fact, it is much easier to attain a trained memory than, say, to learn to play a musical instrument. If you can read and write English, and have a normal amount of common sense, and if you read and study this book, you will have acquired a trained memory! Along with the trained memory, you will probably acquire a greater power of concentration, a purer sense of observation, and perhaps, a stronger imagination.

Remember please, that there is no such thing as a bad memory. This may come as a shock to those of you who have used your supposedly "bad" memories as an excuse for years. But, I repeat, there is no such thing as a bad memory. There are only trained or untrained memories. Almost all untrained memories are one-sided. That is to say that people who can remember names and faces, cannot remember telephone numbers, and those who remember phone numbers, can't, for the life of them, remember the names of the people they wish to call.

There are those who have a pretty good retentive memory, but a painfully slow one; just as there are some who can remember things quickly, but cannot retain them for any length of time. If you apply the systems and methods taught in this book, I can assure you a quick and retentive memory for just about anything.

As I mentioned in the previous chapter, anything you wish to remember must in some way or other, be associated in your mind to something you already know or remember. Of course, most of you will say that you have remembered, or do remember, many things, and that you do not associate them with anything else. Very true! If you were associating knowingly, then you would already have the beginnings of a trained memory.

You see, most of the things you have ever remembered, have been associated subconsciously with something else that you already knew or remembered. The important word here, is, "subconsciously." You yourselves do not realize what is going on in your subconscious; most of us would be frightened if we did. What you subconsciously associated strongly, will be remembered, what was not associated strongly, will be forgotten. Since this tiny mental calisthenic takes place without your knowledge, you cannot help it any.

Here then is the crux of the matter — I am going to teach you to associate anything you want to, consciously. When you have learned to do that, you will have acquired a trained memory.

Keep in mind that the system that I teach in this book is an aid to your normal or true memory. It is your true memory that does the work for you, whether you realize it or not. There is a very thin line between a trained memory and the true memory, and as you continue to use the system taught here, that line will begin to fade.

That is the wonderful part about the whole thing; after using my system consciously for a while, it becomes automatic and you almost start doing it subconsciously!

CHAPTER THREE
Test Your Memory

Some college students were taking an examination just prior to their Christmas vacation. This was an exam they hadn't looked forward to, since they knew it would be a tough one. It was! One student handed in his paper with this remark on it:
"God only knows the answers to these questions. Merry Christmas!"
The professor marked the papers, and returned them to the students. One had a message on it:
"God gets an A, you get an F. Happy New Year!"

I don't think you'll find the tests in this chapter quite as difficult. Even if you do, it doesn't matter, since no one will know how badly you do on them. In a previous chapter, I gave you a few examples showing how conscious associations are a great help in remembering anything. Such a simple aid to our memories, and yet so effective. The fact that those of you who learned the phrase, "Never believe a lie" never misspelled the word, "believe" again, proves their effectiveness. The more important fact that you can retain these simple associations over a period of years, proves it still more.

It is my contention that if you can remember or retain one thing with the aid of a conscious association, you can do it with anything else. That's my contention and I intend to prove it with you; I also intend to prove it to you. After you've learned the methods, I'm sure you'll agree that conscious associations will be more useful and valuable to you than you ever imagined they could be. If I were to tell you now, that after reading and studying the system in this book, you would be able to remember as high as a fifty digit number, and retain it for as long as you liked, after looking at it only once — you would think me mad.

If I told you that you could memorize the order of a shuffled deck of fifty two playing cards after hearing them called only once, you would think me mad! If I told you that you would never again be troubled by forgetting names or faces, or that you would be able to remember a shopping list of fifty items, or memorize the contents of an entire magazine, or remember prices and important telephone numbers, or know the day of the week of any date — you would surely think I had "flipped my lid." But read and study this book, and see for yourself!

I imagine that the best way for me to prove it to you is to let you see your own progress. In order to do that, I must show you first how poor your untrained memory is. So take a few moments out, right now, and mark yourselves on the tests that follow. In this way you will be able to take the same tests after reading certain chapters, and compare your scores.

I feel that these tests are quite important. Since your memory will improve with almost every chapter you read, I want you to see that improvement. That will give you confidence, which in itself is important to a trained memory. After each test you will find a space for your present score and a space which is to be used for your score after reading those particular chapters.

One important point, before you take the tests —don't flip through the book and read only the chapters that you think will help you. All the chapters will help you, and it is much better if you read from one to the other. Do not jump ahead, of me, or yourself!

Test #1

Read this list of fifteen objects just once — you can take about two minutes to do so. Then try to write them, without looking at the book, of course, in exactly the same order in which they appear here. When scoring yourself, remember that if you leave out a word, that will make the remaining words incorrect, for they will be out of sequence. I will remind you to take this test again, after you've read Chapter 5. Give yourself 5 points for each correct one.

Book, ashtray, cow, coat, match, razor, apple, purse, venetian blind, frying pan, clock, eyeglasses, door knob, bottle, worm.

Write your score here _20_.

Score after learning Chapter 5 _____.

Test #2

Take about three minutes to try to memorize the twenty objects listed here, by number. Then try to list them yourself without looking at the book. You must remember not only the object, but to which number it belongs. You'll be reminded to take this test again, after you've read Chapter 6. Give yourself 5 points for every object that you put with the correct number.

1. radio	6. telephone	11. dress	16. bread
2. airplane	7. chair	12. flower	17. pencil
3. lamp	8. horse	13. window	18. curtain
4. cigarette	9. egg	14. perfume	19. vase
5. picture	10. tea cup	15. book	20. hat

Write your score here_____25_____.
Score after learning Chapter 6_____.

Test #3

Look at this twenty digit number for about two and a half minutes, then take a piece of paper and try to write it from memory. Give yourself 5 points for every number that you put down in its correct place or sequence. Understand please, that the important thing here is retentiveness, which you cannot test until you have read Chapter 11.

72443278622173987651

Write your score here_____65_____.
Score after learning Chapter 11 _____.

Test #4

Imagine that someone has taken five cards out of a shuffled deck of playing cards. Now the rest of the cards (47) are called off to you just once. Could you tell, by memory, which five were not called, or were missing? Let's try it. Look down this list of forty-seven cards only once. After you've done so, take a pencil and jot down the names of the five cards that you think are missing. You must not look at the book while you are writing. Don't take more than four and a half minutes to look at the list of cards. I will ask you to take this test again, after you have read and studied Chapter 10. Give yourself 20 points for every missing card you list correctly.

Jack Hearts	Ace Clubs	Eight Clubs	Six Hearts
Ace Diamonds	Nine Spades	Queen Clubs	Four Hearts
King Hearts	Four Clubs	Seven Spades	Ten Spades
Seven Diamonds	Five Hearts	Seven Clubs	King Diamonds
Ten Clubs	Three Hearts	Two Diamonds	Ten Hearts
Jack Spades	Nine Clubs	King Clubs	Queen Diamonds
Three Spades	Ten Diamonds	Eight Hearts	Eight Diamonds
Nine Hearts	Eight Spades	Six Spades	Five Clubs
Seven Hearts	Five Spades	Four Spades	Two Clubs
Queen Hearts	Ace Spades	Queen Spades	Five Diamonds
Three Diamonds	Six Diamonds	Three Clubs	Two Hearts
Two Spades	Jack Diamonds	Jack Clubs	

Ace Hearts & Diamonds

Write your score here _____.
Score after learning Chapter 10 _____.

Test #5

Take about six or seven minutes to look at the fifteen faces and names pictured on the following page. Towards the end of this chapter you'll find them pictured again in a different order, without their names. See if you can't give the right name to the right picture. I'll remind you to take this test again, after you've read through Chapter 17. Give yourself 5 points for every name and face that you match up correctly.

Write your score here _____.
Score after learning Chapter 17 _____.

Test #5

Miss Sitler

Mr. Gordon

Mr. Hunt

Mr. Enlove

Mr. Donahue

Miss Palmer

Mr. Daegenshine

Miss Ralstone

Mr. Shaw

Mr. Koransky

Mr. Zacaria

Mr. Talman

Miss Carson

Mr. Smallowitz

Mr. Rubin

Test #6

Take seven to nine minutes to look at this list of ten people and their telephone numbers. Then copy all ten people onto a piece of paper, close the book, and see if you can write the telephone number next to each one, from memory. Remember that if you were to dial one wrong digit, you would get the wrong party — so, if only one digit in the number is wrong, you get no score on that particular one. I will remind you to take this test again, after you've read through Chapter 19. Give yourself 10 points for each telephone number that you list correctly.

Baker	TA 5-3174	Banker	SU 9-4281
Tailor	RH 3-8205	Mr. Karpel	RE 8-9714
Shoemaker	JU 6-0746	Doctor	TA 7-1015
Dentist	WA 4-6904	Mr. Goldberg	WA 6-8222
Mr. Bookman	CO 5-1127	Mr. Corrigan	CA 9-4132

Write your score here _20_____.

Score after learning Chapter 19 _____.

Do not feel discouraged because of the poor marks that you may have received on the foregoing tests. I have given them to you for a definite purpose. First, of course, as I stated above, that you would be able to see your own progress as you read through this book. Also, to show you how unreliable an untrained memory really is.

It does not take a lot of work and study to be able to get 100% on all these tests. I like to refer to the system in this book as the "lazy man's" way of remembering!

CHAPTER FOUR
Interest In Memory

The true art of memory is the art of attention.

—*Samuel Johnson*

Please read the following paragraph very carefully:

You are driving a bus which contains fifty people. The bus makes one stop and ten people get off, while three people get on. At the next stop seven people get off the bus, and two people get on. There are two more stops at which four passengers get off each time, and three fares get on at one stop, and none at the other. At this point, the bus has to stop because of mechanical trouble. Some of the passengers are in a hurry and decide to walk. So eight people get off the bus. When the mechanical trouble is taken care of, the bus goes to the last stop, and the rest of the people get off.

Now, without re-reading the paragraph, see if you can answer two questions about it. I feel pretty sure that if I asked you to tell me how many people were left on the bus, or how many got off the bus at the last stop, you would have the answer immediately. However, one of the questions I want you to answer is: How many stops did the bus make altogether?

I may be wrong, but I don't think that many of you can answer this question. The reason, of course, is that you all felt sure that the question I would ask, after you read the paragraph, would pertain to the amount of people. Therefore you gave your attention to the amount of people that were getting on and off the bus. You were interested in the amount of people. In short, you wanted to know or remember how many people would be left on the bus. Since you didn't think that the number of stops was important, you didn't pay much attention to that. You weren't interested in the amount of stops, therefore they didn't register in your mind at all, and you didn't remember them.

However, if some of you did feel that the amount of stops was important or if you felt you would be questioned on that particular point; then you surely did know the answer to my first question, or remembered the number of stops that the bus made. Again, simply because you were interested or wanted to know that particular information.

If you feel elated because you did answer my question, don't. Because I doubt if you will answer the second one. A good friend of mine who is employed at Grossingers, a large resort hotel, at which I perform quite often, uses this in his afternoon quizzes. I know that a very small percentage of the guests ever answer this correctly, if at all. Without looking at that first paragraph again, you're to answer this question: What is the bus driver's name?

As I said, I doubt if any of you can answer this correctly, if at all. Actually, this is more of a trick question on observation than it is a memory test. I use it here only to impress upon you the importance of interest in memory. Had I told you before you read that "bus" story, that I would ask for the driver's name
—you would have been interested in the name. You'd have wanted to notice and remember it.

Even so, it is sort of a tricky question, and you may not have been observant enough to be able to answer it. This, incidentally, is a principle that many professional magicians have been using for years. It is called "misdirection." It simply means that the important move in a trick, the move that actually is the "modus operandi," is kept in the background. Or, it is covered with another move, one that has nothing to do with the trick, but which you are led to believe is the important move. This is the move that you will observe and remember. The one that actually worked the trick is not even noticed, and that is why you are completely fooled. Most people, when describing a magician's trick, will make the effect so impossible that if the magician himself were listening, he wouldn't believe it. Only because they leave out the all important move in their description. Aside from "box" tricks, or tricks that mechanically work themselves, magicians would have a tough time fooling their audiences if it weren't for the art of "misdirection."

Well, I "misdirected" you by making you think I was going to ask about one thing, and then I asked about something you didn't even notice. I guess I've kept you in suspense long enough. You probably are anxious to know the answer to my second question. Well, actually the first word of the paragraph tells you who the driver is. The first word of the paragraph is, you. The correct answer to the question, "What is the bus driver's name?" is your own name! You were driving the bus. Try this one on your friends and see how few of them can answer it correctly.

As I've said, this is more of an observation test than a memory test. But memory and observation do go hand in hand. You cannot possibly remember anything you do not observe; and it is extremely difficult to observe or remember anything that you do not want to remember, or that you are not interested in remembering.

This, of course, leads to an obvious memory rule. If you want to improve your memory immediately, force yourself to want to remember. Force yourself to be interested enough to observe anything you want to remember or retain. I say, "force yourself," because at first a little effort may be necessary; however in an amazingly short time, you'll find that there is no effort at all required to make yourself want to remember anything. The fact that you are reading this book, is your first forward step. You wouldn't be reading it if you didn't want to remember, or if you weren't interested in improving your memory. "Without motivation there can hardly be remembrance."

Aside from intending to remember, confidence that you will remember is also helpful. If you tackle any memory problem with the thought, "I will remember," more often than not, you will. Think of your memory as a sieve. Each time that you feel or say, "I have an awful memory," or, "I'll never be able to remember this," you put another hole in the sieve. If, on the other hand, you say, "I have a wonderful memory," or, "I'll remember this easily," you're plugging up one of those holes.

A lot of people I know, invariably ask me why they can't remember a thing, even though they write down everything they wish to remember. Well, that's like asking why they can't swim well, even though they tie a twenty pound stone around their necks. The very fact that they do write it, is probably why they forget; or rather, why they didn't remember in the first place. As far as I'm concerned, the phrase, "I forgot" should not be in the language. It should be, "I didn't remember in the first place."

You cannot forget anything you ever really remembered. If you were to write things down with the intent of aiding your memory, or with the conscious thought of helping you to be exact with the information, that would be fine. However, using pencil and paper as a substitute for memory (which most people do), is certainly not going to improve it. Your handwriting may improve, or the speed of your writing might improve, but your memory will get worse through neglect and non-use. You see, you usually write things down only because you refuse or are too lazy to take the slight effort or time to remember.
Oliver Wendell Holmes put it this way:

"A man must get a thing before he can forget it."

Please keep in mind that the memory likes to be trusted. The more you trust it the more reliable and useful it will become. Writing everything down on paper without trying to remember, is going against all the basic rules for a stronger and better memory. You're not trusting your memory; you haven't the confidence in your memory; you're not exercising the memory, and your interest is not strong enough to retain it, if you must write it down. Remember that you can always lose your paper or notebook, but not your mind. If I may be allowed a small attempt at humor, if you do lose your mind, it doesn't matter much if you remember or not, does it?

Seriously, if you are interested in remembering, if you have confidence that you will remember, you have no need to write everything down. How many parents continually complain that their children have terrible memories, because they can't remember their school work, and consequently get poor marks? Yet, some of these same children can remember the batting averages of every baseball player in the major leagues. They know all the rules of baseball; or who made what great play in what year for which team, etc. If they can remember these facts and figures so easily and so well, why can't some of them retain their lessons at school? Only because they are more interested in baseball than they are in algebra, history, geography and other school subjects.

The problem is not with their memories, but with their lack of interest. The proof of the pudding is in the fact that most children excel in at least one particular subject, even though they have poor marks in all the others. If a student has a good memory for one subject, he is a good student in that subject. If he can't remember, or has a poor memory in that subject, he will be a poor student in that subject. It's as simple as that. However, this proves that the student does have a good memory for things that he likes, or is interested in.

Many of you who went through High School had to take a foreign language or two. Do you still remember these languages? I doubt it. If you've traveled in foreign countries, or to places where they speak these particular languages, you've wished many times that you had paid more attention in school. Of course, if you knew that you were going to travel to these places, when you were in school, you would have been interested in learning the language; you would have wanted to do so. You'd have been amazed to find how much better your marks would have been. I know that this is true in my case. If I had known then that I would want to know these languages, I'd have learned and/or remembered much more easily. Unfortunately, I didn't have a trained memory then.

Many women will complain that their memories are atrocious, and that they can't remember a thing. These same women will describe and remember in detail what a lady friend was wearing when they met weeks ago. They usually can spot another woman in a car traveling up to forty miles an hour, and tell you what she's wearing; the colors, her style of hairdo, whether the hair was natural or bleached, and the woman's approximate age!

They'll probably even know how much money this woman had. This, of course, goes out of the realm of memory and starts to touch on psychic powers. The important thing, the thing that I have been trying to stress in this chapter, is that interest is of great importance to memory. If you can remember things that you are interested in to such a tremendous degree, it proves that you do have a good memory. It also proves that if you were as interested in other things, you would be able to remember them just as well.

The thing to do is to make up your mind that you will be interested in remembering names, faces, dates, figures, facts, anything; and that you will have confidence in your ability to retain them. This, alone, without the actual Systems and Methods of associations in this book, will improve your memory to a noticeable degree. With the Systems of association as an aid to your true memory, you are on your way to an amazingly remarkable and retentive memory. You can start to prove this to yourself in the next chapter.

CHAPTER FIVE
Link Method Of Memory

A man's real possession is his memory.
In nothing else is he rich, in nothing else is he poor.
—Alexander Smith

I want to show you, now, that you can start, immediately, to remember as you've never remembered before. I don't believe that anyone with an untrained memory can possibly remember twenty unassociated items, in sequence, after hearing or seeing them only once. Even though you don't believe it either, you will accomplish just that if you read and study this chapter.

Before going into the actual memorizing, I must explain that your trained memory will be based almost entirely on mental pictures or images. These mental pictures will be easily recalled if they are made as ridiculous as you can possibly make them. Here are the twenty items that you will be able to memorize in sequence in a surprisingly short time.

carpet, paper, bottle, bed, fish, chair, window, telephone, cigarette, nail, typewriter, shoe, microphone, pen, television set, plate, donut, car, coffee pot, and brick.

A famous man once said that method is the mother of memory. So, I'll teach you now, what I call the Link method of memory. I've told you that your trained memory will consist mostly of ridiculous mental images, so let's make ridiculous mental images of the above twenty items! Don't be alarmed! It is child's play; as a matter of fact it is almost like a game.

The first thing you have to do is to get a picture of the first item, "carpet," in your mind. You all know what a carpet is, so just "see" it in your mind's eye. Don't just see the word, "carpet," but actually, for a second, see either any carpet, or, a carpet that is in your own home and is therefore familiar to you. I have already told you that in order to remember anything, it must be associated in some way to something you already know or remember. You are going to do that right now, and the items themselves will serve as the things you already remember. The thing that you now know or already remember is the item, "carpet." The new thing, the thing you want to remember will be the second item, "paper."

Now then, here is your first and most important step towards your trained memory. You must now associate or link carpet to, or with, paper. The association must be as ridiculous as possible. For example, you might picture the carpet in your home made out of paper. See yourself walking on it, and actually hearing the paper crinkle under foot. You can picture yourself writing something on a carpet instead of paper. Either one of these is a ridiculous picture or association. A sheet of paper lying on a carpet would not make a good association. It is too logical! Your mental picture must be ridiculous or illogical. Take my word for the fact that if your association is a logical one, you will not remember it.

Now, here is the point which I will keep reminding you of throughout this book. You must actually see this ridiculous picture in your mind for a fraction of a second. Please do not just try to see the words, but definitely see the picture you've decided on. Close your eyes for a second; that might make it easier to see the picture, at first. As soon as you see it, stop thinking about it and go on to your next step. The thing you now already know or remember is, "paper," therefore the next step is to associate or Link, paper to the next item on the list, which is, "bottle." At this point, you pay no attention to "carpet" any longer. Make an entirely new ridiculous mental picture with, or between bottle and paper. You might see yourself reading a gigantic bottle instead of a paper, or writing on a gigantic bottle instead of on paper. Or, you might picture a bottle pouring paper out of its mouth instead of liquid; or a bottle made out of paper instead of glass. Pick the association which you think is most ridiculous and see it in your mind's eye for a moment.

I cannot stress, too much, the necessity of actually seeing this picture in your mind's eye, and making the mental image as ridiculous as possible. You are not, however, to stop and think for fifteen minutes to find the most illogical association; the first ridiculous one that comes to mind is usually the best to use. I'll give you two or more ways in which you might form your pictures with each pair of the twenty items. You are to pick the one that you think is most ridiculous, or one that you've thought of yourself, and use that one association only.

We have already linked carpet to paper, and then paper to bottle. We now come to the next item which is, "bed." You must make a ridiculous association between bottle and bed. A bottle lying on a bed, or anything like that would be too logical. So you might picture yourself sleeping in a large bottle instead of a bed, or you might see yourself taking a Snort from a bed instead of a bottle. (I can get pretty ridiculous.) See either of these pictures in your mind for a moment, then stop thinking of it.

You realize, of course, that we are always associating the previous object to the present object. Since we have just used "bed," this is the previous, or the thing we already know and remember. The present object, or the new thing that we want to remember, is "fish." So, make a ridiculous association or link between bed and fish. You could "see" a giant fish sleeping in your bed; or a bed made out of a gigantic fish. See the picture you think is most ridiculous.

Now — "fish" and "chair" — see the gigantic fish sitting on a chair, or a large fish being used as a chair. Or, you're catching chairs instead of fish while fishing.

• **Chair and Window**—See yourself sitting on a pane of glass (which gives you a pain) instead of a chair. Or, you might see yourself violently throwing chairs through a closed window. See the picture before going on to the next one.

• **Window and Telephone**—See yourself answering the phone, but when you put it to your ear, it's not a phone you're holding, but a window. Or, you might see your window as a large telephone dial, and you have to lift the dial to look out the window. You could see yourself sticking your hand through a window pane in order to pick up the phone. See the picture you think is most ridiculous, for a moment.

• **Telephone and Cigarette**—You're smoking a telephone instead of a cigarette; or you're holding a large cigarette to your ear and talking into it instead of a telephone. Or, you might see yourself picking up the phone and a million cigarettes fly out of the mouthpiece and hit you in the face.

• **Cigarette and Nail**— You're smoking a nail; or hammering a lit cigarette into the wall instead of a nail.

• **Nail and Typewriter**—You're hammering a gigantic nail right through a typewriter, or all the keys on your typewriter are nails and they're pricking your fingertips as you type.

• **Typewriter and Shoe**—See yourself wearing typewriters instead of shoes, or you're typing with your shoes. You might want to see a large shoe with keys and you're typing on that.

• **Shoe and Microphone**—You're wearing microphones instead of shoes, or, you're broadcasting into a large shoe.

• **Microphone and Pen**—You're writing with a microphone instead of a pen, or you're broadcasting and talking into a giant pen.

• **Pen and Television Set**— You could "see" a million pens gushing out of the television screen, or pens performing on television, or there is a screen on a gigantic pen and you're (I can't resist this pun) watch-ink a television show on it.

• **Television Set and Plate**—Picture your television screen as one of your kitchen plates, or see yourself eating out of the television set instead of out of a plate, or you're eating out of a plate, and seeing a television show in the plate while you eat.

• **Plate and Donut**—"See" yourself biting into a donut, but it cracks in your mouth for it's a plate. Or, picture being served dinner in a gigantic donut instead of a plate.

• **Donut and Automobile**—You can "see" a large donut driving an automobile; or, see yourself driving a gigantic donut instead of a car.

• **Automobile and Coffee Pot**—A large coffee pot is driving a car, or you're driving a gigantic coffee pot instead of a car. You might picture your ear on your stove, with coffee perking in it.

• **Coffee Pot and Brick**—See yourself pouring steaming coffee from a brick instead of a coffee pot, or "see" bricks pouring from the spout of a coffee pot instead of coffee.

That's it! If you have actually "seen" these mental pictures in your mind's eye, you will have no trouble remembering the twenty items in sequence, from "carpet" to "brick." Of course, it takes many times the length of time to explain this than to simply do it. Each mental association must be seen for just the smallest fraction of a second, before going on to the next one.

Let's see now if you have remembered all the items. If you were to "see" a carpet, what would that bring to mind immediately? Why, paper, of course. You saw yourself writing on a carpet, instead of paper. Now, paper brings bottle to mind, because you saw a bottle made of paper. You saw yourself sleeping in a gigantic bottle instead of a bed; the bed had a gigantic fish sleeping on it; you were fishing, and catching chairs and you were flinging chairs through your closed window. Try it! You will see that you will go right through all the items without missing or forgetting any of them.

Fantastic?? Unbelievable?? Yes! But, as you can see, entirely plausible and possible. Why not try making your own list of objects and memorizing them in the way that you have just learned.

I realize, of course, that we have all been brought up to think logically, and here I am, telling you to make illogical or ridiculous pictures. I know that with some of you, this may be a bit of a problem, at first. You may have a little difficulty in making those ridiculous pictures. However, after doing it for just a little while, the first picture that comes to mind will be a ridiculous or illogical one. Until that happens, here are four simple rules to help you.

1. Picture your items out of proportion. In other words, too large. In my sample associations for the above items, I used the word, "gigantic" quite often. This was to make you get the items out of proportion.

2. Picture your items in action whenever possible. Unfortunately, it is the violent and embarrassing things that we all remember; much more so than the pleasant things. If you've ever been acutely embarrassed, or been in an accident, no matter how many years ago, you don't need a trained memory to remember it vividly. You still squirm a bit whenever you think of that embarrassing incident that happened years ago, and you probably can still describe in detail the facts of your accident. So get violent action into your association whenever you can.

3. Exaggerate the amount of items. In my sample association between telephone and cigarette, I told you that you might see millions of cigarettes flying out of the mouthpiece, and hitting you in the face. If you saw the cigarettes lit and burning your face, you'd have both action and exaggeration in your picture.

4. Substitute your items. This is the one that I, personally, use most often. It is simply picturing one item instead of another, i.e. smoking a nail instead of a cigarette.

1. Out of Proportion.   2. Action.   3. Exaggeration.   4. Substitution.
     Try to get one or more of the previous into your pictures, and with a little practice you'll find that a ridiculous association for any two items will come to mind instantly. The objects to be remembered are actually linked one to the other, forming a chain, and that is why I call this the Link method of remembering. The entire Link method boils down to this: associate the first item to the second, the second to the third, third to the fourth, and so on. Make your associations as ridiculous and/or illogical as possible, and most important, **SEE** the pictures in your mind's eye. In later chapters you will learn some practical applications of the Link system, how it can help you to recall your daily schedule or errands, and how you can use it to help you remember speeches. The Link system is also used to help memorize long digit numbers and many other things.

However, don't jump ahead of yourself; don't worry about those things now.

Of course, you can use the Link immediately to help you remember shopping lists, or to show-off for your friends. If you want to try this as a memory stunt, have your friend call off a list of objects; have him write them down so that he can check you. If when you try this you find that you are having trouble recalling the first item, I suggest that you associate that item to the person that's testing you. For example, if "carpet" were the first item, you could "see" your friend rolled up in your carpet. Also, if on first trying this as a stunt, you do forget one of the items, ask what it is and strengthen that particular association. You either didn't use a ridiculous enough association, or you didn't see it in your mind, or you would not have forgotten it. After you've strengthened your original association, you'll be able to rattle off the items from first to last. Try it and see!

The most impressive part of it, is that if your friend asks you to call off the items two or three hours later, you will be able to do it! They will still be brought to mind by your original associations. If you really want to impress your listeners, call the items off backwards! In other words, from the last item called, right up to the first one.

Amazingly enough, this works for you automatically. Just think of the last item, that will recall the next to last item, and so on down, or rather, up the line.

By the way, why not try Test #1 in Chapter #3 again. Compare your score now, with the score you had before you read this chapter on the Link method.

CHAPTER SIX
Peg System of memory

A certain organization, whose membership consisted of gag-writers only, was having its annual dinner at a swank hotel in New York City. One of the membership rules of the organization was that the members would never actually tell a joke or a gag to each other. They had memorized all the standard gags by numbers, and instead of telling the joke, they would save time by simply calling the number of that particular one.

During the dinner, as a situation would present itself, and any of the comedy writers thought of a gag to fit the situation, he would call the number, and shouts of laughter would invariably go up. "Number 148," called one—peals of laughter. "Number 204," shouted another—more laughter. Towards the end of the dinner, one of the new members shouted "Number 212," and was greeted by a loud silence. Whereupon his neighbor turned to him and said, "You'll soon learn, my friend, that it's not the joke that's important, but the way you tell it."

Although the story is pure fiction, most people would say it is impossible to remember so many jokes by number. Let me assure you that it is possible, and I will teach you how, in a later chapter. First, however, you must learn how to remember the numbers. Numbers themselves are about the most difficult things to remember because they are completely abstract and intangible. It is almost impossible to picture a number. They are geometric designs and they mean nothing in our minds, unless they have been associated to something you know, over a period of time. Of course, your own address or your own telephone number does mean something to you. The problem is to be able to associate any and all numbers easily, quickly, and at any time.

If you were to try to hang a painting on your bare living room wall, what would happen? Why, the painting would fall to the floor, of course. However, if you had a tiny peg in that wall, then you would be able to hang the painting on it. What I'm going to do, is to give you some "pegs" no, not for your wall, but to keep in your mind, always. Anything you wish to remember from now on, having to do with numbers in any way, you will be able to "hang" on these pegs! That is why I call this the PEG system of memory.

The PEG system will show you how to count with objects (which can be pictured) instead of numbers. This is not a particularly new thought. It was first introduced by Stanislaus Mink von Wennsshein along about the year 1648. In the year 1730, the entire System was modified by Dr. Richard Grey, of England, who called the idea, letter or "number equivalents." The idea was great, but the method just a bit clumsy, because he used vowels as well as consonants in the system. Since 1730, however, many changes have been made, although the idea is basically the same.

In order for you to learn the method, you must first learn a simple phonetic alphabet. No need for dismay — it consists of only ten sounds, and with my help, it shouldn't take you more than ten minutes to learn them. This will be the most worthwhile ten minutes you've ever spent, since this phonetic alphabet will eventually help you to remember numbers, or numbers in conjunction with anything else, in such a way that you never would have thought possible.

I will give you now, a different consonant sound for each of the digits 1, 2, 3, 4, 5, 6, 7, 8, 9 and 0. These you must commit to memory. I'll make this simple for you by giving you a "memory aid" for remembering each one. Read them carefully and with your full attention.

The sound for #1 will always be—T or D. The letter t has one downstroke.
The sound for #2 will always be—N. Typewritten n has two downstrokes.
The sound for #3 will always be—M. Typewritten m has three downstrokes.
The sound for #4 will always be—R. Final sound of the word, "four" is R.
The sound for #5 will always be—L. Roman numeral for 50 is L.
The sound for #6 will always be—J, eh, sh, soft g, etc. The letter J turned around is almost like the number 6. (J6)
The sound for #7 will always be—K, hard c, hard g. The number 7 can be used to form a K. One seven right side up, and the other upside down.
The sound for #8 will always be—F or V. Written f and figure 8 both have two loops, one above the other. (f 8)
The sound for #9 will always be—P or B. The number 9 turned around is P.
The sound for 0(zero)will always be—S orZ. First sound of the word, "zero."

If you will attempt to picture the little memory aid that I have given with each one, you should remember them easily. Please keep in mind that the letters are not important; we are interested in the sound only. That's why I call this a phonetic alphabet. With some of the digits I've given more than one letter, but the phonetic sounds of these letters are the same, in each case. Your lips, tongue and teeth are used in the same identical way to sound P and B, or F and V, or J, sh, ch, etc. The sound of the letter G in the exclamation, "gee"would, according to the phonetic alphabet, represent #6, whereas the same letter in the word, "go" would represent #7. The letter C in the word "coat" represents #7, the same letter in the word "cent" would represent zero, since it is pronounced with the S sound. The letters kn in the word, "knee" or "knife" would stand for #2, because the K is silent. Remember then, it is the sound that's important, not the letter.

Now, look this over once:

1. T, D	**6. J, sh, ch, g**
2. N	**7. K, c, g**
3. M	**8. F, v**
4. R	**9. P, b**
5. L	**10. Z, s**

Turn away from this page and see if you remember the sounds from one to zero. Test yourself on remembering them out of order, too. You should know them all by now. I could give you one more aid for memorizing these sounds, by telling you to remember this nonsense phrase: TeN MoRe LoGiC FiBS. This will help you to memorize the sounds in order from one to zero. It is necessary, however, to know them out of sequence, so you shouldn't have to rely on the nonsense phrase too long. The original memory aids that I gave you, should suffice.

This simple phonetic alphabet is of utmost importance, and the sounds should be practiced until they are second nature to you. Once they are, the rest of the Peg system will be a cinch for you. Here is a method of practice to help you learn the sounds thoroughly: anytime you see a number, break it down into sounds in your mind. For example, you might see the number 3746 on a license plate; you should be able to read it as m, k, r, j. You might see an address 85-29, and be able to read it as fl-np. You can look at any word and practice breaking it down into numbers. The word "motor" would be 314. The word paper is 994, and "cigarette" would break down to 0741. (The double tt is the same sound as a single t, therefore it represents #1, not #11.)

None of the vowels, a e i o or u have any meaning at all in the phonetic alphabet; neither do the letters w, h or y. (Remember the word, "why").

Before going any further, complete the following exercises. The first column of words should be changed to numbers, and the second column of numbers must be broken into sounds.

climb_____	6124_____
butler_____	8903_____
chandelier_____	2394_____
sounds_____	0567_____
bracelet_____	1109_____
hypnotize_____	8374_____

You are ready now to learn some of those "pegs" I mentioned. I would suggest however, that you know the sounds thoroughly before you go on to the pegs themselves.

All right, since we now know a certain phonetic sound for all the digits from one to zero, you can see that we can make up a word for any number, no matter how many digits it contains. For example, if we wanted to make up a word for #21, we could use any of the following: net, nut, knot, gnat, nod, neat, note, knit, etc., because they all begin with the n sound (#2) and end with the t or d sound (#1). For #14 we could use tear, tire, tore, door, tier, deer, dire, dray, tree, etc., because they all begin with the t or d sound for #1, and end with the r sound for #4. Remember that we are interested in the consonant sounds only.

Do you get the idea of how I formed those words? If you do, then I can go ahead and give you the first few "pegs." Each one of the peg words that I will give you has been specially chosen because it is comparatively easy to picture in your mind, and that is important.

Since the number 1 contains only one digit, and that one digit is represented by the t or d sound, we must use a word that contains only that one consonant sound. So, we will use the word, "TIE." From here on in, the word, "tie" will always represent the number 1 to you.

As I said, it is important to be able to picture these objects, so I will give explanations of all those where I think an explanation is necessary. The word, "NOAH" will always represent #2. Picture an old, white haired man on an ark.

The word, "MA" will always mean #3. Here I suggest that you always picture your own mother.

The word, "RYE" will always represent the number 4. You can picture either a bottle of rye whiskey Or a loaf of rye bread. Once you decide on a particular mind picture for this, or for any of the pegs, use that particular picture always. You can see how I arrive at these words. They all have only one consonant sound, and that one sound is the one representing the digit of the number.

The word, "LAW" will always represent #5. The word "law" itself, cannot be pictured; I suggest that you picture any policeman, in uniform, because they represent the law.

Number 6 is the word "SHOE."
Number 7 is the word "COW."
Number 8 is the word, "IVY." For this one, you can picture either Poison Ivy or ivy growing all over the sides of a house.
Number 9 is the word, "BEE."
Number 10 has two digits, the digit 1 and a zero. The peg word for #10 therefore must be made up of a t or d sound and an s or z sound, in that order. We'll use the word, "TOES" — picture your own toes.

Ordinarily it would be a little difficult to remember ten completely unassociated words as I have just given you. Since the peg word for any number must contain certain sounds only, you'll find that it is easy. As a matter of fact, if you have read the ten words once, with a little concentration, you probably already know them. Try it!
When you say the number to yourself, think of its sound first, then try to remember the peg word. Test yourself in and out of order. You should know that #3 is "ma," without repeating, "tie," "Noah," ma!

To show you how fantastic your memory can be with my little memory aids, you can do this until the words become second nature to you; if you come to a number, and you think you can't remember its peg — think of the sound for that number, and say any words that come to your mind, starting with, and containing that particular consonant sound only. When you say the right one, it will sort of "ring a bell" in your mind, and you'll know that's the right one. For instance, if you couldn't think of the peg word for #1, you might say to yourself, "toy, tow, tea, tie"; as soon as you say "tie," you'll know that it is the correct word.

You can see, now, what I've done. I have built you up slowly with each item. First I gave you an aid to remember the phonetic sounds, now those sounds are your aid to remember the very important peg words; and the peg words will help you to remember anything where numbers are involved, so make sure you know them well.

1. tie	6. shoe
2. Noah	7. cow
3. ma	8. ivy
4. rye	9. bee
5. law	10. toes

Now, if you feel that you know the first ten peg words thoroughly, I'll show you how to use them for remembering objects in and out of order. I'll give you ten objects, out of sequence, and prove to you that you can remember them after reading them only once!

9—purse	5—typewriter
6—cigarette	2—TV set
4—ashtray	8—wrist watch
7—salt-shaker	1—fountain pen
3—lamp	10—telephone

The first one listed is **#9—purse**. All you have to do is to make a ridiculous and/or illogical association of the peg word for #9, which is "bee," and purse. If you have realized the importance of actually "seeing" these ridiculous associations in your mind, you'll have no trouble. For this first one, you might see yourself opening a purse and a swarm of bees fly out of it, stinging you. Just "see" the picture for a moment, then go to the next one.

#6(shoe)—cigarette. You can see yourself smoking a shoe instead of a cigarette, see millions of cigarettes falling out of a shoe, or you can see yourself wearing gigantic cigarettes instead of shoes.

#4(rye)—ashtray. You might see yourself dropping ashes into a scooped out loaf of rye bread instead of an ashtray, or, you're buttering an ashtray instead of a slice of rye bread.

I am giving you one or more ways that each object can be associated ridiculously with its peg word. You are to use only one of these pictures for each one. Use one that I give, or one that you think of yourself. The first illogical picture that comes to mind is usually the best one to use, because that is the one that will come to mind later on. I'll help you with all ten of them, since it is the first time you are attempting this method; but after this you should be able to do it without my help.

#7(cow)—salt-shaker. Picture yourself milking a cow, but the cow has salt-shakers instead of udders. Or, see salt-shakers coming out instead of milk.

#3(ma)—lamp. You can picture your mother wearing a gigantic lamp for a hat. See the lamp going on and off. (Action-Rule #2.)

#5(law)—typewriter. You might "see" a policeman putting handcuffs on a typewriter, or you can see a typewriter walking the beat, swinging a club, like a cop.

#2 (Noah)—Television set. You might picture Noah sailing on a television set instead of an ark.

#8 (ivy)—wrist watch. You can see millions of wrist watches growing all over the side of your house, instead of ivey; you can see yourself wearing ivy on your wrist instead of a watch.

#1 (tie)—fountain pen. Picture yourself wearing a gigantic fountain pen instead of a tie, or you might see yourself writing with your tie, instead of a fountain pen.

 # 10 (toes)—telephone. See yourself dialing with your toes, or, you pick up the telephone, but it turns out that you're holding your toes. (Probably talking to a heel.)

Now, take a piece of paper, number it from one to ten, and try to fill in the objects in order, without looking at the book. When you come to #1, just picture your peg word, tie, and the ridiculous picture of you wearing a fountain pen instead of a tie will come back to you immediately. So you know that #1 is fountain pen. When you picture Noah, you will see him on a television set instead of an ark; so you know that #2 is television set.

You will remember them all quite easily. The wonderful part about it, is that you also know them out of sequence. You can see, of course, that it makes no difference. You can also call them off backwards — just think of the peg word for #10 (toes) and work up to "tie."

You should now be thoroughly amazed at your own ability. But wait! Why not memorize twenty-five objects instead of only ten? Well, at the end of this chapter you will find the peg words for numbers 11 through to 25. Please learn those just as you learned the first ten. When you know them perfectly, try this on your friends. Have them number a sheet of paper from one to twenty or twenty-five, or as many as you wish to show-off with. Then have him call out any of those numbers, haphazardly, and then name any tangible object. Ask him to write that object alongside the number called. Have him do that until every number has an object next to it. Now call them right back to him from #1 right down to the last one. Then have him call any number, and you immediately give him the object, or have him call any object and you tell him what number it is!!

Don't let that last part throw you, there is nothing to it. If I was to ask you now what number salt-shaker was, you would "see" the ridiculous picture of a you know that salt-shaker was #7.

Watch the look of astonishment on your pal's face when you're through!
Please do not go on to the next chapter until you are sure that you know all the peg words from 1 to 25.

11. tot	**15. towel**	**19. tub**	**23. name**
12. tin	**16. dish**	**20. nose**	**24. Nero**
13. tomb	**17. tack**	**21. net**	**25. nail**
14. tire	**18. dove**	**22. nun**	

For "tot," it is best to picture a child that you know. For #12, you can see the object called, made out of "tin." For "tomb," picture a gravestone. For #20, you can see the object called, on your face in place of your "nose." For "net," you can use either a fishing net, a hair net, or a tennis net.

For #23, you can see the object you wish to remember forming your "name." For instance, if the object were cigarette, you would picture your own name printed out very large with cigarettes. If you don't care for that idea, you might picture one of your business cards for "name," or any other possession that has your name on it. Whatever you decide on, you must use it all the time. For "Nero," I always picture a man playing a fiddle.

Remember, please, that once you decide on a particular picture for any of the peg words, you are to use that picture all the time.

If you know the pegs from 1 to 25 thoroughly, (and I suggest that you go no further until you do), and if you feel confident, (or even if you don't) why not take test #2 in Chapter #3 once again. Try it, and then compare your present score with the original one!

CHAPTER SEVEN
Uses of the Peg and Link Systems

*New Patient: "Doctor, I don't know what to do. You've got to help me;
I just can't remember a thing. I've no memory at all. I hear something
one minute, and the next minute, I forget it! Tell me, what should I do?"
Doctor: "Pay in advance!"*

I can't blame the doctor for wanting his fee in advance in the above anecdote; but I guess that most of us who forget to pay bills, do so because we don't want to remember them. According to Austin O'Malley, "A habit of debt is very injurious to the memory." Unfortunately, we are usually soon reminded of debts.

If you've grasped the idea behind the Link and the Peg systems of memory, you have learned two of the three things that your trained memory will be based upon. The third is the system of substitute words or substitute thoughts, which I will discuss in later chapters.

You can start applying what you've learned immediately, if you want to. Not particularly for remembering debts, which I'm sure you'd rather forget, but perhaps for memorizing the errands that you have to do for each day. If you usually write out your shopping list, why not try to memorize it with the help of the Link system. Simply link the first item to the second item, the second to the third, and so on, down the list. You can memorize an entirely different list the next time you go shopping without fear of confusion. The beautiful thing about the Link method is that you can forget a list whenever you wish. Actually, when you memorize the second shopping list, the first one fades away. You can, of course, retain as many lists or links as you desire.

The mind is a most fantastic machine; it can be compared to a filing cabinet. If you have memorized a list of items with the Link system, which you want to retain, you can. If you want to forget the list, you can. It is merely a question of desire. The list that you want to remember is one which you probably intend to use, or you would have no reason to retain it. The use of the list itself will tend to etch it into your memory. If it happens to be a list that you do not intend to utilize right away, but which you feel you want to retain for future use, you can do that, too. You would have to go over the list in your mind the day after you memorized it. Then go over it again a few days later. After doing this a few times, you have filed the list away, and it will be ready when you need it.

We all realize, of course, that it is sometimes necessary to forget! Benjamin Disraeli, when asked about the favor shown him by royalty, said, "I observe a simple rule of conduct; I never deny; I never contradict; I sometimes forget." This, however, is a question of diplomacy, not memory; and I know that you're reading this book not to be taught how to forget, but how to remember. I will show you soon, how to use the Link system to remember speeches, articles, anecdotes, etc.

The main difference between the Link and the Peg methods is that the Link is used to remember anything in sequence, while the Peg is for memorizing things in and out of order. You may feel that you have no need for the Peg system since you don't have to remember anything out of order. Believe me when I tell you that you definitely should learn the Peg system thoroughly. It will be extremely useful for remembering telephone numbers, style numbers, long digit numbers, addresses —as a matter of fact, the Peg system will aid you in remembering anything that has to do with numbers in any way. Besides, it will enable you to do some fantastic memory stunts for your friends.

Although I intend to go deeper into memorizing schedules or appointments for the week, day or month in later chapters, I can show you how to apply what you have already learned to this problem, right now. You can use either the Peg or Link methods, or one, in conjunction with the other.

Let's assume that you have the following errands to do on one particular day: You have to have your car washed (now we know that it must rain today); make a deposit at the bank; mail a letter; see your dentist; pick up the umbrella that you forgot at a friend's house (you hadn't read the chapter on absent-mindedness, as yet); buy some perfume for your wife; call or see the television repairman; stop at the hardware store for bulbs, a hammer, a picture frame, an extension cord and an ironing board cover; go to the bookstore to buy a copy of this book for a forgetful friend; have your watch repaired; and finally, bring home one dozen eggs. (My, but you've got a busy day!)

Now, as I've said, you can use the Link or Peg systems to enable you to remember to do each of the above errands. Using the Link method: Simply make a ridiculous picture between car and bank — you might see yourself driving into the bank in your recently washed car; you're depositing letters instead of money; now picture your dentist pulling letters out of your mouth instead of teeth, or he's using a letter instead of a drill. To remember the errand concerning the umbrella, picture your dentist working over you while he's holding an umbrella over his head; make a ridiculous picture between umbrella and perfume, now, perfume to television; television to hardware; hardware to book; book to watch; and finally, watch to eggs.

I've given you examples with the first few errands only, because I want you to use your own imagination for forming ridiculous mental links. You simply do the same as if you were linking a list of objects. Actually it is the same thing — when you come to the watch repairing and the purchase of the dozen eggs, it isn't necessary to get the repairing or amount of eggs into the picture. Just use watch and egg for your ridiculous picture: i.e. you're breaking an egg, and a wrist watch falls out; or, you're wearing an egg instead of a wrist watch. The one item will bring the entire errand to mind, of course. These are just memory aids or reminders; you already have remembered that you must repair the watch or that it is a dozen eggs that you need. Thinking of, or being reminded of watch and egg is all that is necessary to start you off on your errand.

When you get to the hardware store, you have to buy five items. Make a separate link of these five: you can start by "seeing" a large bulb as the proprietor of the store; you break him with a hammer; you frame a hammer and hang it on your wall, and so on, to ironing board cover.

After you have linked all your errands for the day, all you have to do, is complete one, and that will remind you of the next, and so on. However, you needn't do all these errands in sequence just because you used the Link method to remember them. That might make it a little inconvenient, unless you've arranged your errands accordingly. No, you can do them in any order you like. Each time you complete an errand, go over the link in your mind, in order to remind yourself if there is one that is convenient to take care of at that moment, considering the time and place. When you think you have attended to all your duties for the day, go over the Link, and if there is one you've missed, you'll know it immediately.

You can utilize the Peg system, of course, for the same thing. Just associate washing the car with your peg word for #1 (tie). You might picture yourself wearing a car instead of a tie.

Now, associate:

bank to Noah	(#2)	television to cow	(#7)
letter to ma	(#3)	hardware to ivy	(#8)
dentist to rye	(#4)	book to bee	(#9)
umbrella to law	(#5)	watch to toes	(#10)
perfume to shoe	(#6)	eggs to tot	(#11)

Use the link to remember the different items you want at the hardware store. You could even use the Peg for this by making another set of associations, i.e. bulb to tie; hammer to Noah, etc. They wouldn't conflict at all, but it is easier to use the Link.

Now, again, when you're ready to start the day, think of your peg for #1 (tie). This will remind you that you have to get the car washed. When that's done, think of your peg for #2 (Noah) and that will remind you to go to the bank, etc. You don't have to do these in order, either; simply keep going over the pegs, and if you've forgotten something, it'll stand out like an eagle in a canary cage.

There you have it! No more excuses to the wife that you forgot to wash the car, or that you forgot to buy the eggs. As I mentioned before, we'll go further into methods for remembering schedules and appointments in another chapter; wherein you will learn to remember appointments for definite times and days. For the time being what you've learned in this chapter will suffice for simple errands. Before going to bed each night, list your errands and appointments for the following day. Memorize them as explained, then go over them in the morning just to make sure. **That's all there is to it.**

Before completing this chapter, please learn the pegs for #26 through to #50. These, of course, follow the rules of the phonetic alphabet, as do all the pegs.

26. notch	32. moon	38. movie	44. rower	50. lace
27. neck	33. mummy	39. mop	45. roll	
28. knife	34. mower	40. rose	46. roach	
29. knob	35. mule	41. rod	47. rock	
30. mice	36. match	42. rain	48. roof	
31. mat	37. mug	43. ram	49. rope	

If the item to be associated with #26 were cigarette, you could see a gigantic cigarette with a "notch" in it. For "mower," picture a lawnmower. For "mug," picture a beer mug. You can use either a fishing rod or a curtain rod for #41. In associating the word for #42, "rain," I usually picture it raining the particular item that I want to recall. For "roll," you might use a breakfast roll.

Be sure that you know all the words from one through fifty, thoroughly, before reading any further. You should know the higher numbered words as well as the lower ones. A good way to practice this would be to remember a list of twenty-five objects, in and out of sequence, using the peg words from 26 to 50 to do it. Just number the paper from 26 to 50 instead of 1 to 25. After a day or so, if you feel ambitious, you can try a list of fifty items.

If you make sure that you use strong, ridiculous associations, you shouldn't have any trouble remembering all of them.

CHAPTER EIGHT
How to Train Your Observation

PARIS

IN

THE   THE

SPRING

X

Have you looked at the phrase in the box on top of this page? If you have, read it again to make sure that you know what it says. Now turn your head away from the book and repeat the phrase. Check it again to see if you have it right! Some of you will probably think it's a bit silly for me to ask you to keep making sure of a simple phrase like that, but it's important for you to be absolutely aware of what it says.

Now, if you've looked at it closely at least three times; what does it say!?

Does it say, "Paris in the spring?" I guess that most of you are nodding, "Yes, of course, that's what it says." Well, at the risk of being repetitious, check it again, will you?

Have you looked at it again? If you still think it reads, "Paris in the spring," your observation is not as keen as it should be. If you will check it once more, and this time point to each word as you read the phrase, you will be amazed to discover that it reads, "Paris in the the spring!" There is one "the" too many in the phrase!

Now you see why I asked you to look at it repeatedly. I wanted to prove that you could look at it any number of times and still not notice the extra "the." If you did notice it right away, don't feel too elated. I honestly didn't know whether this little stunt would be as effective when it appeared on top of a page of print, as when used by itself. You see, I've tested hundreds of people with this, and only one or two spotted it quickly.

Prove it to yourself by printing it just exactly as I have it, on a 3 x 5 index card, or on a piece of paper of similar size. The little x under the word, "spring" is just misdirection. It tends to draw the readers' eyes down to it, and their minds jump ahead on the phrase itself, because it is such a familiar one. Make one and try it with your friends. I've had people look at it as many as ten or fifteen times, and they were willing to bet anything that they knew just what it said. You can ask them to read out loud directly from the card, and they still say, "Paris in the spring!"

I am discussing this only to show that the sense of observation could stand a little sharpening, for most of us. As I said earlier in the book, although my systems actually force you to observe, if you apply them, your sense of observation can be strengthened with a little practice. If you're interested in helping your memory, don't sell observation short. You just can't remember anything that you do not observe to begin with. Educator Eustace H. Miles said about the same thing, "What one has never properly realized, one cannot properly be said to remember either." If you haven't observed, then you haven't realized, and what you haven't realized you can't forget, since you never really remembered it in the first place.

If you want to take the time, it is a simple matter to strengthen your sense of observation. You can start right now! You're probably reading this at home, sitting in a room that should be thoroughly familiar to you. Take a piece of paper, and without looking around you, list everything in the room. Don't leave out anything you can think of, and try to describe the entire room in detail. List every ashtray, every piece of furniture, pictures, doodads, etc. Now, look around the room and check your list. Notice all the things you did not put down on your list, or never really observed, although you have seen them countless times. Observe them now! Step out of the room and test yourself once more. Your list should be longer this time. You might try the same thing with other rooms in your home. If you keep at this, your observation will be keener no matter where you happen to be.

You've all heard, I'm sure, of the little experiment that a college professor tried with his students. He had a violent murder scene enacted in front of them, without letting them know that it was just an act. All of the students were told that they must act as witnesses, and were told to describe, in detail, what they saw. Of course, all the descriptions varied, even down to what the murderer looked like. All the students in the class had seen the same thing, but their observation and their memories were faulty.

This was proven again by popular entertainer, Steve Allen, on his TV show, Tonight. Some members of his cast suddenly burst in front of the cameras, enacting a wild, violent scene. Some shots were fired (blanks, of course), clothes were torn, and so on. The whole thing lasted perhaps a minute. Then Mr. Allen had three members of the audience come up to attempt to answer some pertinent questions about the scene. He asked how many shots were fired, who was shooting at whom, color of clothing, etc. All the answers varied and nobody seemed quite sure of anything. As a matter of fact, when Steve asked Skitch Henderson (who had fired the shots) how many shots he had fired —Skitch wasn't too sure himself.

Of course, you can't go around looking for violent scenes to observe, but you can practice in this way: think of someone whom you know very well. Try to picture his or her face; now see if you can describe the face on paper. List everything you can possibly remember. Go into detail — list color of hair and eyes, complexion, any or all outstanding features, whether or not they wear glasses, what type of glasses, type of nose, ears, eyes, mouth, forehead, approximate height and weight, hairline, on which side is the hair parted, is it parted at all, etc., etc. The next time you see this person, check yourself. Note the things you did not observe and those you observed incorrectly. Then try it again! You will improve rapidly.

A good way to practice this is in a subway or bus, or any public conveyance. Look at one person for a moment, close your eyes and try to mentally describe every detail of this person's face. Pretend that you are a witness at a criminal investigation, and your description is of utmost importance. Then look at the person again (don't stare, or you will be in a criminal investigation) and check yourself. You'll find your observation getting finer each time you try it.

One last suggestion as to a form of practice. Look at any shop window display. Try to observe everything in it (without using the Peg or Link systems). Then list all the items without looking at the display. You can wait until you're home to do this; then go back to check, when you can. Note the items you left out and try it again. When you think you've become proficient at it, try remembering the prices of the items also.

Each time you do any of these exercises, your sense of observation will become noticeably sharper. Although all this is not absolutely necessary for the acquiring of a trained memory, it is a simple matter to strengthen your observation. If you take the little time to practice, you will soon begin to observe better, automatically.

Before reading any further, I would suggest that you memorize the Peg Words from 51 to 75. I might also suggest that for the time being, you use the words that I give you. You could, of course, make up your own words, as long as they stay in the phonetic alphabet system. These would probably serve you just as well, but you might pick some words that would conflict with some of the words that you will eventually learn for other purposes. So, wait until you've finished the book, and then change words to your heart's content.

51. lot	57. log	63. chum	69. ship	75. coal
52. lion	58. lava	64. cherry	70. case	
53. loom	59. lip	65. jail	71. cot	
54. lure	60. cheese	66. choo-choo	72. coin	
55. lily	61. sheet	67. chalk	73. comb	
56. leech	62. chain	68. chef	74. car	

For "lot," picture an empty lot. For "loom," you might find it easier to picture a spinning wheel. "Lure" is bait for fishing; you might picture a worm. For "chum," you can picture a particularly close friend; if you do, use the same friend each time. "Choo choo" is a train, of course. For "chef," picture a chef's hat. For "case," see a large wooden packing crate, or a suitcase.

CHAPTER NINE
It Pays to Remember Speeches, Articles, Scripts and Anecdotes

The confused and nervous speaker was introduced after dinner.
He approached the microphone and murmured haltingly:
"My f-f-friends, wh-when I arrived here this evening only God and
I knew what I was going to say to you.
And now, only God knows!"

I guess that one of the most embarrassing things that can happen to a person is to forget a speech while in front of his audience. Next to forgetting the speech, is the embarrassment of faltering along as if you're not sure of what you have to say. Actually, it seems to me that anyone who is asked to give a talk on any particular subject, must know that subject pretty well; otherwise why would he be asked to talk about it. No, speakers who falter or hesitate during their speeches do so, I think, because they have forgotten the next word or because they are fearful that they will forget the next word.

There, in my opinion, lies the problem. If a speech is memorized word for word, and then a word, here and there, is forgotten, it surely will not be delivered as it should be. Why should you have to grope for one particular word? If you can't think of it; why, use any other word that serves the same purpose. Isn't that much better than hemming and hawing until you remember the exact phrasing just the way you memorized it?

The people who realized this, felt that the next best thing would be to simply read the speech. This solves the problem of forgetting words, until you lose your place on the paper, and forget what you're talking about altogether. Besides, it seems to me that there is a subtle annoyance evident in an audience that is listening to someone reading a speech word for word. I know I feel that way; he might just as well have given me a printed copy of the speech to read at my own leisure.

So, the next step seems to be not to prepare at all. Well, not quite. Even if you are well versed in your subject, you may forget some of the facts you want to speak about. As in the case of the itinerant preacher who always complained that he made his best speeches on the way home. All that he had forgotten to tell his listeners came to mind then, and his horse usually got the best part of the speech.

I believe that the best way to prepare a speech is to lay it out thought for thought. Many of our better speakers do just that. They simply make a list of each idea or thought that they want to talk about, and use this list in lieu of notes. In this way, you can't forget words, since you haven't memorized any. You can hardly lose your place; one glance at your list will show you the next thought to put into words.

But, for those of you who would rather not rely on pieces of paper, the Link method can help you easily. If you wish to memorize your speech thought for thought, from the beginning to the end, you would be forming a sequence. That's why you would use the Link method of memory to memorize it.

I would suggest that you go about it something like this: first, write out or read the entire speech. When you're satisfied with it, read it over once or twice more to get the "gist" of it. Now, get yourself a piece of paper and start to list your KEY WORDS.

Read the first thought of the speech. This might be contained in one, two or more sentences; it doesn't matter. Now select one word or phrase from these sentences which you think will bring the entire thought to mind. That is not at all difficult. In every sentence or paragraph there must be one word or phrase which will remind you of the entire thought. That one word or phrase is your Key Word.

After you have found the Key Word for the first thought, find one for the next thought, and so on. When you're through with the whole speech, you'll have a list of Keys to remind you of each thing you want to say. Actually, if you were to keep this list in front of you as you made the speech, it would serve the purpose. But, if you've mastered the Link system, you know that it is just as easy to make a link of these Key Words, and then throw away the paper.

You might, for example, be giving a talk on your local school problems at a Parent-Teacher Association meeting. Your list of Key Words might look something like this: crowds, teachers, fire, furniture, subjects, playground, etc. In other words, you wish to start your speech with a reference to the crowded conditions in the class rooms. Then you want to talk about the teachers; perhaps about methods and salaries, etc. Now, you express your thoughts on fire drills and fire precautions, which leads you into your discussion on the state of the school's furniture; the desks, chairs, blackboards, equipment, and so on. Now, you would talk about your ideas on the subjects taught, and finally, the recreation (playground) facilities of the school.

You can see that if you make a link: crowd associated to teacher; teacher to fire; fire to furniture, etc., each thought would lead you to the next one, right through to the end of your speech!

At first, you may have to list, perhaps, two or three Key Words for some thoughts. List as many of them as you need, to remember the entire speech. As you use this idea, the amount of Keys necessary will be less and less. And, most important, the confidence you gain by knowing that you remember your talk, will show when you deliver it. Just keep in mind that you must take care of the thoughts; the words will take care of themselves!

If, for some reason or other, you wish to memorize a speech word for word, use the same method. You'll just have to go over it more often. Remember that all these Systems are aids to your true memory. "If you remember the main, the incidentals will fall into place." You actually never forget anything you've remembered, you just have to be reminded of it; the system in this book will do that for you. So, if you remember the main thoughts of your speech, the incidentals, the if's, ands and buts, will fall into place.

The same ideas are used to memorize any article you read, if you desire. First read the article, of course, to get the "gist" of it. Then pick out the Key Words for each thought; then make a link to remember them, and you've got it. With a bit of practice, you'll actually be able to do this as you read.

Many times while reading for enjoyment, I'll come across some piece of information that I'd like to remember. I simply make a conscious association of it, while I'm reading. This idea can, if used enough, speed up your reading considerably. I think that most people are slow readers because by the time they've reached the third paragraph, they've forgotten what was in the first; so they have to jump back.

There is no need to associate everything; just the points that you feel are necessary to remember. Perhaps, if you use my systems, you will fall into the first class of readers in American educator, William Lyon Phelps' two classes. He once said, "I divide all readers into two classes; those who read to remember and those who read to forget."

The same system of linking Key Words can be used for remembering lyrics and scripts. Of course, in this case it is usually necessary to memorize them word for word. You will have to go over them more often, but the Key Word idea will make the job that much easier for you. If you have trouble memorizing your cues in a play, why not associate the last word of the other actor's line to the first word of your line. Even if your cue tells you that you must perform an action, instead of speaking a line, you can still associate it. If the last word of the line prior to your action happens to be, say, "walk"; and the script calls for you to stoop down to pick up a cigarette butt, make a picture in your mind of yourself walking along and continually stooping to pick up cigarette butts. (In this way you will never walk on another actor's lines.)

I'll mention one other use of the Key Word idea, before leaving it entirely. How many times have you wanted to tell your friends some jokes or anecdotes that you recently heard, only to find that you've forgotten them completely? You can hear a whole batch of really funny stories one day, and have them all, or most of them, slip your mind the next. Well, according to Irvin S. Cobb, "A good storyteller is a person who has a good memory and hopes other people haven't."

Your memory for stories and anecdotes will improve immediately if you use the Key Word system. Just take one word from the story, a word from the punch line is usually best, that will bring the entire joke to mind. When you get your Key Words, you can either link them to each to remember all the stories in sequence, or use the Peg system to remember them by number.

Perhaps you've heard the gag about the Flying Saucer that landed in America. Out stepped a creature from outer space, brushed himself off with one of his six arms, looked around with the one large eye in the center of his forehead, and kept his antennae alert for any sounds.

After exploring a bit, he finally approached a gas station, walked over to the gasoline pump, saluted, and demanded, "Take me to your President!"

Well, if you hadn't heard this before, and wanted to remember it with perhaps ten or twelve other stories, you could use either flying saucer, creature from outer space or, gasoline pump as your Key Word for this story. Any one of these would surely bring the entire story to mind, if you liked it in the first place.

Although many of you will find some practical use for it, one of the memory stunts I sometimes use in my shows is the "magazine test." This usually causes a bit of comment because it seems to be the most amazing of memory feats. Actually it is basic and simple.

What happens is this: — the audience is given some copies of a current magazine. (I usually use Tempo Magazine, which is published by the Enterprise Magazine Management, Inc.) They are then asked to call any page number, and I immediately tell them the highlights of that particular page.

This is merely another use of the Peg system of memory. In some instances the Link method is used in conjunction with the Peg, as will be explained directly. To memorize the pages of any picture magazine, all you have to do is to associate the peg word that represents the page number to the highlight of that page.

For example:

If Page #1 has a picture of an airplane on it, you would make a ridiculous association between "tie" (1) and airplane.

Page #2 might be an advertisement for shoe polish. Associate "Noah" to shoe polish.

Page #3 has a picture of a horse on it. Associate "ma" to horse.

Page #4 might have a picture of a circus scene; just associate "rye" to circus.

Page #5 is an advertisement for a television set. Associate "law" to television set.

Page #6 is a book review. Associate "shoe" to book.

That's all there is to it. If you go over the magazine and your associations two or three times, you will know the highlights of every page. If a page has more than one picture on it, use the Link method to remember them. Assume that page #14 is a fashion page, and it has a picture of a hat, one of gloves and a third of a dress.

First associate "tire" (14) to the first picture, which is of a hat. Now, link hat to gloves, and then gloves to dress. When Page #14 is called, the peg word will remind you of hat; hat will tell you that the next picture is of gloves, and gloves will remind you of dress.

If you have seen my performance, you know that I also tell the audience on what part of the page the picture is located; whether it is on the lower or upper left part of the page, upper or lower right, or center, etc. Well, you can do this too, and without any extra effort.

As I've already mentioned, your normal or true memory does most of the work for you; these systems are just aids that make it easier. As you use my systems you'll find your true memory getting stronger. The best example of this is in memorizing a magazine. In order to make the associations in the first place, you must really see and observe the picture on the page. Because of this, when any page number is called, the peg word for that number acts as an aid to enable you to almost reproduce the entire page in your mind's eye. You will know on what part of the page the picture is located. You can only prove this to yourself by trying it.

The only thing you will not be able to do as yet, is to remember the names of any people pictured on the pages. This problem will be solved for you after you've read the chapters on remembering names and faces, and how to utilize substitute words or thoughts.

Before continuing, learn the last of the one hundred peg words.

76. cage	82. phone	88. fife	94. bear
77. coke	83. foam	89. fob	95. bell
78. cave	84. fur	90. bus	96. beach
79. cob	85. file	91. bat	97. book
80. fez	86. fish	92. bone	98. puff
81. fit	87. fog	93. bum	99. pipe
			100. thesis or disease

For "cob," picture corn on the cob. For "fit"' you can picture an epileptic fit, or a girdle (tight fit). For "file," you can use either a filing cabinet or a nail file. "Fob" is a watch fob. For "bat" picture a baseball bat. For "puff," picture a ladies' powder puff, and for "pipe" see a man's smoking pipe.

After learning these, you should be able to count from one to one hundred quickly, with your peg words only. The beauty of it is that you don't have to take time out to practice them. If you're traveling to work or doing anything that doesn't require thought — you can go over all the pegs in your mind. If you go over them just every once in a while, they'll soon be as familiar to you as the numbers from one to one hundred.

CHAPTER TEN
It Pays to Remember
Playing Cards

"Yes, my grandfather was a gambler, and he died at a very early age."
"Gosh, that's too bad. How did it happen? "He died of five Aces!"

Since I want you all to stay healthy, the memory feats in this lesson utilize a regular deck of cards; not with five, but with the usual four Aces. Truthfully, although this chapter is devoted entirely to remembering playing cards, I am stressing the demonstrations you can do with a deck of cards and your trained memory. The systems, however, can be applied to many card games. Please don't think that after you've mastered these you can always win at cards. Keep in mind that you can't beat a man at his own game. I will leave the applications of the systems up to you; I use them for demonstration purposes only.

The late Damon Runyon used the following in one of his stories: "Son," the old guy says, "no matter how far you travel, or how smart you get, always remember this: someday, somewhere, a guy is going to come to you and show you a nice brand new deck of cards on which the seal is never broken, and this guy is going to offer to bet you that the Jack of Spades will jump out of this deck and squirt cider in your ear."

"But, son," the old guy says, "do not bet him, for as sure as you do you are going to get an ear full of cider."

The memory stunts you will do with cards after studying these methods will seem almost as amazing to your friends. Aside from that, they are also wonderful memory exercises. I suggest that you read and learn the contents of this chapter whether or not you indulge in card playing.

Cards, of course, are difficult to picture, just as numbers were before you started reading this book. In order for you to be able to remember them, I'll show you how to make them mean something; something that you can picture in your mind. Some years ago I read an article in a popular magazine about a professor who was trying some sort of experiment. He was attempting to teach people how to memorize the order of a shuffled deck of cards. The article mentioned the fact that he had accomplished his goal. After six months of training, his students were able to look at a mixed deck for twenty minutes or more, and then call off the cards. I don't know the exact system that was used, but I do know that it had something to do with seeing the cards actually laid out in order, in the mind. I have nothing against this; it's just that it shouldn't take you more than a day or two at the most to learn my system. When you have mastered it, it won't take twenty minutes to memorize a shuffled deck of cards. It might take about ten minutes at first, and with time and practice, you'll cut it down to five minutes!

There are actually two things that you must know in order to remember cards. First, is a list of at least fifty-two peg words for the numbers 1 to 52; these you already know. You also have to know a peg word for every card in a deck of cards. These card peg words are not chosen at random. As with the number pegs, they are selected because they are easy to picture, and because they follow a definite system. Here it is, in a nutshell:

Barring a few exceptions which will be discussed later, every card peg word will begin with the initial letter of the card suit. i.e., all the words for the Spade suit will begin with the letter, "S"; all the words for the Diamond suit will begin with the letter, "D"; the Club suit, with "C," and the Heart suit with "H." Each word will end with a consonant sound; this sound will represent the numerical value of the card, according to our phonetic alphabet.

You can see then, that the word you use must represent only one particular card. The first letter will give you the suit, the last sound will give you the value. Let me give you some examples: — the peg word for the Two of Clubs must begin with the letter, "C," and must end with the N sound, which represents 2. Of course, there are many words that would fall into this category: cone, coin, can, cane, etc. I've selected the word, "can." "Can" will always represent the Two of Clubs! Which card would the word, "hog" stand for? Well, it could represent only one card. It begins with "H," therefore it's a Heart; it ends with the hard "g" sound, which represents #7 "hog" is the peg word for the Seven of Hearts. Can you think of a word for the Six of Diamonds? Well, it has to begin with a "D" and end with the J or sh sound—we'll use the word, "dash" to represent the Six of Diamonds.

Here are all fifty-two card peg words. Look them over carefully, and I assure you that you can know and retain them with no more than perhaps twenty minutes to a half hour of study. Look them over once, then read on for the explanation of the exceptions, and how to picture some of the words. Towards the end of this chapter I'll give you a method to enable you to learn these words thoroughly.

CLUBS	HEARTS	SPADES	DIAMONDS
AC - cat	AH - hat	AS - suit	AD - date
2C - can	2H - hone	2S - sun	2D - dune
3C - comb	3H - hem	3S - sum	3D - dam
4C - core	4H - hare	4S - sore	4D - door
5C - coal	5H - hail	5S - sail	5D - doll
6C - cash	6H - hash	6S - sash	6D - dash
7C - cock	7H - hog	7S - sock	7D - dock
8C - cuff	8H - hoof	8S - safe	8D - dye
9C - cap	9H - hub	9S - soap	9D - deb
10C - case	10H - how	10S - suds	10D - dose
JC - club	JH - heart	JS - spade	JD - diamond
QC - cream	QH - queen	QS - steam	QD - dream
KC - king	KH - hinge	KS - sing	KD - drink

The exact system for forming the card pegs has been used for the Aces to Tens only. The reason for this should be obvious to you. If we were to follow the same system for the court, or picture cards, each court card peg word would have to contain two consonant sounds aside from the first letter. This is so because the Jack represents #11, the Queen, #12 and the King, #13. It would be a bit difficult to find words that are easy to picture, and which would still fit into the system. So, for the four Jacks I simply use the name of the suit itself for the peg word; each of which is a word that is easily pictured. The King of Clubs and Queen of Hearts will always be represented by the words, "king" and "queen" respectively. For the remaining court cards I have chosen words that begin with the initial suit letter, and that rhyme as closely as possible to the sound of the card itself, i.e. King (Spades) – sing: Queen (Diamonds) – dream.

Don't let these exceptions throw you, they'll stick in your mind because of the fact that they are exceptions.

If you have looked at the list of card pegs, you have undoubtedly recognized some of them as being the same as your number words. This will not create any confusion since the duplications only occur with words over #52 in your pegs. Being that there are only fifty-two cards in a deck, the words will never conflict.

You are to do the same with the card words as you did with the number pegs. Select a certain mind picture for each word, and use that picture all the time. For the word, "core," you might picture the core of an apple. For, "cuff," picture a pair of trousers, or just the cuff of the trouser. For the King of Clubs, picture the item to be associated as sitting on a throne, being the "king." The same goes for the Queen of Hearts — be sure that in your pictures for "king" and "queen" you have something to distinguish one from the other. (Picturing "queen" in a long flowing gown, and the "king" in knee breeches would do it.) If you had to remember that the King of Clubs was the 19th card, you could picture a "tub" (19) sitting on a throne, wearing a crown, and being a "king." Another idea would be to see a king wearing a tub instead of a crown. Either picture is a good one.

For the word, "hoof," it's best to picture a horseshoe; for "hose" you can see either a garden hose, or ladies' hose; for "hinge," picture the associated item being hinged. If you wanted to remember that the Two of Spades was the 29th card, you might see a gigantic door "knob" (29) instead of the "sun" (2S) shining in the sky with a tremendous brilliance. For "sum," picture a sheet of paper covered with numbers; or, an adding machine. For the word, "sore," I usually picture the associated item with a large bandage, as if it had a wound or sore. "Sash" — picture a window sash. "Steam" — picture a radiator. For "sing," you can picture a sheet of music, or you can see the associated item singing. "Date" — picture the fruit, or a calendar. "Dash" — picture the associated item running the 100 yard dash. "Dive" — picture the item diving into a body of water. "Deb" — is the abbreviation of debutante. For "dose" it is best to picture a spoonful of medicine.

The few suggestions above, are just that — suggestions. You must decide which picture you will "see" for each card word, just as you did with the number words. After you've decided, use that picture only. Use any picture that the word brings to mind; but be sure that the mental picture for any card word does not conflict with the mental picture of any of your number pegs from 1 to 52.

You now have all you need to memorize a complete deck of cards. Since each card is represented by an object, you simply use the Peg system as if you were memorizing a list of fifty-two objects. If the first card is the Five of Spades, you might see a large tie (1) acting as a Sail on a boat; or, you're wearing a sailboat instead of a tie.

If the second card were the Eight of Diamonds, you could see Noah (2) diving into the water. Third card — Two of Spades — see your ma (3) in the sky instead of the sun. Fourth card — Queen of Diamonds — see a bottle of rye (4) sleeping and dreaming; or, you are dreaming of a bottle of rye. Fifth card — Three of Clubs — see a gigantic comb walking the beat like a cop (law-5), or a policeman is arresting a comb, and so on.

When you are demonstrating this for your friends, have the peg word for #1 in your mind before he starts calling the cards. As soon as you hear the first one, associate the card word for that particular card with the peg word, "tie." Then immediately get the peg word for #2 in your mind, etc. When you've memorized the entire deck in this fashion, call the cards off in order, from one to fifty-two! You can have your friend call any number and you tell him the card at that position, or, have him call any card and you tell him at which number it is in the deck.

Of course, you don't have to memorize the entire deck to impress your friends. If you wish to present a faster demonstration, you can remember half the deck. This is just as effective, because it is just about impossible for anyone with an untrained memory to remember twenty-six cards, in and out of order.

However, if it is a fast demonstration you want, the one that follows is the fastest, most impressive, and yet, the easiest of them all! This is called the "missing card" stunt. You have anyone remove, say, five or six cards from a complete deck, and have them put them in a pocket. Now, let your friend call the remaining cards to you at a fairly rapid pace. After he has called all of them, you tell him the names of the five or six missing cards!!

I told you that this was easy to accomplish, and it is. Here is all you have to do: as soon as a card is called, transpose it to the representative card peg word, and then mutilate that object in some way! That's it! Let me explain. Assume that the Four of Hearts is called — just "see" a picture of a hare with no ears. If the Five of Diamonds is called, see a doll with an arm or leg missing. If you hear the King of Diamonds, see a spilled drink. That's all you have to do. Don't linger over your associations, just see the picture for the merest fraction of a second, and you're ready for the next card.

This can be done quickly because you are cutting out one mental calisthenic, so to speak. You're not using your number pegs at all. Of course, the speed with which the cards can be called is just a matter of practice. I can assure you that after a while, you will practically "see" the picture in your mind, before your friend is through naming the card!

Now — after all the cards have been called, go over the words for the cards in your mind. The best way to do this, is to go from Ace to King of one suit at a time. When you come to an object that is not mutilated or broken in any way, that must be one of the missing cards! For example, you start down your list of words for the Club cards: cat — you had pictured the cat without a tail. Can — you had seen a tin can that was crushed. Comb — you had pictured a comb with all its teeth missing or broken. Core — you do not recall anything wrong with the core, therefore, the Four of Clubs is one of the missing cards. The unmutilated words will stand out in your mind like a sore thumb as soon as you come to them. You need only try it once, to be convinced.

I suggest that you always use the same suit order when going over your card words mentally. It doesn't matter which order you use, as long as you can remember it easily. I use Clubs, Hearts, Spades and Diamonds because it's easy to remember. Just think of the word, CHaSeD. If you wanted to use Hearts, Spades, Diamonds and Clubs order, you could remember that by thinking of the phrase — HiS DeCk.

Incidentally, if you wanted to demonstrate your Bridge playing technique, you could do the missing card stunt with thirteen missing cards. The amount of cards taken from the deck before the deck is called to you doesn't make any difference. You could even have half the deck called, and then name all the cards in the other half!

After my own performances, I think that the thing my audiences talk about the most, except perhaps names and faces, are the card demonstrations that I do. They are very impressive to most people, whether or not they play cards.

I'm sure that most of you have read this far without actually learning the card words. Now that you see the things you can do with them, I hope you will learn them. By the way, do any of you see how you can apply the missing card idea to games like Gin Rummy, Bridge, Pinochle, Casino, or for that matter, to any game where it is to your advantage to know which cards have or haven't been played? I will leave that to you.

In a later chapter, you will find some more stunts and ideas with cards. However, one more thought before I close this chapter — if you wanted to remember a deck of cards in order only, you could do it quickly by using the Link method alone! You would simply link the card pegs to each other as they were called. Of course, you wouldn't know them out of sequence with this method.

I keep telling you to have the cards called off to you; but it's just as good to look at the cards to remember them. It just adds a little to the effect upon your spectators, if you do not look at them.

After going over the card words mentally, a few times, you can use a deck of cards to help you practice. Shuffle the deck, turn the cards face up, one at a time, calling out or thinking of the peg word for each one. When you can go through the entire deck at a fairly brisk pace without hesitating, then you know your card words.

And when you do, would you try your new found ability on test #4 in Chapter #3? I think you will be pleased at the difference in your scores.

CHAPTER ELEVEN
It Pays to Remember Long Digit Numbers

The memory is a treasurer to whom we must give funds,
if we are to draw the assistance we need.

—Rowe

Once, during my performance at the Concord Hotel in upstate New York, a "friend" in the audience asked me to memorize the number, 414,233,442,475,059,125. I did, of course, using my systems. The reason I mention this now, is because I had forgotten the little stunt I used as a child. I would boast to my friends of what a marvelous memory I had, and ask one of the boys (a stooge, of course) to call out a long digit number. He would then proceed to call out the subway stops of the New York Sixth Avenue Subway. We all knew these stops, and it would have been quite obvious if he had said, "4," then "14" and then "23," and so on. However, hearing the numbers in groups of three made them unrecognizable to the uninitiated.

In those days the Sixth Ave. express stopped at West 4th Street, then 14th Street, 23rd Street, 34th Street, 42nd Street, 47th and 50th Streets, 59th Street, 125th Street, etc. I would simply call off these stops and leave my pals exclaiming over my prodigious memory. This all proves that numbers can be remembered if they are made to represent or mean something to us. I have helped you to do just that by utilizing the peg system. Now, any number, whether it represents subway stops or not, can be made to mean something to you. And, in my personal opinion, that is the only way to memorize and retain a number. Yes, I've heard of the few rare cases of people who could memorize numbers instantly. I've heard of one person who could remember and retain long numbers as they were flashed before his eyes. (I wish I could do it!) These people don't know how they remember, they just do. Unfortunately, these are the few exceptions that strengthen my belief.

How would you go about memorizing the number 522641637527? Here is the way a memory expert of the 19th century did it. He told his students to separate the number into four sections of three digits each: 522 641 637 527.

Now, I quote:

"Bring the first and fourth groups into relation, and you see at once that the fourth group is larger than the first by only five. Bringing the second group into relation with the third section, we find they differ only by four. Again, the third group is larger than the fourth by 100 and by 10, that is 527 becomes 637, the seven alone remaining steadfast. Beginning with the fourth group and passing to the third, we have the fourth group with 110 added. The second group is the third group with only four added, and the first group is the fourth group with only five subtracted."

This system, without any modification is also taught by some modern memory experts. When I first heard of the above method of memorizing numbers, I felt that one would have to have a trained memory in the first place, just to remember the instructions! As far as retaining the number is concerned — well, I think it highly improbable that you would retain it for any length of time, if you memorized it at all. There were no ridiculous pictures or associations made to remind you of it. I believe, however, that I see the point that these memory experts were probably driving at. If you do try to follow their instructions, you must concentrate on the number. This, of course, is half the battle won. Any method that forces the student to be interested in, and to observe the number, and to concentrate on it, must meet with some success. It's just that it is too much like swatting a fly with a sledge hammer; the means are almost too burdensome to justify the end.

The Peg system of memorizing long digit numbers is actually a combination of the Peg and the Link methods. It forces you to concentrate on the number; it is easy to do, and the retentiveness is amazing! If you have learned the list of Peg words from 1 to 100 this should be a cinch for you. If you haven't learned them yet, this will make you want to do so. For the time being, you can make up the words as you go along. I'll use the same number as used above to explain the method.

First, let's break the number down into two digit numbers. 52 26 41 63 75 27. Now, each of these two digit numbers should represent or suggest a peg word to you:

52	26	41	63	75	27
lion	notch	rod	chum	coal	neck

All you have to do is to make a link of the six peg words! Or, any words you happen to be using. Picture a lion with a large notch in him.

Picture yourself whittling notches into a gigantic curtain rod. See yourself throwing your arms around the rod as if it were your chum, or, your
chum is being used for a curtain rod. Picture yourself embracing a large
piece of coal as if it were your chum; and, finally, see yourself or anyone
with his neck made of coal.

You should be able to make this link in about thirty seconds. After
you've made it, go over it once or twice in your mind to see if you've
memorized it. In repeating the number, all you do is transpose your peg
words back to numbers. You'll know the number now, forwards and
backwards! In actual practice, you should form your peg words and link
them as you move your eyes from left to right across the number.

There you have it! You merely linked six objects to memorize twelve
digits, and you will retain them for as long as you desire. If you have
tried this while I explained it, and if you remember the number, you
should feel proud of yourself. I say this because, according to some of our
intelligence quotient tests, the adult should remember a six digit number
forwards and backwards, after hearing or seeing it once. The superior
adult should do the same with an eight digit number. You've just
accomplished it with a twelve digit number, and there is no limit to the
retentiveness.

Don't let anyone talk you out of it, either, by telling you "no fair"
because you used a "system." Those that do say this, are surely envious
of you because they can't do it, system or not. There are always those that
scream, "It's unnatural to remember with a system; you have to do it by
normal memory." Well, who's to say that this method is unnatural? It is
surely more natural to remember than to forget. And, by using any of my
systems you're simply aiding your true memory! As I explained earlier,
anything that anyone remembers must be associated to something they
already know and remember. People do it all the time, sometimes
consciously, sometimes without realizing it; all we are doing is
systemizing it. There's a "method" to our madness! Those that say
memory systems are unnatural, really mean, I think, that they don't
know about them, or how to use them.

Now that I've defended your recently acquired facility to remember,
let's go a step further. If you've grasped the idea, which I'm sure you
have, why not use your imagination and make it even easier. If you like,
you can link only four words in order to memorize a twelve digit
number. Just make up words to fit three of the digits at a time, and link
those. For example, you could picture a bolt of linen (522) riding a
chariot (641) which is dragging a shoemaker (637). The last consonant
sound is disregarded since you know that the word represents only three

digits) who is very lanky (527).

Here is another example:

<table>
<tr><td>**994**</td><td>**614**</td><td>**757**</td><td>**954**</td></tr>
<tr><td>**paper**</td><td>**ashtray**</td><td>**clock**</td><td>**bowler**</td></tr>
</table>

If a long digit number that you wish to remember falls into line for words that fit four digits at a time, why not use them! In that way you can sometimes memorize and retain a twenty digit number, by linking only five words:

42109483521461279071

Doesn't that number look formidable? But look at it now:

<table>
<tr><td>**4210**</td><td>**9483**</td><td>**5214**</td><td>**6127**</td><td>**9071**</td></tr>
<tr><td>**rents**</td><td>**perfume**</td><td>**launder**</td><td>**cheating**</td><td>**basket**</td></tr>
</table>

Link rents to perfume, perfume to launder, launder to cheating, cheating to basket and you've memorized a twenty digit number!

If, in your particular business, you find it necessary to memorize long numbers very often, you'll soon use the first word that pops into your mind to fit either the first two, three or four digits. There is no rule that says you must use words to fit the same amount of digits in any long digit number. To memorize the number quickly, you use any words at all. Usually you will have time to think for a moment to find the best words for the number to be memorized. I have to leave this to your own imagination. However, until you've become proficient at it, I would suggest that you use the peg words for two digits at a time.

You can see now, the importance of knowing the ten basic sounds of the phonetic alphabet thoroughly. If you haven't learned them yet, reread the chapter on how to learn and practice them. If you are not sure of how to make ridiculous or illogical associations, reread that chapter. If you do know the sounds, the peg words and how to make your associations, try your knowledge on test #3 in Chapter #3, and see the progress you have made.

CHAPTER TWELVE
Some Pegs For Emergencies

The memory is always present; ready and anxious to help if only we would ask it to do so more often.

—Roger Broille

Many times when I've been challenged to prove that anyone can remember by using something similar to the Peg system, I would use a method which taught the skeptic to memorize ten miscellaneous objects forwards and backwards, and in and out of order, in about five minutes. What I did was to put ten small items, in a row, on a table; items like a ring, a watch, a cigarette, a match book, a comb, etc. I then told the person that these ten objects were to represent the numbers from one to ten.

Now I taught him to associate the item I called to the object on the table which represented the number called. In other words, if I called "typewriter" as #7, and the seventh item on the table was the ring; he would associate "typewriter" to ring. Later on, when I asked if he remembered #7, he would count to the seventh object, the ring, which would remind him of the typewriter.

This usually convinced the skeptic that he could remember better than he thought he could, but he always wanted to know if he'd have to carry those ten items with him. Of course, if he memorized those ten things he would have had a list of ten pegs to which to associate any other ten objects. But, it is a bit difficult to memorize ten completely unassociated items to use for a peg list; and, in this case, would hardly be worth the trouble.

However, as I mention elsewhere in the book, it was Simonides who first used the rooms of his house, and the furniture in the rooms as a peg list. And, this idea will work just as well today, except that it is a bit limited. Also, there is too much sameness in pieces of furniture to make a useful list. There is the possibility of becoming confused, and, it would take time to know which number each piece represented.

There have been a great many ideas thought up on how to devise peg lists. I've heard of one man who used twenty-six women that he knew, whose names each began with a different letter of the alphabet. This gave him a list of twenty-six pegs. If he wanted to remember that, say, typewriter, was # 16, he would associate typewriter to Pauline. This will work; but again — too much sameness; each peg must create a distinctly different picture in your mind if it is to work properly.

There are some ideas besides the phonetic alphabet which can be used just as well, except that they are limited in length. For instance, I have had occasion to need a few short peg lists to help me recall up to twenty or twenty-six items. Well, there are two methods that I've used quite often. The first is to use the twenty-six letters of the alphabet. All you have to do is to make up a word for each letter which sounds like the letter itself. Look at this list:

A—ape	N—hen
B—bean	O—eau (water)
C—sea	P—pea
D—dean	Q—cute
E—eel	R—hour (clock)
F—effort	S—ass
G—jean	T—tea
H—ache	U—ewe
I—eye	V—veal
J—jail	W—Waterloo
K—cake	X—eggs
L—el (elevated train)	Y—wine
M—ham	Z—zebra

If you go over this list once or twice, you'll have it. Decide on a picture for each one, and use that all the time. Now you have a list which will enable you to memorize up to twenty-six objects. For "B," I used "bean" only because "bee" would conflict with your basic peg word for #9. Of course, there are other words that can fit for some letters, and you can use any that you like. Just be sure that they do not conflict with your basic list of pegs. The words listed above are the ones that I use.

Incidentally, if you made a link from zebra to ape, you would be able to recite the alphabet backwards, which is quite a feat in itself. If you want to, you can associate each letter word to your regular peg word for that particular number. In this way you would know the numerical position of each letter immediately: ape to "tie"; bean to "Noah"; sea to "ma," and dean to "rye," etc.

Another idea I use is to make a list of nouns, each of which look like the number they represent. You can do this with many numbers, and for those that you can't, you can make up any picture to remind you of it. For

#1, you might picture a pencil, because a pencil standing upright looks like the numeral one. For #2, you can picture a swan; a swan on a lake is shaped something like the numeral two. I usually picture a three leaf clover for #3. A table or chair, or anything with four legs can represent #4. For #5 you can see a five pointed star. A yo-yo on a string, with a little stretch of the imagination, looks like a numeral six.

A golf club held upside down is similar in shape to #7. For #8, you could picture an hourglass. For #9, I use a tape measure. I mean the tape measures that are made of metal and unroll from a round container. If you pull the tape out about six inches, the thing looks like a numeral nine. A bat and ball pictured side by side can represent #10; the bat is the digit 1, and the ball is the zero. I picture spaghetti for #11; my original picture was of two pieces of raw spaghetti lying side by side, which looked like #11. For #12, you can think of 12:00 o'clock and picture a clock.

You can use either a black cat or walking under a ladder for #13. My original picture for #14, was a straight running river or stream to represent the 1, and a farm that looked like the numeral four from the air. If you can create this picture in your mind, looking from an airplane and seeing this farm adjacent to the river, they would look like the #14. You can then use either farm or river, or both, to represent the number.

I pictured myself stepping into an elevator and saying, "Fifteenth floor, please," for #15. I now use elevator to represent the number. For #16, I pictured a road sign that said, "Route 16."

I have used this list for years, to help me memorize sixteen objects. There is no reason for you to stop at sixteen. You can use the same idea to bring the list up to twenty, or higher if you like. No thought or picture is too far fetched, if it suggests a certain number to you, then it will serve the purpose. Just get your imagination working. Anyway, here is the list as I've used it, up to # 16:

1 — pencil	9 — tape measure
2 — swan	10 — bat and/or ball
3 — clover	11 — spaghetti
4 — table	12 — clock
5 — star	13 — black cat (or ladder)
6 — yo-yo	14 — farm (or river)
7 — golf club	15 — elevator
8 — hourglass	16 — sign

There are other ideas which I could list; but I won't. If you need any more lists, you can use your imagination to help you form them. I'm sure you realize that the phonetic alphabet, and the letter or number equivalent method taught in this book, is far superior to any of the methods mentioned in this chapter. Your basic list of peg words can be brought up to a thousand, or over, if you wanted to, and the beauty of it is that as soon as you heard one of them, the sounds in the word would tell you immediately which number it represented. The phonetic alphabet makes it possible for peg words to be at your fingertips for any number; you don't have to make them up and remember them in advance, either, you can make them up when, or as, you need them.

The two ideas I've suggested to you here, however, can be useful if you need a short list quickly, or, if you want to use one of them in conjunction with your basic peg words. The latter idea can be used for some amazing memory feats, as you will learn in a later chapter.

Before closing this chapter, I just want to remind you again that none of these ideas are too far fetched. Any one of them will work for you if you make up your mind to use them. The two listed here, are as far as I'm concerned, the best of the lot; but any list of words that you happen to know in sequence, can serve as a peg list. I know one man who uses his own body for this purpose. From head down, he uses hair, forehead, eyes, nose, mouth, chin, neck, chest, all the way down to toe, for his peg list So, if an object to be remembered were #3, he would associate it to "eyes," if it were #7, he would associate it to "neck," and so on.

Some of the old time memory experts who performed in vaudeville would use the theater itself to help them do the stunt of memorizing objects called by the audience. They might have used the stage for #1, the footlights for #2, the orchestra for #3, divans for #4, balcony for #5, etc. Anything in the theater was utilized; the draperies, chandeliers, exit signs, men's room, ladies' room, etc.

And, of course, one of the most common, and most limited, peg lists is the one which uses words that sound like the numbers. Such as, gun for one, shoe for two, tree for three, door for four, and so on, up to hen for ten, which is about as far as you can go.

Well, I guess my main reason for telling you about all these other ideas for word lists, was to show off the effectiveness of the phonetic alphabet. As far as I know, there is no other idea that approaches it for its unlimited qualities and for its versatility.

In the next chapter you will see how either one of the lists you learned here, or parts of them, can be used in conjunction with the phonetic alphabet.

CHAPTER THIRTEEN
It Pays to Remember Dates

"What day is today?"
"Gosh, you've got me, I don't know what day it is."
"Well, why don't you look at that newspaper
you have in your pocket - that should tell us."
"Oh, no, that won't do us any good, it's yesterday's paper!"

Although all of us can tell what day today is by looking at yesterday's paper, how many of you can tell quickly, or slowly, for that matter, the day of the week that any date this year will fall on? Not many, I'm sure. If you feel that having this information at your fingertips, with hardly any effort, is worthwhile, then read on. There are, of course, many different methods for calculating the day of the week for any given date, not the least of which is counting on your fingers.

Some of the Systems are so involved that it seems much simpler to take the time to find a calendar, and get your information there. On the other hand, there are ways of actually knowing the day of the week for any date in the twentieth century! This doesn't seem to me to have any particular practical value; although it may have for some of you. Used as a memory stunt however, it is quite impressive.

I intend to teach you how to do that in this chapter, but first, for practical use, I have come across a very simple way to find the day of the week for any date of the current year. This idea is so easy, that most of you will wonder why you didn't think of it yourselves. This is it: —

All you have to do is memorize this twelve digit number, 633752741631, the way you've been taught to do. You can break the digits down into your peg words and link them, or make up words to take in more than two digits at a time. For example, you can remember this number by making a link of these four words, chum, mug, linger and dishmat. Once you have memorized the number, you can tell the day of the week for any date of the year, say, 1957! Each digit in the number represents the first Sunday of the month for one of the twelve months! The first Sunday in January falls on the 6th of January; the first Sunday in February falls on the 3rd of February; the first Sunday in March is the 3rd of March; April 7th is the first Sunday in April; May 5th is the first Sunday in May, and so on.

All right, so now you know the day of the month upon which the first Sunday falls for each month. How can this help you to know the day of the week for any date of the current year? Simple! You wish to know the day of the week for August 22nd, 1957 and you know that the first Sunday of August is the 4th of the month. Knowing this, your calculations are elementary. If the 4th is a Sunday, then the next Sunday is the 11th and the following Sunday, the 18th. The 18th is a Sunday, so the 19th is Monday, the 20th is Tuesday, the 21st is Wednesday, and, of course, August 22nd is a Thursday!

Do you want to know the day of the week on which Christmas fell in 1957? Well, thanks to the twelve digit number, you know that the first Sunday of December was the 1st of the month. Therefore the 8th must be a Sunday, the 15th was a Sunday, and the 22nd was a Sunday. If the 22nd of December was a Sunday, then the 23rd was Monday, the 24th was Tuesday, and the 25th of December (Christmas) must have fallen on Wednesday!

Here is the way my mind actually works when I want the day of the week for any date in 1957: I use the words, chum, mug, linger and dishmat to remember the twelve digits. I know that the word, "chum," gives me the first Sunday of the month for January and February. The word, "mug" tells me the first Sunday of March and April. "Linger" gives me the same information for May, June, July and August, and I know that "dishmat" represents September, October, November and December.

Now, if I wanted to know the day of the week for, say, November 9, 1957—I immediately think of "dishmat." I know that the third consonant sound of this word represents the first Sunday of November. The first Sunday is the 3rd, therefore the 10th of November is also a Sunday; and, if the 10th is a Sunday, the 9th of November must be a Saturday.

If, in your particular business, it would be a help if you knew the day of the week for the present year and the following year. Get a hold of next year's calendar, and memorize the twelve digits for that year by making up a link of four or five words. You could do this for as many years as you want to, but I don't believe it's practical for more than two years. However, the memory feat that follows is also a practical method of knowing the day of the week for any date in the twentieth century.

As a stunt, you would tell your friends that you've memorized all the calendars of the twentieth century. To prove it, ask them to call out any date; a date of which they themselves know the day of the week. This is necessary, of course, so that they can check your answer. Most people remember the day of the week of their weddings, graduations or other important anniversaries. When the date is called, you almost immediately tell them the day of the week for that particular date!

To accomplish this you must know two things besides the month, day and year: a certain number for the year, which I will refer to as the "year key," and a certain number for the month, which I'll call the "month key."

Perhaps, if I explained the method and procedure before going into the technicalities, you would find it easier to understand. This is it: let's assume that you want to know the day of the week for March 27, 1913. Let's also assume that you know the "year key" for 1913 is 2, and that the "month key" for March is 4. You would add these two keys, arriving at #6. Now you add this number (6) to the day, in this particular case, #27 (March 27). This gives you a total of 33. The last step is to remove all the sevens from your total. Seven goes into 33 four times, (4 x 7 = 28); remove 28 from 33, which gives you a final total of 5. That is your day — the fifth day of the week is Thursday! For this stunt we must consider Sunday as the first day, Monday the second day, Tuesday the third day, Wednesday the fourth day, Thursday the fifth day, Friday the sixth day and Saturday the seventh day.

March 27, 1913 did fall on a Thursday! Please don't consider this complicated; it isn't. Actually you will never have to add any numbers higher than seven. The keys for the years and the months are all either 0, 1, 2, 3, 4, 5, or 6. Sevens are always removed as soon as possible. If you had to add a "year key" of 5 to a "month key" of 6, you would arrive at 11; but immediately remove one seven, which leaves you with 4. The 4 is all you would have to keep working with. If the day that is given you is higher than seven, you remove all the sevens, i.e., the date is the 16th; remove the two sevens (2 x 7 = 14) and use the remainder of 2 only. In the above example, you would simply add 4 to 2, which tells you that the day of the week is the sixth, or Friday.

I will give you a few more actual examples, after I acquaint you with the year and month keys, and my methods for remembering them. These are the month keys, which will always remain the same: —

January—1	July—0
February—4	August—3
March—4	September—6
April—0	October—1
May—2	November—4
June— 5	December—6

I'll give you a memory aid for remembering each of these keys. The method that follows is one way, and I'll explain one other. You can use whichever you like best, or one which you think of yourself.

January is the first month of the year; therefore it is easy to recall that the key for January is 1.

February is a cold month, it usually has plenty of snow; both the words, "cold" and "snow" have four letters, so the key for February is 4.

In **March** the wind blows. Both "wind" and "blow" have four letters, which will help you to remember that the key for March is 4.

April is known for its showers. "Showers" has seven letters, so all the sevens must be removed; (7 - 7 = 0) so we know that the key for April is zero.

The key for **May** is 2. Do you recall the game we used to play when we were children, the one in which we would say, "May I take 2 giant steps?" Well, if you remember that phrase, you will recall that the key for May is 2. Or, you might think of "May Day" or "May Pole," consisting of two words.

"**June** Bride" is a common phrase; "bride" has five letters, so you will remember that the key for June is #5.

For **July**, you could use this for a memory aid: we all know that July 4th is a celebration of the signing of the Declaration of Independence in 1776. Take the two sevens from the year 1776, leaving 1 and 6. One and six are seven; remove this seven, leaving 0. Or, July 4th is usually associated with fire crackers; the word "cracker" has seven letters; remove the seven, leaving 0. The key for July is zero.

August is a hot month. The word "hot" has three letters; the key for August is 3.

September is the month during which the leaves start turning brown. "Leaves" has six letters; the key for September is 6.

Octo means eight, remove the seven (8 - 7 = 1) leaving one. The key for October is 1.

November is the election month. We vote in November; the word, "vote" has four letters, so the key for November is 4. Or, November is the 11th month of the year, remove seven, leaving four.

Finally, the big holiday in **December** is Christmas. Christmas is the anniversary of the birth of Christ. "Christ" has six letters, so we know that 6 is the key for December.

Although some of the above may seem a bit far fetched, they will help you remember the keys. Another way would be to form a substitute word for each month, (the system of substitute words will be explained thoroughly in the following chapter) and associate that to the peg word

that represents its key number. For zero, use any word that contains the s or z sound only; "zoo" is good because it is easy to picture.
Here are some suggested substitute words for all twelve months:

January-Jan.-Abbreviation of "janitor." Associate janitor to "tie."
February-Fed.-Federal man. Fib or fob. Associate these to "rye."
March-See the object associated (rye) marching.
April - Ape.
May - Use a person whose name is May, or picture a May Pole.
June - Picture a June Bride.
July - Jewel.
August - Gust of wind. Picture "ma" being blown by a gust of wind.
September - Scepter or sipped.
October - Octopus or oboe.
November - Ember, new member.
December - Decimal, deceased or descend.

   You can use either one of the two methods, or one of your own.
Now we come to the year keys. I'll give you all the keys for the years 1900 to 1987. All the years that have 1 for a key, are listed together; the years with 2, are listed together, and so on.
   I would suggest the use of another peg list to help you remember these keys. All you actually need is six words, representing the numbers 1 to 6, which will not conflict with your basic peg list. You can use any of the lists that I suggested in the previous chapter (the alphabet idea: ape, bean, sea, etc., or, pencil, swan, clover, table, star, yo-yo, etc.). For zero, use "zoo" or "sue."
   Since every year listed begins with 19, you don't have to try to remember that. Just associate the peg word for the last two digits of the year, to the word that you are using to represent the key numbers.
   For instance, the key for 1941 is 2. Associate "rod" (41) to either "swan"

1900	1901	1902	1903
1906	1907	1913	1908
1917	1912	1919	1914
1923	1918	1924	1925
1928	1929	1930	1931
1934	1935	1941	1936
1945-0	1940-1	1947-2	1942-3
1951	1946	1952	1953
1956	1957	1958	1959
1962	1963	1969	1964
1973	1968	1975	1970
1979	1974	1980	1976
1984	1985	1986	1981
			1987

1909	1904	1905
1915	1910	1911
1920	1921	1916
1926	1927	1922
1937	1932	1933
1943-4	1938-5	1939-6
1948	1949	1944
1954	1955	1950
1965	1960	1961
1971	1966	1967
1982	1977	1972
	1983	1978

or "bean," according to the list you're using. Make your associations for all of them. Before you know it, you'll have memorized them all.

You now have all the information necessary to do the calendar stunt, except for one thing. If it is a leap year and the date you are interested in is for either January or February, then the day of the week will be one day earlier than what your calculations tell you. For example: if you wanted to find the day of the week for February 15th, 1944: the key for 1944 is 6. Add this to the key for February, which is 4, to get a total of 10. Remove the seven, leaving 3. Add the 3 to the day minus the sevens, (15th day minus 14) which is 3 plus one, giving you a final total of 4. Four would ordinarily represent Wednesday, but in this case, you know that it is actually one day earlier, or Tuesday.

Remember that you do this only for January and February of a leap year. You can tell if a year is a leap year by dividing four into the last two digits. If four goes in evenly, with no remainder, then it is a leap year. (1944-4 into 44 is 11, no remainder). The year 1900 is not a leap year. Two more examples of the system:

June 2, 1923— 0 plus 5 is 5   **January 29, 1937—** 4 plus 1 is 5
             5 plus 2 is 7   5 plus 29 is 34
             7 minus 7 is 0   34 minus 28 is 6
                 0 is Saturday.   6 is Friday.

See if you can find the day of the week for the following dates:—
September 9, 1906, January 18, 1916 (leap year), August 20, 1974, March 12, 1931 and December 25, 1921.
I don't intend to tell you that this system is a snap to learn to do quickly; it does take some time and study, but, as I'm sure most of you know, nothing worthwhile comes too easily.

By the way, if you like this idea better than the one at the beginning of this chapter, and would like to use it for practical purposes, you could remember the "year keys" of only the years you're interested in. That might be the previous year, the present year and the following year. With that, and your "monthkeys," you would be able to know the day of the week for any date within those three years.

CHAPTER FOURTEEN
It Pays to Remember Foreign Language, Vocabulary and Abstract Information

The more intelligible a thing is, the more easily it is retained in the memory, and contrariwise, the less intelligible it is, the more easily we forget it.

—*Benedict Spinoza*

You may not think that the above quote shows any particular brilliance on the part of Mr. Spinoza. You may feel, "Sure, anyone knows that if something is intelligible, or makes sense, it is easier to remember." Well, that's true, it is an obvious thought, but it took Mr. Spinoza to say it, or put it down on paper just that way, as far back as the 17th century.

I'm making a fuss about this particular quote because it tells you in one sentence what this entire book is about. Almost all the systems in the book are basically that, they help make unintelligible things intelligible. One example, of course, is the Peg system; numbers by themselves are usually unintelligible, but the use of the Peg system makes them mean something to you.

Perhaps the best example is in trying to memorize foreign language vocabulary. A word in a foreign language is nothing but a conglomeration of sounds to remember.

To make them easier to remember you will use the system of SUBSTITUTE WORDS. Substitute words or thoughts are used whenever you want to remember anything that is abstract, intangible or unintelligible; something that makes no sense to you, can't be pictured, yet must be remembered. Be sure you read this chapter carefully, because substitute words will also help you to remember names.

Making up a substitute word is simply this: upon coming across a word that means nothing to you, that is intangible and unintelligible, you merely find a word, phrase or thought that sounds as close to it as possible, and that is tangible and can be pictured in your mind's eye.

Any word you may have to remember, foreign language or otherwise, that is meaningless, can be made to mean something to you by utilizing a substitute word or thought. Years ago I was a tropical fish hobbyist for awhile, and I was trying to learn the technical names of the fish fins. Since

I couldn't picture their names at that time, I used substitute words to remember them.

For example: — The tail fin of a fish is called the caudal fin. In order to remember this, I made a picture of a fish with a long cord instead of a tail fin. The picture of a cord was enough to help me recall the word, "caudal." The fin on the back of the fish is known as the dorsal fin. The first thought that came to my mind when I heard, "dorsal," was Tommy Dorsey, (dorsal — Dorsey). I automatically associate Tommy Dorsey with a trombone. So, I simply made a picture in my mind of a man playing a trombone on the fish's back!

This may sound like a long procedure to you; it isn't. The association from "dorsal" to Tommy Dorsey to trombone to the actual forming of the picture is the work of the merest fraction of a second. The thing for you to keep in mind is that tile thought or picture that comes to you when you hear any intangible word, is the one to use. I used Dorsey for dorsal, but you, perhaps, would have thought of "door-sill," which would have served the purpose just as well.

The Spanish word for "bird" is "pajaro," (pronounced pa-kar-ro). Can you think of a substitute word for it? It's easy, because the word almost sounds like "parked car." Parked car, of course, is something that is tangible and which you can picture in your mind. So, why not make a ridiculous or illogical association, as you've already learned, between "parked car" and "bird"? You might "see" a parked car crammed full of birds, or a bird parking a car, etc.

The next time you try to recall the Spanish word for "bird," your ridiculous association will help you to recall that the word is "pajaro." The substitute word you select does not have to sound exactly like the foreign word you're trying to remember. For "pajaro," you might have used pa carrying eau (water), or, parks in a row, either of which would have also helped you to remember the word. As long as you have the main part of the word in your picture, the incidentals, the rest of the word, will fall into place by true memory.

This is strictly an individual thing; there are some substitute thoughts I use that I couldn't possibly explain in words, but they do help me recall the foreign word. The words I use may be great for me, but not for you; you must use the substitute thoughts that you think of.

I am explaining this so thoroughly because it is one of the most useful things you will learn in this book, and I want you to understand just what I'm talking about. To remember a foreign word and its English meaning, associate the English meaning to your substitute word for the foreign word.

Let me give you some concrete examples of the system, using a few simple Spanish and French words: —

Ventana means "window" in Spanish. You might picture a girl (one you know) whose name is Anna, throwing a vent through a closed window. If you wanted to remember the French word for window, which is "fenetre," you might picture a window eating a raw fan, or a fan eating a raw window. Fan-ate-raw--fenetre!

The Spanish word, hermano (pronounced air-mon-o) means "brother." Just picture your brother as an airman.

The Spanish word for "room" is cuarto (pronounced quart-o). Picture a room piled high with quarters.

Vasa means "glass" in Spanish. See yourself drinking from a vase instead of a glass.

The word for "bridge" in French, is pont. See yourself punting a football on or over a bridge.

Pluma means "pen" in Spanish. See yourself writing with a gigantic plume instead of a pen; or, you're writing on a plume with a pen.

The word meaning "father" in French, is pere. Associate father to pear and you'll always remember it.

The sample associations given above are those that I might use, it is always best to make up your own pictures.

Try this method with any foreign language vocabulary, and you'll be able to memorize the words better and faster, and with more retentiveness than you ever could before. Aside from languages, this system can be used for anything you may be studying which entails remembering words that have no meaning to you, at first. A medical student who has to memorize the names of the bones in the human body, may have some trouble with femur, coccyx, patella, fibula, sacrum, etc. But if these were made into substitute words or thoughts like this: — fee more-femur; rooster (cock) kicks or cock sics-coccyx; pay teller or pat Ella-patella; fib you lie-fibula; and, sack of rum-sacrum, then the student could link them to each other, or associate them to whatever it is they must be associated to.

A pharmaceutical student could picture someone pushing a large bell down over him while he throws pine trees from under it, to help him remember that atropine (I throw pine) comes from the belladonna (bell down) root or leaf.

I am actually making up these substitute words as I write; with a little thought you could find much better substitute words for them. You might want to picture a giver (donor) of a bell to remember belladonna, etc.

The point is that the substitute word or thought has meaning while the original word does not. Therefore you make it easier to remember by using the substitute word. You will get some more pointers and practice on this in the chapter on how to remember names.

So—I started this chapter with a quote by Benedict Spinoza, so may I be presumptuous enough to end it with a quote of my own. "Anything that is intangible, abstract or unintelligible can be remembered easily if a system is used whereby the unintelligible thing is made to be tangible, meaningful and intelligible."

CHAPTER FIFTEEN
It Pays To Remember Names and Faces

*Two men approached each other on the street with a look of recognition in
their eyes. One said to the other, "Now wait a minute, don't tell me, I know I
know you, but I'm not sure of where we met. Let me see if I can think of your
name. I've got it! We met in Miami Beach two years ago."*
"No, I've never been to Miami Beach."
*"Hold it' don't tell me. Oh, yes, it was on the boardwalk of
Atlantic City that we met."*
*"Sorry, I've never visited Atlantic City." "I've got it now!
Chicago in 1953!"*
"Nope, I was not in Chicago in 1953."
"Well, I know we've met, where do I know you from?"
"Idiot! I'm your brother!!"

"Oh, I know your face, but I just can't remember your name!"
Although I doubt if any of you are as bad as the fellow in the
anecdote, how often have you been embarrassed because you had to say
this? I'm sure it has happened to you many times. If I were to take a poll
as to why most people want to take my memory course, I think it would
show that at least 80% want to because they can't seem to be able to
remember names and faces.

Usually, of course, it is the name that has been forgotten, not the face.
The reason for this is quite simple. You see, most of us are what we call
"eye-minded." In other words, things that we see register upon our
brains with much more emphasis than what we hear. You always see the
face, but usually only hear the person's name. That's why most of us,
time after time, have to say, "I recognize your face, but I can't remember
your name."

Not only can this be embarrassing, but can sometimes hurt in
business, and ultimately cost you money. Some people try to avoid this
embarrassment by trying to trick people into giving their names before
they themselves realize that their name has been forgotten. This might

work occasionally, but not usually, and it still pays to remember the names. I'm sure you have all heard the old story about the man who met a business acquaintance whose name he couldn't recall. He tried to avoid embarrassment by pretending he knew the name, but wasn't sure of the spelling; so he asked, "How do you spell your name again?" The reply was, "The only way it can be spelled, J,O,N,E,S!" You see, this trick didn't work in this particular case.

Another sneaky way of pretending you didn't forget the name of someone you should have remembered, is this: merely ask the person what his name is. If he tells you his second name, you say, "Oh, I wouldn't forget that, it's your first name I meant." If the person tells you the first name first, you, of course, say that you knew that, but it was the second name you wanted. In this way, you get the person's full name, and it seems as if you only forgot one of the names. There is only one thing wrong with this little bit of hocus-pocus. If the person gives you his full name as soon as you ask for the name in the first place, you're out of luck.

Then there is the classic example of the fellow who always asked people whose name he had forgotten, whether they spelled it with an e or an i. This was fine, until he tried it with Mrs. Hill.

No, I'm afraid it still pays to remember the name, instead of resorting to trickery. Not only does it pay to remember it, but believe me, it's easier than resorting to subterfuge because it takes much less effort.

People have tried various Systems and methods to help their memory for names. Some use the alphabet, or first initial method. That is to say, they make a tremendous effort to retain only the initial of the person's name. This is more wasted effort, since they usually forget the initial anyway; and even if they remember the initial, how can that tell them the person's name? If you address Mr. Adler as Mr. Armanjian, or vice versa, he isn't going to be pleased just because the name you called him has the same first letter as his own.

Although writing things down on paper can sometimes be helpful in remembering, it cannot be depended upon as far as memorizing names is concerned. In conjunction with a good system of association, perhaps, as I will explain later, but not by itself. If you were able to draw an exact replica of the person's face, this would be better, since you would then know which name belongs to which face. You'd have your two tangibles with which to make some sort of ridiculous association. But, unfortunately, most of us can't draw that well, and if we could, it wouldn't be that helpful that it would make up for the time it would take.

Some memory teachers will tell their students to keep a memory book and write down the name of every person they want to remember. As I've said, this might help a little if used together with a good system of association, but not otherwise. It might help some, of course, if you wanted to run down the list of names each time you meet a person, with the hope that the name will come to mind when you see it written in your book. If it did, I don't think you would feed the ego of the person whose name you "fished" out of a book instead of out of your memory.

It isn't necessary, I'm sure, for me to tell you how important it is to remember names and faces. Yet, here is one of the most common memory complaints of modern times: "I just can't remember names!" Our way of life today makes it almost unavoidable to meet many new people every day. You meet people continually, people you want to remember, and people that you do not think are important enough to bother remembering until you meet them again. Then when it is too late, you realize that you should have tried to remember.

Would it not be an asset for any salesman to remember the names of his customers? Or for a doctor to remember the names of his patients; a lawyer, his clients, etc.? Of course, it would. Everybody wants to be able to remember names and faces, but many times an important sale is nipped in the bud, money is lost, someone is caused to be embarrassed or a reputation is stained, because someone forgot an important person's name. Yet, even as far back as early Greek and Roman civilization, Cicero remembered the names of thousands of his villagers and soldiers, by using a memory system.

There is a young lady that I've heard of, who is the hat check girl in a popular New York night club. She has gained a reputation, because she never issues a check for your hat or coat. She simply remembers which hat or which coat belongs to whom. It is said that she never yet has given anyone the wrong article. This may not seem so important to you, since it would be just as easy to do it with hat or coat checks, the way all checkroom attendants do it. But this young lady has made herself into sort of an attraction at this night club, and her sizable tips prove it. Of course, this is not exactly remembering names and faces, since she doesn't remember the name, but it is similar enough. She must associate the hat or coat, or both, to the person's face.

I've been told that the bellboy of a large hotel down south has gained a similar reputation. Whenever someone checks into the hotel that has been there even once before, this bellboy addresses them by name. The last I heard, he is well on his way to saving enough money out of his tips to buy the hotel.

This should prove to you, if proof were necessary, that people love to be remembered, they even pay for it. This particular hat check girl and bellboy surely made more money than the others who worked at the same jobs.

A person's name is his most prized possession, and there is nothing more pleasing to him than hearing his own name or having it remembered by others.

Some of my students and myself have remembered as many as three hundred names and faces at one meeting; and you can do it too!

Before getting into the actual systems and methods for remembering names and faces, I'd like to show you how you can improve your memory for them by at least 25% to 50% without the Systems! Read the next few paragraphs very carefully.

The main reason that most people forget a name is because they never remembered it in the first place! I'll take that a step further, and say that they never even heard the name in the first place. How often have you been introduced to someone new, something like this: "Mr. Reader, meet Mr. Stra-ph-is?" All you hear is a mumbled sound instead of the name. Possibly because the person who is doing the introducing doesn't remember the name himself. So, he resorts to double-talk. You, on the other hand, probably feel that you will never meet this person again, so, you say, "Nice to meet you," and you never bother to get the name right. You may even spend some time talking to the person and finally say good-bye, and still not hear the name properly.

The only thought most people will give to this situation, is a self-questioning, "Gosh, what was that person's name. That nice gentleman I spoke to the other day?" When no answer is forthcoming, the entire thing is shrugged off with an, "Oh, well," and that's that!

This is how people find themselves talking to others, and addressing them as, Buddy, Old Pal, Fella, Sweetheart, or Honey — anything you can think of to keep from finding it necessary to use the person's name, while you squirm with embarrassment because you don't know the name. Oliver Herford put it this way when he gave his definition of the word, "darling" — "The popular form of address in speaking to a person of the opposite sex whose name you cannot at the moment recall."

Here, then, is your first rule for remembering names: Be Sure You Hear The Name In The First Place! As I said before, you see the face, so the odds are you will recognize it when you see it again. You can only hear the name, so get it right. I have yet to hear anyone complain, "I know your name, but I can't seem to remember your face." It is always the name that creates the problem. So, to repeat, Be Sure You Hear The Name!

Don't let the fellow that's doing the introducing get away with double-talk. If you haven't heard the name, if you're not absolutely sure of it, ask him to repeat it. Sometimes, even after hearing a name, you may not be sure of the pronunciation; if that's the case, ask the person to spell it for you. Or, try to spell it yourself; he'll correct you if you spell it incorrectly, and, he'll be flattered by your interest in his name.

Incidentally, if you make a habit of trying to spell the name of every new person you meet, you'll soon become accustomed to the spelling of most any kind of name. You'll be surprised as to how many of them you'll spell correctly. Eventually, you will be able to recognize how certain sounds are spelled for certain nationalities. You'll learn that the Italian language has no letter, "J," so the j sound in an Italian name is always spelled with a "g." The J or the soft G sound, and sometimes, the "sh" sound in a Polish name is usually spelled, "cz," while the sound, "eye" is sometimes spelled with the letters, "aj." The ch or tz sound in an Italian name is sometimes spelled with a double "c"; the sh sound in a German name, particularly at the beginning of the name, is usually spelled, "sch," etc. Of course, it doesn't always work. I recently came across a name that sounded like, "Burke," but was spelled, "Bourque." However, many of the people who have seen my performance will vouch for the fact that I spell their names correctly almost 85% of the time. Or, closely enough to impress them, anyway. So, you see, it can be done. I mention this because spelling a person's name correctly or almost correctly, will impress them almost as much as remembering it.

If after making sure of the spelling, you realize that the name is the same or similar to that of a friend or relative of yours, mention that fact. This all serves to impress the name on your mind. If it is an odd name, one that you have never heard before, say so. Don't feel shy, or as if you're imposing when you do these things, because everybody is flattered when you make a fuss over their names. Just as they would be if you showed an interest in any of their prized possessions, or in any of their particular interests. This, I suppose, can be put down to human nature.

While talking to the person, repeat his name as often as you can in the course of the conversation. Don't keep jabbering it like an idiot, of course, just use it whenever you feel it is apropos and necessary. I am not mentioning this to be facetious. I've read some "memory experts" instructions on this point, and they have given sample conversations: — "Why, yes, Mr. Greenpepper, I do sail to Europe every season, Mr. Greenpepper. And, oh, Mr. Greenpepper, don't you just adore Rome, Mr. Greenpepper? Mr. Greenpepper, tell me this, etc., etc.," and so on into the night. This will not impress Mr. Greenpepper, it will scare him out of his wits.

No. Just use it, as I said, wherever and whenever you feel it fits. Do use the name when you say good-bye or good night. Don't just say something about hoping to meet again, say, "Good-bye Mr. Johnson, I hope we'll meet again soon, etc." All this will etch the name more firmly and definitely into your mind.

The only effort involved here, as usual, is just in doing this the first few times. After that it will become habit and you won't even realize that you are doing it. Make up your mind to follow the hints suggested in the last few paragraphs. Read them over, if you feel you're not sure of them.

For some people, all this in itself comprises a system for remembering names. It is simply because by following the above hints and suggestions you make names interesting, you act interested, and in so doing you actually create interest. And interest, as I've explained, is a large part of memory.

All the above will help your memory for names and faces by 25% to 50%, if you apply yourself; but keep reading, and I'll help you take care of the remaining 50% to 75%!

CHAPTER SIXTEEN
What's in A Name?

This fellow was very proud of the way he could remember names by association, until he met Mrs. Hummock. Mrs. Hummock was quite heavy, and had a large stomach, so he decided to use "stomach" as his association.
Three weeks later, he met the same lady, glanced at her stomach, and, feeling very pleased with himself, said, "Good day, Mrs. Kelly!"

Not too long ago I had the pleasure of performing for the executive club of a well known department store in New York City. This was their annual dinner, and everyone was seated at tables in banquet style. The one demonstration in my performance that probably hits home for more people than any other, is the one in which I remember everyone's name.

The way I usually do it is to introduce myself to all the guests as they arrive, or, meet them while they're having dinner. I simply walk from table to table getting everyone's name (and getting hungry). I'll meet all the people at one table, then the next, and the next, and so on, until I've met everyone in the room. I work as quickly or as slowly as time suggests. Many's the time that I've had to meet one hundred to two hundred people in fifteen minutes or less, without forgetting a single name! I give credit and praise to my methods and systems, of course, not to myself.

After I've met everyone, and after coffee and dessert, the show goes on. During the performance, I ask everyone who has given me their name at any time during the evening to please rise at their seats. This most often consists of the entire audience. I then proceed to call the names of everyone standing; pointing to each particular person as I call his or her name. During the remainder of my lecture-demonstration, I allow anyone in the audience to interrupt me by shouting, "What's my name?" and, of course, I immediately comply with the person's name.

The reason I am explaining all this is because I was amused at the explanation given by one of the department store executives, revealing how I did the "trick" of remembering everyone's name at this particular affair. This, by the way, was not his idea of a joke, he was firmly convinced that this was how it was done.

The affair was held at the Capitol Hotel in New York City. The room we were in, happened to have had a circular balcony completely surrounding it. Following is the explanation given by the executive. He said:

Mr. Lorayne has a photographer working with him. You know, one of those fellows who takes pictures at banquets and develops them in a few minutes so he can sell them to the people there and then. This photographer and Mr. Lorayne both have tiny microphones and receiving sets hidden somewhere on their persons. The photographer is somewhere on the balcony, hidden, of course. There must be a hole up there, through which he can put the lens of his camera. Now, when everyone is seated, ready for dinner, he snaps a picture of the entire audience, which he develops and dries immediately.

When Mr. Lorayne approaches a table and asks for the names, the photographer hears them too, thanks to the tiny microphones and receivers. He, the photographer, that is, has the picture in front of him; he spots the table that is giving the names, (he can see through the hole) spots the particular person and listens to the name. He then writes that name on the picture, across the face of the person who gave it! He does this with every person in the room.

Now, you see how simple (author's note: simple??) it is? When Mr. Lorayne is performing, he always points to a person before he calls his or her name. The reason for the pointing is so that the photographer can spot that person on the picture, read the name, and quickly whisper it into his microphone. Of course, Mr. Lorayne hears it and calls the person by name.

That's it. That was this gentleman's explanation of my method. (Say, maybe it's not such a bad idea at that!) Of course, he completely discarded all the other demonstrations that I did during my performance. He also forgot that many of the people change places after dinner, (most of the time I will meet the people in one room, and do the show in another) and that after the show, I spoke to the people away from the tables, in the elevator, and even in the street, and called them by name. Perhaps he didn't forget; he may have thought that the photographer was still whispering the names into his little microphone. If that were the case, the photographer had a trained memory.

I relate this incident only to show how difficult it is for some people to believe that you actually can remember the names and faces of an entire audience. They simply take the path of least resistance and the negative attitude, and feel that if they can't do it, no one else can; it's just impossible. After reading my methods on how to remember names and faces, I'm sure you will agree with me that it is not impossible. On the contrary, it is much, much easier than the method so emphatically believed by the department store executive.

I would have been happy to send a copy of this book to this particular gentleman, to prove it to him, too, only I don't know his name; you see, I forgot where I put that picture!

In previous chapters I've mentioned how important it is to be interested in a person in order to remember his or her name. If you were to be introduced to four hundred people in one evening, and then perhaps meet these four hundred people two or three more times, you would still forget most of their names. If, however, you were to enter a room in which there were four hundred celebrities, such as movie stars; you'd probably be able to call them all by their full names. Not only that, but you could tell them at least one of the movies in which you have seen them perform. You'll agree, I'm sure, that this is because people are interested in celebrities and usually want to remember them. Well, I've already stressed the fact that being interested in and wanting to remember, is half your battle won over a supposedly poor memory. Remember to use the rules that I gave you in the last chapter.

- Be sure you hear the person's name in the first place.
- Spell it or have him spell it if you're not sure of it.
- If there is any odd fact about the name, or if it is similar to a name you know, mention it.
- Repeat the name as often as you can during the course of the conversation.
- Use the name when you say good night or good-bye.

If you use these rules in conjunction with what I am about to teach you, you should never again forget a name or a face. To simplify the process, you will learn first, what to do with the name, and then, how to associate the name to the face. Actually they go hand in hand; the name will conjure up the face, and the face will bring the name to mind.

All names can be separated into two categories; names that mean something, and names that have no meaning (to you) at all. Names like Cook, Brown, Coyne, Carpenter, Berlin, Storm, Shivers, Fox, Baker, King, Gold, Goodman, Glazer, and many others, all have a meaning. Names like Krakauer, Conti, Sullivan, Mooney, Littman, Carson, Linkfeld, Smolensky, Morano, Morgan, Resnick, Hecht, and so on, have no meaning at all to most of you. Of course, the lists are almost endless; these are just a few examples of each.

There are some names that fall into the "no meaning" category, that do, however, suggest or create a picture in your mind. When you hear the name, Sullivan, you might think of, or picture, a rubber heel, since a very popular brand name of a rubber heel is O'Sullivan. You might picture or think of John L. Sullivan, the champion fighter. The name, Lincoln would, of course, create or suggest a picture of our sixteenth president, Abraham Lincoln. Mr. Jordan might suggest a picture of the River Jordan, while the name Di Maggio would make you think of baseball. So, we arrive at three categories of names; those that actually have a meaning, those that have no meaning in themselves, but do suggest something to you, and finally, names that have no meaning and do not suggest or create a picture in your mind.

It is with the third Category that you must use your imagination. You must, in order to remember the name, make it mean something to you. This is already so with the first two categories, so they are no particular problem. The names that have no meaning at all should present no problem either, if you have read the chapter on how to remember foreign language vocabulary. If you've read this chapter carefully, you know that you must utilize my system of "substitute words or thoughts" in order to make the names mean something to you. No matter how strange the name sounds upon first hearing it, it can always be broken down to a substitute word or thought. Simply think of a word or phrase that sounds as much like the name as possible. If you were to meet a Mr. Freedman, you might picture a man being fried. Fried man-Freedman. If the name were Freeman, you could picture a man holding or waving an American flag; he's free. You might want to picture a man escaping from prison; he's a free man. Remember please, that whatever you decide on for your substitute word, phrase or thought, is the one to use. Ten people given the same name to remember, may all use a different substitute word in order to remember it.

The name Fishter might make you picture a fish stirring something, or stirring something with a fish. Fish stir-Fishter. Someone else may feel that picturing just a fish would be enough to recall the name. If you want to picture someone tearing a fish in half, or a fish tearing something in half, that would do it too. Fish tear—Fishter. You could picture yourself fishing and catching a toe instead of a fish. Fish toe-Fishter. Any one of these would suffice to help you remember the name.

It is not important to strain yourself to find a substitute word that sounds exactly like the name; or to use words for every part of the name. Remember what I told you some chapters ago; if you remember the main, the incidentals will fall into place by true memory. The very fact that you are thinking of and with the name, in this fashion, will help impress it on your mind. You have automatically become interested in the name merely by searching for a substitute word for it. That's why the anecdote that heads this chapter may be good for a laugh, but can't happen in actual practice.

Recently I had to remember the name, Olczewsky, pronounced ol-hew-sky. I simply pictured an old man (I always picture a man with a long, flowing white beard to represent an old man) chewing vigorously, while he skied; old-chewski-Olczewsky. The name Conti might suggest soap, (Conti Castile), or you might picture someone counting tea bags. Count tea-Conti. For the name Czarsty, you could picture a Russian Czar with a sty on his eye; the name Ettinger might suggest someone eating, or someone who has "et" and injured himself, perhaps hurt a tooth, etc. Et injure — Ettinger.

It doesn't matter how silly you get; more often than not, the sillier the better. I've often said that if I could explain on stage, the silly associations that I've made to remember names, among other things, I'd have a very funny routine.

A name like D'Amico, pronounced Dam-e-ko, is not too unusual a name. I've come across it a few times, and I've remembered it by picturing a woman seeing a dam overflow and screaming, "Eek" and "Oh." Or, picturing myself going towards an overflowing dam (the overflowing gets action into the picture) and saying, "me go." Dam eek oh, dam me go-D'Amico. This all sounds quite ridiculous. Good. The more ridiculous, the easier to tie the picture onto the face, as I will explain in a moment, and the easier to remember and retain the name.

After meeting a lot of new people, and using my systems, you will find that you'll have certain pictures or thought for names that you come across very often. I, for example, always picture an ice cream cone for the name Cohen or Cohn. I see a blacksmith's hammer for Smith or Schmidt. Yes, I use the same picture for Smith and Schmidt; true memory tells me the difference. You can prove this to yourself only through your own experience.

Here are some other "standards" that I employ:

The name Davis always makes me think of the Davis Cup in Tennis. So when I meet a Mr. Davis, I always picture a large loving cup. If the name were Davison, I would picture the large loving cup and a tiny one next to it; the large cup's son. Sure, it's silly, but it works! Of course, the name Davis may bring an entirely different picture to your mind. If it does, use it. For the names ending with either "itz" or "witz," you can picture itch or brains (wits). i.e., Horowitz-you might picture yourself being horrified at the sight of brains. Horror wits-Horowitz.

Many names end in either "ly" or "ton." A lea is a meadow, so I always get a meadow into my association to help me recall "ly." "Ton," of course, has a meaning. You might picture a weight, a barbell or a dumbbell to always represent "ton." There are many names that either end or begin with "berg"; for these, I always use iceberg. The suffix or prefix "stein" always makes me picture a beer mug or stein. I come across the suffix, "ler," quite often, as in the name, Brimler. "Ler" sounds like law to me, and I always picture a judge's gavel to represent law. You might decide to picture a policeman or a jail or handcuffs to represent law; that's okay, just use the same picture for the ending "ler" each time. Eventually you will fall into a pattern with most endings or entire names. This will make it easier and will cut down on time if you have to meet and remember people quickly.

The knowledge of a foreign language will sometimes help in creating a picture or association. The name Baum, means "tree" in German. The name, Berg, means "mountain." If you know this, you can use it in creating your substitute words or thoughts. Just recently I met a Mr. Zauber. When I remarked that it was an odd name, he told me that in German, Zauber meant "magician." I had already pictured myself sawing a bear. Saw bear-Zauber. Either that, or "magician," would have helped me remember Mr. Zauber.

I have a very close friend whose last name is Williams. His hobby happens to be playing billiards, at which he is exceptionally proficient. I have fallen into the habit of picturing someone shooting or playing billiards whenever I meet a Mr. Williams. This works just as well as actually breaking down the name to yams (sweet potatoes) writing their wills. Will yams-Williams. The first time I met a Mr. Wilson, the first thought that came into my mind was the slogan for a whiskey, "Wilson, that's all." Now, whenever I meet a Mr. Wilson, I picture a bottle of whiskey to help me remember his name.

So, as I pointed out, you will eventually fall into certain habits and use certain standards with particular names. Just keep in mind that there isn't a name that can't be made to mean something (to you) which will sound like the name itself and help in bringing it to mind, when necessary.

Although your best method of practice is to go ahead and use the system, here are some names which ordinarily are completely abstract; have no meaning at all. Why not see if you can create a substitute word, phrase or thought for each one.

Steinwurtzel	McCarthy	Pukczyva
Brady	Gordon	Hulnick
Arcaro	Briskin	Platinger
Moreida	Casselwitz	Kolcyski
Kolodny	Hayduk	

If you had any trouble with any of the above names, here's the way I might have created substitute thoughts for them.

Steinwurtzel—a beer stein worth selling. Stein worth sell — Steinwurtzel.

McCarthy—I always picture the famous ventriloquial dummy, Charlie McCarthy for this name.

Brady—You could picture a little girl's braids for this. If you want to get the entire name in your picture, see yourself braiding the lines of a large letter, "E." Braid E—Brady.

Gordon—I always picture "garden" for this name.

Arcaro—I usually see the famous jockey of the same name. If you want to break the name down, see yourself carrying an "O." I carry O—Arcaro.

Briskin—You might want to picture someone briskly rubbing their skin. Brisk skin—Briskin.

Moreida—You could see yourself reading and calling for more and more books to read. Some of you may have thought of your mother (Maw) being a reader. More reader or Maw reader—Moreida.

Casselwitz—A castle completely stocked with brains (wits). You might see the brains actually oozing from all the windows. Castle wits—Casselwitz.

Kolodny—I would picture a large knee being all different colors. Colored knee —Kolodny.

Hayduk—Ducks eating hay, or a hayloft or haystack full of ducks.

Platinger—Picturing a plate with a bandage would suffice. Plate injure —Platinger.

Kolcyski—Either a piece of coal skiing in a sitting position, or calling your friend Sid to ski would do it. Or, it is too cold to stand up and ski, so you sit and ski. Coal sit ski, call Sid ski, cold sit ski—Kolcyski.

Hulnick—You might see a little child being very happy because she has a whole nickel. A picture of a ship whose hull is made up of nickel or nickels, would also do it. If you saw yourself nicking a hole in something, you would still recall the name. Whole nickel, hull nickel, hole nick—Hulnick.

Pukczyva—This name is pronounced puck-shiv-va. I would see a hockey puck shivering with cold. Puck shiver—Pukczyva.

There you are. If you thought of entirely different pictures, don't worry about it. The point is, that no matter how strange a name sounds, or how long it is, or how difficult to pronounce, you can always find a substitute word or thought for it If the substitute word brings the name back to you, then that's the one to use, and in the next chapter, I'll show you how to use them.

CHAPTER SEVENTEEN
More About Names and Faces

Ruth was a sweet and lovely girl and had many boy friends,
but her mother felt it was time she was married.
While reading a book on the meanings of names, Ruth said,
"Mother, it says here that Philip means 'lover of horses,' and
James means 'beloved.' I wonder what George means?"
"I hope, my dear," said Mother, "that George means business!"

Now that you know how to make any name have meaning by using a substitute word or thought, you have to know how to associate the name to the face in such a way as to remember both of them. Many memory Systems teach the student to make a jingle with the name; something like, "Mr. Baker is a faker" or "Mr. Cold is old," or "Mr. Radcliffe had a mad tiff," or "Mr. Lillienkamp is a carnival tramp."

This is fine, until you meet a Mr. Nepomosimo or a Mr. Smolensky. Even if you could create a rhyme with those names, what I never could quite grasp is how this would help you to remember the person's face, or rather, how one would bring the other to mind. No, I don't think that this jingle system is of too great a help. In my opinion, the only way to remember a person's name is to would bring the other to mind. No, I don't think that this jingle system is of too great a help. In my opinion, the only way to remember a person's name is to associate that name to the person's face in some ridiculous way. And here's how to go about it:—

Whenever you meet someone new, look at his face and try to find one outstanding feature. This could be anything; small eyes, large eyes, thick lips, thin lips, high forehead, low forehead, lines or creases on the forehead, long nose, broad nose, wide nostrils, narrow nostrils, large ears, small ears, ears that stand away from the head, dimples, clefts, warts, mustache, lines on the face, large chin, receding chin, type of hairline, jutting chin, small mouth, large mouth, teeth-just about anything.

You are to pick the one thing that seems most outstanding to you. It may not be the most outstanding feature; someone else may choose something entirely different. This isn't important; the thing that stands out to you is the thing that will be obvious and outstanding when you meet this person again. The point that is important is that as you're looking for this one outstanding feature, you must pay attention to and be interested in the face as a whole. You're observing and etching this face into your memory.

When you have decided on the outstanding feature, you are ready to associate the name to that particular part of the face. For example, Mr. Sachs has a very high forehead. You might "see" millions of sacks falling from his forehead, or see his forehead as a sack instead of a forehead. You can see, of course, that you're to use the same laws and principles as you've been taught in the early chapters of the book. The most important principle being that you must actually see this picture in your mind's eye. Look at Mr. Sachs' face, and "see" those sacks falling from every part of his forehead. That's all there is to it! If Mr. Robrum had a large nose, I would picture his nose as a bottle of rum and a robber stealing it!

Mr. Horwick might have very bushy eyebrows, so I would see wicks in them, as in candles, and see a woman trying to take them because they are her wicks. Her wick—Horwick.

The original publisher of this book was Mr. Frederick Fell. The moment I met Mr. Fell, I noticed a cleft in his chin. I simply saw things falling from this cleft, and that's all I needed to help me remember that his name was Mr. Fell. Remember that in these examples, I give the substitute thought and the outstanding feature that I personally think is best. The name, "Fell" could have meant "feel," or the material, "felt" to you, and you could have associated that to any other feature on Mr. Fell's face. The substitute word and the outstanding feature chosen is an individual thing; the things you choose are the right ones to use.

At first, some people may feel that it takes too long to find a substitute word for a person's name, and then associate it to his face. They think that it would be embarrassing to have people notice that they are staring at them. Please believe me, it does not take any time at all. After a minimum of practice, you'll find that you've found a substitute word for the name (if it's necessary) and associated it to an outstanding feature on the person's face in less time than it takes to say, "Hello." As in everything else, it's the very first effort that is the most difficult. Sure, it's easier to be lazy and just go on forgetting names, but, try my system and you'll soon agree that it is just as easy to remember them.

The best way to practice remembering names and faces is to just start doing it. However, to give you a bit of confidence, let's try this: I'm sure that before you started reading this book, most of you felt that you definitely couldn't remember and retain the names of fifteen people if you met them all at once. If you took the little test in Chapter #3, you probably proved it. Well let me introduce you to the pictures of fifteen people right now, just to prove that you can do it, with the help of my systems. Of course, it isn't as easy with pictures, since you see the faces in only one dimension, whereas ordinarily you see people in three dimensions. It may be a little difficult to find outstanding features of a face in a picture, but I'll try to help you with each one.

No. 1 is Mr. Carpenter. This name is no problem because it already has meaning. The next step is to find an outstanding feature on Mr. Carpenter's face. You might decide on his very small mouth. If you look closely, you'll see a sort of scar on his right cheek. Pick one of these (the one that's most obvious to you) and associate Carpenter to that. You might see a carpenter working on the small mouth (get the carpenter's tools into the picture) trying to make it larger; or, have the carpenter working on the scar, trying to repair it. Now, and most important, look at the picture of Mr. Carpenter and actually see this picture, see your association in your mind's eye for at least a split second. You must make yourself "see" this picture or you'll forget the name. Have you done that? If so, to picture #2.

No. 2 is the Mr. Brimler we spoke about awhile ago. Notice the long dimples in his cheeks. Can you see the heavy character lines from his nose to the corners of his mouth? As in every face, there are many outstanding features that can be used. I would use the dimples, and see them brim full of judges' gavels. Remember, I use a gavel to represent law or "ler." If you want to use policeman, jail or handcuffs, go ahead. You might "see" police brimming all over the dimples. Whichever way you want to do it, is fine; but look at Mr. Brimler and see the picture you've decided on.

No. 3 is Miss Standish. I would select her "bang" hairdo. You could "see" people standing on the bangs and scratching themselves violently because they itch. Stand itch-Standish. Of course, a dish standing would serve the same purpose, but I like an association into which I can inject some sort of action. Now look at Miss Standish and see the picture you've decided on, in your mind's eye.

No. 4 is Mr. Smolensky. Don't let the name scare you, it's easy to find a substitute thought for it. I would see someone skiing on Mr.

1. Mr. Carpenter

2. Mr. Brimler

3. Miss Standish

4. Mr. Smolensky

5. Mr. Hecht

6. Mrs. Bjornsen

7. Miss Van Nuys

8. Mr. Hamper

9. Miss Smith

10. Mr. Kannen

11. Mr. D'Amico

12. Miss Forrester

13. Mr. Pfeffer

14. Mr. Silverberg

15. Miss Kornfeld

Smolensky's very broad nose, and taking pictures (while skiing) with a small camera (lens). Small lens ski — Smolensky. See how simple it is? I have chosen Mr. Smolensky's broad nose; you might think that the receding chin is more obvious. Choose whichever you think is most obvious, and see the picture of the skier taking pictures with a small lens.

No.5 is Mr. Hecht. I would see his mustache being hacked from his face with an axe. See the association violently if you can. Violence and action make it easier to recall. Hacked-Hecht. Be sure you see the picture.

No. 6 is Mrs. Bjornsen, pronounced, Byorn-son. The way I would remember Mrs. Bjornsen is to see a boy (son) being born in the very wide part in her hair. You might think that either her full cheeks or wide mouth, or dark eyes are niore outstanding, if so, use those in your association. But look at Mrs. Bjornsen and actually see the picture for a fraction of a second.

No. 7 is Miss Van Nuys. The first thing that I notice when I look at Miss Van Nuys are her bulging eyes. I would see moving vans driving out of Miss Van Nuys' eyes, and making terribly loud noises. So loud that you have to hold your ears. (Get the action in the association.) Van noise —Van Nuys. Be sure you see the picture!

No. 8 is Mr. Hamper. Notice the very wide mouth. I would see myself throwing all my dirty clothes into his mouth because it's a hamper. Remember to look at Mr. Hamper and see the picture in your mind's eye.

No. 9 is Miss Smith. This is a common name, but don't think you'll remember it if you do not make an association. The names, Smith, Jones and Cohen, are forgotten just as often as the longer and less common names, and there's less excuse for doing so. Miss Smith has very full lips, they almost appear to be swollen. I would see a blacksmith using a gigantic smith's hammer on Miss Smith's lips. The blows of the hammer are causing the lips to swell. You might want to utilize Miss Smith's long eyebrows, it doesn't matter. What does matter is that you look at Miss Smith and see that picture or association.

No. 10 is Mr. Kannen. Pick an outstanding feature. You might notice the ear standing out from the head, or the lines in the corner of the eye, or the thin long mouth. You can see a cannon shooting off the outstanding feature, or cannons shooting from the feature. Pick the association you like, and see it in your mind's eye.

No. 11 is Mr. D'Amico. You can't miss the full head of wavy hair. See the hair as a dam, and it is overflowing while you scream, "eek" and "oh." Or, you are running towards the dam, shouting, "me go." Look at Mr. D'Amico, and see the picture.

No.12 is Miss Forrester. I would see trees (forest) growing out of those heavy, definite lines on her lower cheeks. If you want to be sure of the entire name, see the forest growing wild and tearing her checks. Forest tear — Forrester. Be sure you see the picture.

No. 13 is Mr. Pfeffer. The "p" is silent. The first thing that hits my eye is the cleft in Mr. Pfeffer's chin. I would see lots of black pepper pouring out of this cleft. So much, in fact, that it's making me sneeze. "Pepper" would be enough to tell me that this is Mr. Pfeffer. If you want to make sure, hear yourself sneezing like so: "fffft," with an "f" sound. Silly? Yes, but this will come back to you later, and you'll know that the name is Pfeffer, not Pepper. See the picture.

No. 14 is Mr. Silverberg. See a large silver iceberg instead of Mr. Silverberg's jutting chin. Actually see it glittering, so you get the idea of silver in there. If you want to use the laugh lines around the Corners of Mr. Silverberg's mouth, that's okay, too. See a silver iceberg on each side. Whichever feature you use, be sure to actually see the picture.

No. 15 is Miss Komfeld. I would see millions (exaggeration) of ears of corn falling from Miss Komfeld's wide mouth. Make sure that you look at Miss Komfeld, and actually see the picture or association in your mind's eye.

I have purposely used a wide assortment of names to prove that it just doesn't make any difference as to the type of name. You might want to go over these faces once, quickly, to make sure you've made a strong enough association. Now, here are the same faces in a different order without their names. See if you can't fill in the fifteen spaces under the pictures. When you've done so, check yourself and be amazed at the improvement in your memory for names and faces!
If you had any trouble at all recalling any of the names, the reason is that you didn't make your association vivid enough; you didn't actually see

the association in your mind's eye. If you did miss any, just look at the face again, strengthen your association and try it again. You'll surely remember them all on your second try. If you feel confident, why not try that test in Chapter #3, and compare your score now, with the score you originally made. Tomorrow, or the day after, look at the fifteen faces pictured in this chapter, and in Chapter #3, and you'll see that you still know the names of all the people!

Keep in mind that if you can remember the names of faces in pictures, you'll find it much easier to do when actually meeting people. Aside from finding an outstanding feature more easily, there are many other things that can be taken into consideration, such as: manner of speech, speech defects, character, type of walk, manner of bearing, and so on.

If you happened to be at an affair, and wanted to show off by memorizing the names of everyone present, you could do it now, by using the systems you've just learned. You would probably find it helpful to review the names every so often. Each time you look at a person, his name should spring to mind. The name coming to mind in this fashion serves as a review, and serves to etch the name more firmly into your memory. If you were to spot someone you've met, and the name didn't come to mind, ask for the name again, or ask someone else to give it to you. Then strengthen your original association. Try it! You'll amaze yourself and your friends.

For practical purposes, for those of you who meet people, and would like to retain the names, writing the names would help, as far as review is concerned. As I said in the preceding chapters, writing in conjunction with a system of association is fine. This is a good example of that fact. You would, of course, use the Systems learned here, upon meeting these people. Then at the end of theday, think of each new person you've met and as the name comes to mind, jot it down. The next day go over this list of names. As you look at each one, a picture of the person's face will come to mind. Just picture the person for a moment, and see your original association of the name to face. That's all. Do the same thing a few days later; then again, a week later, and so on until the faces and names are indelibly etched in your memory.

Of course, all this is theoretical, because if you wanted to remember these people, it is probably because you intend to meet them again. If you do meet them often and recall their names, well, then that serves the purpose of review, and writing the names isn't necessary at all.

The thing to do is to use whatever is best for you or your particular circumstances. Just make up your mind to get over the initial hump of actually putting my Systems to work, and they will diligently work for you.

CHAPTER EIGHTEEN
It Pays to Remember Facts About People

It is the common wonder of all men, how among so many millions of faces there should be none alike.

—Sir Thomas Browne

Yes, fortunately, there are no two faces exactly alike. If all faces did look alike, we couldn't remember them, or the names, memory system or not. I have been challenged many times, to remember the first names of a set of identical twins. So far, I have always been able to spot one difference, however minute, in their faces. It is to this difference that I would associate their names. So, as the French say, "Vive la difference!"

If you have studied the previous chapters on how to remember names and faces; and if you have tried the methods, you should be greatly improved by now. Although in most cases it is the second, or family names that most of us want to remember, some of you may be interested in remembering first, or given names as well. This too, can be done with a conscious association. You can use a substitute word for the first name, and get that into your original mental picture; or, you can picture someone you know very well, having the same first name, with the person you wish to remember.

Substitute words for first names are easy to find; Harry could be "hairy;" Clark could be "clock;" for William, I always picture a man with a bow and arrow as William Tell, while money or "rich" always means Richard, to me. Anne could be "ant;" Marion could be "marrying;" for Gloria, you might see the American Flag (Old Glory), etc.

If you use the substitute word idea for remembering first names, after a while you will have one at your fingertips for any one that you meet. The system of picturing a friend of yours whose first name is the same as the person whom you want to remember, might work just as well for you. If you meet a Mr. John Sitrous, you could use the substitute word "citrus" to associate to an outstanding feature; then put your friend, John, into the picture somehow, (in a ridiculous way) and you'll remember that Mr. Sitrous' first name is John.

Again, it is not for me to tell you which idea to use, you may use one or both, as the circumstances demand. This is entirely up to you. If you find that you can remember first names with one system better than with the other, then by all means, use the one that helps you most.

If at first, you have a bit of trouble remembering the first names, don't let it bother you; just use the second name. Keep at it for a while and you'll soon be able to remember first names just as well as you do second names, and vice versa. You won't insult anyone by remembering only his or her last name. Benjamin Disraeli had an out even if he forgot both names; he once said, "When I meet a man whose name I cannot remember, I give myself two minutes, then if it is a hopeless case, I always say, 'And how is the old complaint?'" Since most of us have some sort of old complaint or other, Disraeli probably flattered everyone he used this on, making them believe that he remembered them quite well. However, no need for subterfuge; use my systems and you will remember names and faces.

More important, I think, than remembering first names, is to be able to remember pertinent facts about the people you meet This holds true for business and social life. Business-wise, particularly, since it is often helpful to remember what items or style numbers you sold to a certain customer, or, if you're a doctor, to remember patients' symptoms and ailments, etc. It is also very flattering to meet a person whom you haven't seen in some time and have him ask about things that are close to you, but would ordinarily have no interest to him. This will not only make people like you (people always like you if you show an interest in their interests) but can be quite an asset in business.

The method is the same as for remembering first names. Just put the thing into your original association when you're memorizing the name and face. If I met a Mr. Beller, whom I wanted to impress and I knew he was an avid stamp collector, I might associate "bell" to an outstanding feature on his face, and then associate stamps to that bell.

Some of you may feel that this might confuse you into thinking that the man's name is Bellstamp; but again, true memory tells you the difference. You'll know that the name is Beller (to make sure, you could use bell—law in the original association) and you'll be able to flatter him by asking, or talking, about his stamp collection.

During my own performances, I will usually meet doctors, judges, commissioners, mayors, and many people with titles other than "Mister." It is essential for me to address them correctly, because even though I remember their names, people with titles may be insulted if I do not use that title, or if I forget it. The same idea applies; I simply put something into my original association which will remind me of the title. Anything will do; the first object that comes to mind when you hear the title is usually best. I always picture a stethoscope to remind me of "doctor," because that's the first thing with which I associate a doctor. Of course, scalpel, hypodermic, operating table, or anything like that, would suffice.

When I meet a judge, I always put a gavel into my mental picture. This is enough to remind me to address this person as "judge." You might like to picture the judicial robe; that's just as good. Years ago, I recall seeing a picture of New York's mayor Jimmy Walker, wearing a top hat. For some reason, this picture has always stuck with me. Now, whenever I am introduced to a mayor of a town at an affair, I make sure to get a top hat into my association.

I have done quite a few performances for servicemen, and I have had to prepare a substitute word beforehand to remind me as to whether the person was a sergeant, corporal, lieutenant, captain, major, or what have you. As I met each man, I would put this substitute word into my association of name to face, and I did address each man correctly.

So you see that any word can be put into your associations to remind you of things pertaining to the person, as well as his or her name. I have mentioned time and again, the fact that you must use these ideas in order for them to work for you. I do this only because it is important enough to warrant repetition. If you maintain the attitude that nothing can help your terrible memory, then nothing will, because you won't let it. Take a positive view of it all; try these ideas, and you'll be pleasantly surprised. If you've read up to here in this book, and tried all the ideas and systems up to now, I'm sure you've already been convinced.

I've also told you that all these ideas and methods are merely aids to your true memory. If you didn't have the capacity to remember to begin with, you wouldn't remember, no matter how many Systems you used; nor could you remember the systems. If you were to make an extreme effort to remember, you would; there's no question about that. The problem is that we're all too lazy to make that effort. The Systems contained in this book, simply make it easier for you to make the effort. In order to make your associations, you must pay attention to the thing you want to remember; the rest is easy.

It would take far too much time and space for me to tell you how helpful my trained memory has been to me, aside from my public appearances. Of course, people will sometimes carry things to an extreme. I meet and remember approximately one to three or four thousand people every week, sometimes more. It would be a little silly for me to try to retain all those names and faces. But, I never know when I'll be stopped on the street, or in a movie, or while driving my car, or in some small town that I may have played two or three years ago — and have someone demand, "What's my name?"

These people expect me to remember them although I met them with three or four hundred other people, at the time. The amazing part is that in 20% to 30% of the time, my original associations, made, perhaps years ago, will come back to me after thinking for a few moments. Then I do know the person's name. In your case, this is no problem because I'm sure that very few of you have to meet and remember anywhere near three or four hundred thousand people a year.

I think that this book probably would never have been published if it weren't for the fact that I remembered one person's name. I had spoken to Mr. Fell, the publisher, about the book the first time I met him. He said he would think about it, and that was that. About five months later after meeting many thousands of people, I happened to be performing for an all male group at a charity breakfast. A gentleman approached me and asked if I remembered him. After a moment's thought, I realized it was Mr. Fell, who happened to have heard that I was appearing there, and came down to test me. I told him his name; and weeks later he all but confessed that if I hadn't remembered him, he wouldn't have been half as enthused about the book as he was now. You see, he naturally wanted to be sure that my systems really worked.

This is only one instance where remembering one person's name was important to me. Remembering the right persons name at the proper time, may perhaps mean a great deal to you, sometime in the future. It might be the stepping stone to a better job, a bigger opportunity or a much better sales contract, etc. So, try these systems, use them, and I believe you'll be well paid for your efforts.

⋆⋯⟩═⟩ ⟨═⟨⋯⋆

CHAPTER NINETEEN
It Pays to Remember Telephone Numbers

The little girl was trying to get the telephone operator to find a
telephone number for her.
OPERATOR: *You can find that number in your telephone directory.*
LITTLE GIRL: *Oh, I can't, I'm standing on it!*

Although most of you do not have to stand on the telephone directory in order to use the phone, you do have to use it quite often to look up numbers that you've forgotten. Sure, many people feel that it isn't necessary to remember phone numbers since that's just what the directory is for; but the fact remains that the phone companies have to keep information operators on duty continually. Next to forgetting names and faces, I think the most common memory complaint is, "I simply can't remember telephone numbers!" As I mentioned in an earlier chapter, most untrained memories are one-sided. Those who usually do remember telephone numbers, can't remember names, and vice versa. Of course, I intend for you to be able to do both, and more, with equal proficiency.

My good friend Richard Himber, famous musician-magician, realized that most people couldn't remember phone numbers, so he did something about it. He made it very simple for everyone to remember his — he just told them to dial his name, R. Himber. Somehow, he managed to obtain an exchange for his telephone that begins with the letters, RH. The rest of the number is 4-6237, which you get when you dial i-m-b-e-r. Now, don't you all dial it just to see if this is true — take my word for it, it is!

This, of course, solved everybody's problem when it came to remembering Mr. Himber's telephone number (if they remembered his name) but unfortunately, we can't all have numbers like this. No, you'll just have to learn to remember phone numbers, and the telephone operators will love you for it.

Telephone numbers in New York and most major cities consist of an exchange name, an exchange number, and four trunk line numbers, i.e. Columbus 5-6695. By making a ridiculous association of two or three words or items, you can memorize any telephone number; and by adding one thought to your association, you can remember to whom the phone number belongs.

Most telephones in use today are dial phones, so all that is necessary to remember is the first two letters of the exchange name; since that is all we have to dial. These two letters are all we will consider. Now then, the first thing you have to learn, is to form one word which will immediately help you recall both the first two letters of the exchange name and the exchange number. The word, of course, should be one that can be pictured easily. The number CO 5-6695 can serve as an example. How can we find one word to represent CO 5? Simple! The word must begin with the letters, "Co," and the very next consonant sound in the word must be the sound that represents the exchange number according to our phonetic alphabet. In this case, it is the "l" sound, representing #5.

Any word that can be pictured will do, no matter which sounds follow the "l" sound; because those will be disregarded. The only things that matter in the word you choose are the first two letters and the next consonant sound. For example, the word, "column" would represent CO 5; the "mn" at the end of the word is disregarded. The words, collar, colt, color, cold or coliseum would also fit the system. If you can think of a word that can be pictured, that has no other letters after the consonant that represents the exchange number, use it. The word, "coal" is an example that fits this case.

Keep in mind that you don't have to use a word that has only the first two letters and the exchange number sound. The first word that comes to you is usually, although not always, the one to use. If the number you wish to memorize begins BEachview 8, you could use the word, "BEef" (BE 8). Here are a few more examples to make sure that you get the idea:

REgent 2—rent—Reynard (The Fox)
ESplanade 7—escape—escalator
GRamercy 8—grave—graph
DElaware 9—deep—deputy
GOrdon 5—gold—goal
CLover 3—clam—climb

I've given only two words for each exchange, but there are many others that would fit.

Do you see how simple it is? There's no reason why you shouldn't be able to find a word, immediately, to represent any exchange and exchange number. Let me remind you that the word you select has to have a meaning for you only. Probably, if I gave ten people an exchange and exchange number, they would each use a different word to help remember it. Although nouns are usually best, that doesn't mean that you have to use a noun. Some of you may find that a foreign word you know, is just right for a certain exchange and exchange number; if so, use it; it doesn't matter. What does matter is that it recalls the exchange for you. I could give you a list of all the exchange names used in New York City and the exchange numbers used with these names, and also give you a word that would represent each of them. I could do that, but I won't. I don't believe it would help you any. It's much better if you make up the words as soon as you find it necessary to do so, instead of memorizing a long list of them.

At the risk of being repetitious, I must say, again, that the picture created in your mind is something that I cannot help you with. One word may create an entirely different picture in your mind, than it would in mine. Actually, sometimes it is not even a word that I use, but a thought. I purposely used one in the above examples. For REgent 2, I gave "Reynard" as a word to help remember it. Now, Reynard creates a definite picture in my mind because Reynard the Fox was a favorite character of mine when I was a child. If you never read those wonderful stories, then Reynard would mean nothing to you. If I had used Reynard in my association, I would simply picture a fox. True memory would tell me that the telephone number began RE 2, and not FO 7 (fox). I'm telling you all this just to show you that even if you can't think of a word to fit a particular exchange name and number, you can always find something, even a nonsense phrase or word, to recall it for you later on. The same thing holds true, not only for phone numbers, but for anything that makes it necessary for you to make up a word for an association.

All right, now to go on with the rest of the telephone number. If you understand the idea of how to make up a word for the exchange name and number; the rest is easy. All you have to worry about now are the four trunk line numbers. Well, any four digit number can be broken into two of your peg words. If you simply associate the two you'll remember the four digits. For the number 4298, you would associate rain (42) to puff (98); for 6317 — chum (63) to tack (17); for 1935 — tub to mule, and so on. You now have all the ingredients for remembering phone numbers, all that remains is to mix them. Let's use CO 5-6695 as an example. To remember this number simply associate coal (CO 5) to choo choo (66) to bell (95)! For the number AL 1-8734, you could use altar to fog to mower; and for OX 2-4626 — oxen to roach to notch.

Now, before showing you how to remember whose phone number you're remembering, let me point out that there is one fly in the ointment, so to speak, involved here. Were you to make a ridiculous picture in your mind of say, steam, rope and tomb, you would know that the exchange was ST 3 (steam) and that the trunk line numbers were 4913 (rope, tomb). But, would you remember whether it was 4913 or 1349? Therein lies the problem! You might be confused a week or so after memorizing a phone number, as to which peg word was first and which was last. Of course, if you use a telephone number that you memorize, then this is really a theoretical problem. Once you've used it a few times, you'll know which pair of digits comes first. As I've said many times before, the systems are wonderful aids to your true memory. Without the use of the system for remembering phone numbers, you probably wouldn't know any of the digits in the number.

However, for numbers that you do not intend to use right away, there are many methods of avoiding this confusion, some good and some, not so good. I'll give you three or four ways right now, and you can pick the one or two that you think is best.

The first idea is to make a link of the words, instead of one complete ridiculous picture. For example, for ST 3-4913 you could make one picture of a radiator (steam) lassoing (rope) a tomb; whereas if you made a link you would associate steam to rope, and then rope to tomb. Since the link system makes you remember in sequence, you would know that you've memorized the number in its correct order.

Another idea, and one I use quite often, is to simply make one complete ridiculous picture, but to make the ridiculous picture itself in a logical sequence. Let me explain that for you. Actually I've done it in the example I just gave you. The picture of a radiator lassoing a tomb is quite ridiculous, but it is a good example of a logical sequence in an illogical picture. Having made the association in this way, you couldn't possibly think of tomb being first, or lasso (rope) being second. The words (which, of course, are transposed back to numbers when you want to dial the phone number) are pictured in the correct order to begin with. Let me give you another example of this, so you'll know just what I'm talking about. For the phone number DE 5-3196, the words deal, mat and beach would suffice in aiding your memory. If you pictured yourself dealing mats on a beach (getting sand all over the mats and yourself) you've got a logical illogical association. The word mat definitely comes before the word beach, so you know that the number is 3196 and not 9631.

The above idea is the one I use most often, followed by this one: I always try to find a word to fit more than two of the four digits of the trunk line numbers. For example — ST 3-4913 — I might picture a radiator ripping the hem of a girl's dress. Steam — ripped — hem. Or, steam — repaid — me, etc. And, there will be some numbers wherein you can find a word to fit all four of the trunk line digits.

I believe that most of you will want to use one or more of these three methods. However, to give you a wider choice, here are one or two other ways of avoiding the possibility of mixing your numbers. You can always use your peg word for the first two digits of the four; and any word that is not a peg word, but does fit phonetically, for the second pair of digits, i.e. the trunk line number to be memorized is 6491, use cherry for 64 but don't use bat in your association for 91. Use any other word for 91, like beet, or boat. Now, after any length of time, when you want to remember this particular number, you would know that 64 is first because cherry is a peg word; beet or boat are not peg words, therefore 91 is the second pair of digits! For the number IN 1-4084, you might associate Indian-rose-fairy. Fairy is not a peg word, so 84 must be the last or second two digits.

I devised this last method quite recently and I find that it works like a charm. Its use definitely dismisses the possibility of exchanging the numbers. There are other thoughts on the subject, of course, such as picturing one of your items much larger than the other, etc., but I don't hold too much stock in them.

I have taken all this space to explain these ideas because the same thoughts hold true for remembering prices, addresses, time schedules, style numbers and anything that requires that you memorize four digit numbers. As far as telephone numbers are concerned, the worst that could happen if you exchanged the digits in the trunk line numbers, is that you would dial the wrong number the first time, but get your party the second time.

By the way, if a zero should be the first of the two digits, simply make up a word for the digits. For 05 — use sail, cell or sale; for 07 — sick, sock or sack, etc. If you run across two zeros in a row, you could use seas, sews or zoos.

Well, now you should know how to memorize any telephone number! In order to remember whose phone number it is, it is necessary to add only one word to your association. If the number belongs to someone with whom you deal, say, the tailor, butcher, grocer, doctor, or anyone that can be pictured, just put that person into your association. For example, the tailor's phone number is FA 4-8862. Just make an association of tailor-farm-fife-chain. If you're using my suggestion of not using a peg word for the last two digits, you could use chin instead of chain. You might picture the tailor (a man sewing) growing fifes on his farm, which he plays with his chin. If you like the link idea, simply link the four items.

Since a tailor, doctor, dentist, etc. can be pictured, all you have to do is get that picture into your association. If you want to remember names in conjunction with phone numbers, you must use the substitute word system as you learned in Chapter 16..

Mr. Hayes' telephone number is OR 7-6573 — you might picture a bale of hay (Hayes) playing an organ (OR 7) in jail (65) while it combs (73) its hair. If you are using the link idea, link hay to organ, organ to jail, jail to comb. If you like my last suggestion on how to avoid mixing the trunk line numbers; change comb to coma, game or comma, etc.

Let's say that you wanted to remember that Mr. Silverberg's phone number was JU 69950. You might "see" a picture of a shiny silver iceberg sitting in a courtroom as judge (JU 6) smoking a gigantic pipe that's covered with lace. This is a logical illogical sequence in one ridiculous picture. I'll use this same number to show how you would handle it using any of the methods for keeping the trunk line numbers straight.

Link method — associate iceberg to judge, (the iceberg is pounding his gavel) then judge to pipe, ("see" a gigantic pipe as a judge) and then pipe to lace, (picture yourself smoking a pipe filled with lace, or see a pipe making lace).

If you want to use less items in your association for this particular phone number, you could picture the iceberg as a judge with a lot of pupils (9950)!

To use the last method, simply change lace, to any other word that would represent 50; like lass, lose, lies or lasso.

I have given you examples of memorizing phone numbers using the different ideas, because I feel that it is up to you to use the method that comes easiest to you. As with anything else in this book, I can only give you theoretical examples, your imagination must do the rest for you, and only you can decide which of certain methods are best for you.

I doubt if you would ever find it necessary to memorize a phone number that you didn't intend to use for any great length of time. The fact that you want to remember it means that you intend to use it. And, as I mentioned before, the association will recall it for you the first few times you have to dial it; after that you can forget your original association, or stop trying to remember it, anyway, because the phone number will probably be permanently etched in your memory.

As usual, the explanation takes much longer than the deed itself. It is but the work of a few moments to memorize a telephone number. Unless you are using it as a memory stunt, and want to do it quickly, you would ordinarily have plenty of time to find the proper words and make your associations. The fact that you must think of the number in order to find these words and make the association helps to set it into your mind in the first place. If all I accomplish with this book, is to make you think of, or concentrate quite a bit, because you will certainly have improved your memory.

You can check your improved memory for phone numbers right now by trying test #6 in Chapter #3 again, and comparing the scores.

CHAPTER TWENTY
The Importance of Memory

A business man traveling in the mid-west was told about an Indian, living in the vicinity, who had a most fantastic memory. Having just completed a memory course, and priding himself on his own newly acquired achievements, he decided to visit this Indian to see whose memory was better.

He introduced himself to the Indian and proceeded to test him. The memory expert answered every question quickly and accurately. His mind was a storehouse of knowledge, containing such information as the populations of nearly all American cities, important dates, scientific theories, etc. The business man couldn't stump him. Finally, he decided to try one last question. "What did you have for breakfast on the morning of April 5th, 1931?" The Indian didn't hesitate for even a second, as he answered, "eggs!"

The business man took his leave, completely stunned by this prodigious memory. When he arrived home, he told all his friends about it, only to have them scoff and say that eggs were usually eaten at breakfast, and that anyone could have answered that.

As the years passed, the man began to believe this, until one day he found himself back in the mid-west on a sales trip. One afternoon he happened to come upon the same Indian he had met here years ago. Wanting to show that his memory for faces was pretty good, he raised his hand in the traditional Indian greeting, and said, "How."

The Indian thought for just a moment, and then answered, "SCRAMBLED!

Although this anecdote is pretty silly, since no one would ask anyone to recall what they had for breakfast years ago, you'd be surprised at the questions some people ask me. If I had a conversation with a person some time ago, they'd ask me to repeat the conversation exactly; or, if I'm spied reading a newspaper, someone is sure to grab it from me and insist that I prove that I've memorized it word for word. They don't realize that the beauty of having a trained and systematic memory, is that I can remember what I want to remember.

It would be kind of ridiculous for me to memorize the daily paper word for word. There is no need for that; however, I can and do remember anything that I come across that I feel is important enough to memorize. I just make an association for it as I read it. When I read a story or novel, I am usually reading for enjoyment only, and I'm not at all interested in remembering what I'm reading. There are some things that we all want to forget; for example, it is diplomatic to remember a woman's birthday but not her age.

After completing this book I hope that all of you will be able to remember anything you read, that is, if you want to. As I've mentioned before, you can remember anything if you so desire. These memory systems just make it easier for you. Perhaps, some of you do not, as yet, agree with that. You may feel that it is much easier to write down a telephone number than to stop and make an association as I've explained. Well, I must admit that it probably would be faster and easier, at first; but you wouldn't be helping your memory.

You might feel that since there are millions of reference books to use whenever you need certain information, why bother to remember. And, of course, most business men have secretaries to remember for them.

Yes, it's true that business men have secretaries, but they probably wouldn't be in the position to hire one if they didn't have good memories for their businesses in the first place. And, how long do you think the secretary would keep the job if she couldn't remember?

Although there are millions of reference books, and we certainly need them, a lawyer pleading a case in court would much rather have the details of a precedent in his memory, than have to stop to look it up. If he could quote pages and laws from certain law books, the judge and jury would most certainly be favorably impressed. A carpenter doesn't stop to look at a book when he has to use a particular tool, he remembers how to use it. If an emergency arises on the operating table, the surgeon acts immediately. All the medical books in existence wouldn't help that patient, if the doctor didn't remember just what to do. When you visit your doctor and tell him the symptoms of your illness, he doesn't have to refer to the notes he wrote while attending medical school, he remembers which ailment has which symptoms.

Those that write new ideas on old subjects, must know or remember all the old ideas first. Could a man like Professor Einstein come up with new formulas and theories if he didn't know or remember all the current ones? Of course not. The telephone would never have been invented if Alexander Graham Bell had not known or remembered all the principles of transporting sound that were then in existence. If it were not for memory, we would never have new inventions.

I could go on, ad infinitum, demonstrating how and why the memory is important; or why it is not always convenient to refer to books or lists. Most everything we do is based on memory. The things we often say we do by "instinct," are really done through memory.

Writing things down just isn't enough in itself to help you remember. Why are some children slow in school, even though they write notes in class? It is not because they are stupid! It is because they don't remember their work. In school they are told they must remember certain things, but unfortunately, they are not taught how to do so.

So, a trained and retentive memory is certainly important.

It is getting over the first hurdle that is always the most difficult in any new thing you learn. The first hurdle in training your memory, is to actually use my system. Use it, and it'll work for you. Just knowing the system and still writing phone numbers on paper, is the same as not knowing the system at all.

Those of you who happen to know how to type fairly rapidly, do you recall how you felt when you first started to learn typing? You thought you'd never get the hang of it, and felt that others, who did type well, were just more suited for it than you were. Now, you probably can't understand why you felt that way; there is nothing more natural than for you to sit down and type rapidly.

Well, it's the same with a trained memory. I believe that I can memorize a telephone number faster than anyone can write it, and, I strengthen my memory each time I do so. When I first started using these systems, I felt as you may feel now; that it is easier to write things down and forget them, than to bother with associations. But, keep at it, and you'll feel the same about this as you do about typing. You'll wonder, after a while, why it took any effort at all, in the beginning.

The thing to keep in mind, above all else, is to make all your associations ridiculous and/or illogical. Many of the systems being taught today, and those in the past, do not stress this nearly enough. As a matter of fact, some of them will teach you to make logical associations. There's only one fault with such systems as far as I'm concerned; they won't work. I do not believe that you can remember logical associations anywhere as well, or as easily, as ridiculous ones.

Some of the old systems taught the student to correlate two objects when he wanted to remember one in conjunction with the other. A correlation meant to link the two objects by means of other words which either sounded alike, meant the same, were the exact opposites or were brought to mind somehow or other. This happens to be an excellent imagination exercise, so let me explain it to you. If you wanted to remember "pencil" and light "bulb" for some reason; you might reason this way:—

pencil—lead—heavy—light—bulb.

Do you see the process? Pencil would naturally make you think of lead; the mineral lead is very heavy; the opposite of heavy is light; and light logically leads you to bulb.

How would you correlate "diamond" to "cigarette"? Well, here's one way: diamond — ring — smoke ring — smoke — cigarette. Actually, you can correlate any two objects to each other; even the most unlikely things. Of course, it's much easier to remember "pencil" and "bulb" by making an association of yourself writing with a light bulb instead of a pencil; or, throwing a switch, and a pencil lights instead of a bulb. As far as "diamond" and "cigarette" is concerned, if you "saw" yourself smoking a diamond instead of a cigarette, you'd certainly recall it with more facility than by making a correlation. I mention the correlations only because it is a good imagination exercise, and because you might have some fun trying it with your friends. The idea, of course, is to use as few words as possible in order to correlate any two items. Correlations are a fair.5ly current idea for memory training, but as I've already told you, memory systems go back as far as early Greek civilization. I believe itwas Simonides, the Greek poet, who first used something like the Peg system in the year 500 B.C. He used the different rooms of his house, and the pieces of furniture in the various rooms, as his pegs. This is limited, but it will work. If you would make up your mind to use the rooms of your house and the furniture in a definite order, you would have a list of peg words. These would be the things you already know or remember, and any new thing to be memorized would be associated to them.

This must have worked for Simonides, because one of the stories about him, tells of the time he was giving a recitation at a banquet, and the roof of the building collapsed. Everyone was killed, except Simonides. Because of the mangled condition of the bodies, they could not be identified for burial. Simonides was able to tell just who each one was; for he had memorized their positions around the banquet table.

Coming back to modern times, General George Marshall received some favorable publicity because of something he did at some of his press conferences. He told the newsmen to interrupt him and ask him any questions, at any time during his talk. The reporters would do that, asking questions pertaining to the topic that the General was discussing at that moment. General Marshall would listen to the question, but would not answer it. He wouldn't break his train of thought, but went right on with his talk. After the talk was completed, he would look at one of the men who had asked a question, and answer that particular one. He would then look at another man, and answer his question. He did this until all or most of the questions were answered. This was always of great amazement to the newsmen; but it is quite easy with the aid of a memory system.

Former Postmaster James Farley has a reputation of knowing some twenty thousand people by their first names.

In a recent article for the N.Y. Times, Mr. Fancy called remembering names the "most effective of all forms of flattery." His marvelous memory for names has certainly been a great help to him. It is even said that Mr. Farley's campaigning and calling people by name was influential towards the late Franklin Roosevelt's first election to the presidency.

I don't expect you all to be influential in the election of presidents, but you can certainly improve your memory beyond your wildest hopes, if you will learn and use the systems taught in this book.

CHAPTER TWENTY ONE
Don't Be Absent-Minded

Towards the conclusion of his lecture on the wonderful sights to be seen
in this world, the famous traveler said,
"There are some spectacles that one never forgets!"
At this point a tiny old lady in the back row, stood up and timidly
inquired, "Oh, my, can you tell me where I could get a pair?
I'm always forgetting mine!"

Are you continually plagued by misplacing certain items? Do you waste precious time searching for your glasses or for the pencil which is usually perched behind your ear? Are you the type that's always scream-ing, "But I just had it in my hands a moment ago I?" Do you always hide your valuable trinkets so well, that you yourself can't find them? Ladies, are you constantly late for a date because you simply can't locate your favorite lipstick? And, men, does your wife rant and scream while you laboriously search for that misplaced cuff link?

If the answer to any of these questions is, "Yes," run, don't walk, to your nearest bookstore.

Well, if this were a radio or television commercial, it might sound something like that, don't you think? But seriously, have I hit the bull's eye with some of the above questions? I'm almost certain that I have, because very few of us are fortunate enough not to be absent-minded at times.

Many people make the mistake of confusing absentmindedness with a poor memory. Actually, I feel that they should be considered as two entirely different things. People with excellent memories can also be absent-minded. You've all heard of the absent-minded professor stories; well, be assured that in order to be a professor you must have a good memory to begin with. The hundreds of gags about the absent-minded professors who wind their wives, kiss the cat good night and put out the clock, may be true for all I know, but it still doesn't signify that they have poor memories.

I believe that you can cure absentmindedness with just a little effort and with the tips contained in this chapter. However, please do not feel that you can do it by just reading it. You have to make it your business to use the information supplied here. Then, and only then, will it help you. I assume that many people will read through a book of this type; never try to use the information given, and then complain that this will never help them. That, of course, will be true, if you just read through this book without attempting to apply the systems. Many adults always claim that they are too old to learn. I believe they mean that they are too late to learn—no one is too old! E. L. Thorndike, an authority on adult education, said that "age is no handicap to learning a new trade, profession, or anything you want to do at any time of life." The italics in this quote are mine; if you really want to learn, you can; so don't use age as an excuse.

Actually, absentmindedness is nothing more than inattention. If you paid attention to where you put your glasses, naturally you would know where they were when you needed them. The American College Dictionary gives "preoccupied" as one of the definitions of absent-minded, and that just about hits the nail on the head. The little things that we do continually, like putting down things, are just not important enough to occupy our minds, so we become absent-minded.

It stands to reason that if you put things away without thinking, or mechanically, you'll forget where they are because you never remembered in the first place. When you leave your house, you usually worry about whether you locked your door or not, simply because you locked it. Unconsciously, without giving it a thought.

So, I've solved your problem! To avoid absentmindedness, think what you're doing. I know, you're thinking, "I knew that. If I were able to think each time I put something away, or locked a door, I wouldn't be absent-minded!" Okay, then, why not use conscious associations to help you remember trivial things? It's easy to do.

For example, one thing that is annoying to all of us, is forgetting to mail letters. You either forget to take them when you leave your house, or, if you do take them, they remain in your pocket for days. If you want to be sure that you take the letter with you when you leave the house, do this: first decide what it is that you do or see at the very last moment upon leaving your house. I personally see the doorknob of my front door, because I check it to see if the door is locked. That is the last thing I do, so I make a ridiculous association between doorknob and letter. When I leave my house the next morning, I'll check the doorknob; once I think of doorknob, I'll recall my ridiculous association and remember that I must take the letter!

The last thing that you do before you leave your house may be entirely different; you may kiss your wife or husband good-bye; well, associate that kiss with the letter. Make sure that your associations are ridiculous and/or illogical.

Now, how can you be sure to mail the letter? One way is to keep it in your hand until you drop it in a mail box. If you'd rather keep it in your pocket, make an association between the person the letter is going to, and the mail box. You might "see" him sitting on top of a mail box, etc. If you do not know the person well enough to picture, use a substitute word as you've already learned. If the letter were going to the telephone company, you would associate telephone to mail box, and so on. When you see a mail box, in the street, it will remind you to mail the letter. (After all that, I hope you remembered to put a stamp on the envelope!)

This idea can be used for all the little things you want to remember to do. If you keep forgetting your umbrella at the office, just associate umbrella to the last thing you do upon leaving the office. If your wife calls and tells you to be sure to buy some eggs on your way home, associate eggs with, say, your front door. This will act as a final reminder. Instead of waiting to be reminded when you're home, associate eggs to grocery store; then when you see a grocery store, it will remind you to go in and buy the eggs.

Of course, all these are theoretical examples: you would know just what to associate to what, in your own particular case.

Now we come to the real petty annoyances of absent-mindedness; such as putting things down, and then forgetting where they are. Well, the method applied to this is exactly the same. You have to make an association between the object and its location. For instance, if the phone rings, and as you reach for it, you put your pencil behind your ear, make a fast mental picture between ear and pencil. When you're through with the phone, and you think of pencil, you will know it's behind your ear. The same thing goes for any small item or small errand. If you're in the habit of putting things down anyplace, get into the habit of making an association to remind you of where it is.

One of the questions usually asked at this point is: "Fine, but how am I going to remember to make these associations for all these petty things?" There is only one answer to this question — use some will power at first, and be sure that you do make the associations. When you see the results, I'm sure you'll manage to keep it up, and before you know it, you will have acquired the habit.

There is no doubt, by the way, that this system must cure absent-mindedness. The reason is obvious; the eyes cannot see if the mind is absent and your mind is absent when you put things away mechanically. The very idea of making an association makes you think of what you're doing for at least a fraction of a second, and that's all that's necessary.

If you make an association between your key and your door, as you lock the door you are no longer doing it mechanically. You are thinking of it; therefore, later on when you wonder if you locked the door, you'll know you did. When setting the alarm on your clock, make an association between clock and hand, or between clock and anything, for that matter. It doesn't matter; the important thing is that you're thinking of it for the moment. And, because you did think of it for the moment, you won't have to get out of bed later to check if the alarm is set.

I say that the association doesn't matter, and it doesn't. As a matter of fact, if you closed your eyes and saw yourself turning off your iron as you were doing it, you wouldn't have to worry about whether it was on or off, while trying to enjoy a movie. Closing the eyes and picturing the action, is just as good as the association. It serves the same purpose; that of forcing you to think of what you're doing at the moment.

That's all there is to it. But I can't stress strongly enough the necessity of using what you've just learned. Please don't read it, nod your head and say it's a great idea, and then forget about it. Put out the bit of effort necessary at first, and you will be glad you did.

Captain of ship talking to sailor: "Don't you ever say 'the back of the ship' again—that's the stern of the ship; and that's port-side, that's starboard, that's the crow's nest, that's the gig, that's the forecastle, etc.
"If you ever say 'back of the ship' again, I'll throw you out of that, that, er, that little round hole over there!"

Just as absentmindedness is often mistaken for a poor memory, so is absentmindedness often blamed for mental blocks. Again, I don't think that one has anything to do with the other. Having something familiar on the tip of your tongue and not being able to remember it, is not absentmindedness. What it is and why it happens, I don't know; but, unfortunately it does happen; to me as well as to you.

There isn't much I can do to help avoid mental blocks. There isn't any system I know of that can stop them. However, I can tell you that when it does happen, try to think of events associated with the name or event you're trying to recall. If it's the name of a familiar person that you can't think of, try to picture the last time you saw that person, where it was, what you were doing and who else was present at the time.

The mind must work in its own devious way; more often than not, just thinking around the fact you want, will make it pop into your mind.

If this doesn't help, the next best thing is to forget about it. Stop thinking about it completely for awhile, and the odds are it will come to you when you least expect it.

That's about all the help I can give you when it comes to mental blocks. Try my suggestions the next time it happens to you; you may be surprised at how helpful they are!

CHAPTER TWENTY TWO
Amaze Your Friends

FARMER (showing off his farm to a friend): "How many sheep would you say were in that flock? See if you can get close with a rough guess."
FRIEND (after short pause): "I'd say there were about 497 sheep there."
"Why, you hit it right on the head, that's exactly right! How in the world did you know?"
"It was simple, really, I just counted all the legs, and then divided by four!"

The memory stunt contained in this chapter may not be as astounding as dividing the legs of sheep by four, but it's certainly easier to do. You'll probably be glad to know that there are no mathematics involved at all, just a trained memory.

A friend of mine in the textile business here in New York has told me that he has gained quite a reputation for himself by remembering numbers. He goes to lunch with a few business acquaintances each day, and he invariably asks them to give him any four or five digit number to memorize. He usually has anywhere from three to six people with him, and he memorizes the numbers they give him. They interrupt him during the luncheon to see if he can still recall the numbers and, of course, he does.

I don't mention this because it's a big deal particularly, but it is a good conversation starter, and it has accomplished a purpose for my friend. He tells me that everyone in his trade is talking about him and his remarkable memory. I do mention it, however, to show you how people are impressed with any sort of memory feat; only because they feel that they could never accomplish it themselves. If folks are so amazed when a man remembers a half dozen four or five digit numbers, you can imagine the fantastic effect upon them, after you've mastered the stunt contained in these pages.

How would you like to be able to memorize this list of numbers:

	1	2	3	4	5	6	7	8	9	10
A—	9491	0261	4850	8210	1427	0214	5390	0141	7450	7590
B—	2195	6140	5827	5197	4270	9401	4260	5014	1395	8150
C—	8520	7461	9511	7157	9420	4532	1950	1404	7841	7410
D—	2116	5152	9470	2154	9750	7471	7220	1941	0191	3102
E—	4595	5891	3944	0182	0594	9414	6720	8227	8527	7480
F—	0137	5814	9950	9427	1285	2754	3662	1540	8927	9521
G—	9015	3145	8195	8540	9514	7040	7312	1211	9227	1270
H—	9210	7427	ozi6	4910	7531	7421	1484	2469	0791	2520
I—	4175	1842	3058	7462	3212	0746	7915	7527	0743	9710
J—	4112	9434	0941	7212	9402	7213	5810	1204	6920	4210

That's right! You can memorize this list of four hundred digits, easily!! Not only will you know them in order, but also out of sequence! The idea is to give anyone a copy of this list, and have them test you on it. They may ask you to give the numbers across for letter G, or the numbers down, for column 4. They can ask for E7 and you will immediately give them the number 6720. In other words, you prove to them that you have thoroughly memorized the list; and so you have!

My good friend and memory expert, Bernard Zufall, was the first one that I know of, to use this type of stunt. He has been using it for many years with three digit numbers instead of the four digit numbers that appear here. He, of course, utilized his own methods to memorize the list. I will teach you here, the method that I use:

You must realize by now that it would be almost impossible to accomplish this without the aid of the phonetic alphabet. Certainly, it would be definitely impossible to memorize and retain the numbers without it. As a matter of fact, this feat is so unbelievable to the uninitiated, that you will find some people examining the list to find some mathematical solution. Let them, since this is not based on mathematics at all, they'll be more impressed and confused than ever.

None of the four digit numbers in the list is repeated at any time, each one is used only once. The numbers have not been chosen at random, I've picked each one because it fits into the system. And, here is the system: if someone were to call E7, here is the way my mind would work. My Key word for E7 must begin with the letter E, and it must have one other consonant sound at the end. That sound (in this particular case) must be the sound that represents #7, which is the k or hard g sound. My Key word for E7 is "egg." Eggs come from chickens and the phonetic alphabet tells me that "chickens" stands for 6720. If you'll check the list, you will see that 6720 is the correct number!

If B5 were called, I would know that the Key word must begin with the letter B, and the ending consonant sound must be the L sound for #5. The Key word for B5 is "bell." A bell rings. Rings—4270! Can you see the simplicity of it? Don't get me wrong, it will take you a bit of time and study to master all the numbers, but the system is easy. Again, may I mention that this is not only a fantastic memory stunt, but a wonderful thinking and memory exercise. Each time you master one of the stunts in this book whether you care to present them or not, you are improving your memory, exercising that muscle and sharpening your wits.

Well then, you know that each time a letter and number are called, you must transpose it into a Key word. It doesn't matter if the number is called first, the system is the same. The letter is always at the beginning and the consonant sound that represents the number is at the end of the word. This Key word is correlated to, or associated with another word; and this word gives you the four digit number, according to the phonetic alphabet. If someone were to call, "8C," you would know that the Key word starts with C and ends with the f or v sound. The Key word is "cuff." Cuff is correlated to trouser. Trouser—1404!

The entire list for the one hundred four digit numbers follows below. After you have looked them over, I'll explain some more about the presentation of the feat.

A1 —ate-burped	B1 —bat-and ball	C1 —cat-felines
A2 —awn-sunshade	B2 —bean-shooters	C2 —can-crushed
A3 —aim-rifles	B3 —burn-loafing	C3 —comb-bald head
A4 —air-vents	B4 —boar-wild pig	C4 —car-cadillac
A5 —ale-drink	B5 —bell-rings	C5 —coal-burns
A6 —ash-cinder	B6 —badge-breast	C6 —cash-real money
A7 —ache-limps	B7 —bag-oranges	C7 —coke-tables
A8 —Ave.-street	B8 —buff-luster	C8 —cuff-trouser
A9 —ape-growls	B9 —baby-dimple	C9 —cap-covered
A10 —ace-dubs	B10 —bass-fiddles	C10 —case-crates

D1 —dot-and dash	E1 —eddy-whirlpool	F1 —fat-stomach
D2 —den-wild lion	E2 —en-alphabet	F2 —fun-laughter
D3 —dam-breaks	E3 —ern-emperor	F3 —foam-bubbles
D4 —deer-antler	E4 —err-is divine	F4 —fur-bearing
D5 —dill-pickles	E5 —eel-slippery	F5 —foil-tinfoil
D6 —dish-cracked	E6 —edge-border	F6 —fish-angler
D7 —dog-canines	E7 —egg-chickens	P7 —fake-magician
D8 —dove-white bird	E8 —eve-evening	F8 —five-dollars
D9 —dope-stupid	E9 —ebb-falling	F9 —fib-fibbing
D10 —dose-medicine	E10 —ess-curves	F10 —fuse-blend

G1 —gat-pistol	H1 —hat-bands	I1—it-article
G2 —gown-material	H2 —hen-crowing	I2—inn-tavern
G3—game-football	H3 —ham-sandwich	I3—I'm-myself
G4 —grow-flowers	H4 —hare-rabbits	I4—Ira-Gershwin
G5 —gall-bladder	H5 —hill-climbed	I5—isle-Manhattan
G6 —gush-geysers	H6 —hash-corned	I6—itch-scratch
G7 —gag-comedian	H7 —hack-driver	I7—Ike-Capitol
G8 —gave-donated	H8 —have-ownership	I8—ivy-cling
G9 —gap-opening	H9 —hop-skipped	I9—(y)ipe-scream
G10—gas-tanks	H10 —hose-nylons	I10—ice-buckets

J1—jot-write down	J5 —jail-prison	J8 —jive-dancer
J2—John-Barrymore	J6 —judge-condemn	J9 —Jap-Japanese
J3—jam-spread	J7 —jack-lifts	J10 —juice-rinds
J4—jar-contain		

You'll notice that there is only one slight exception in the system, at 19. There is no word beginning with I and ending with the p or b sound. So I use the word, "yipe," which serves the purpose just as well. Also, in every possible case, the sounds representing the four digit numbers are contained in one word. There are only eight instances where I found it necessary to use a phrase of two words.

I'm sure that you all can see the simple associations or correlations with each Key word. If you go over them once or twice, concentrating on them as you do, you should remember most of them. Each Key word should lead you logically to the associated word. Coke, for C7, is short for Coca-Cola, which is usually found on dinner tables. En, for E2, is just the name of the letter itself, which is part of the alphabet. I don't think that any of the others need any explaining.

You must learn all these words thoroughly before you can present this feat for your friends. After you've learned them, practice the transposing of the associated words or phrases into numbers. Once you can do that quickly, you're ready to present the feat.

You can have the list printed on a card, if you like, so that you can hand them out to your friends. Then after you've demonstrated your fabulous powers of retention and recall, you can let them keep the card as a souvenir. Let them try to memorize it, if they can!

Aside from simply allowing your spectators to call the letter and number, you can go further. They can ask you to call out all the numbers diagonally from, say, A1 to J10. All you have to do, is give the numbers for A1, B2, C3, D4 etc. They might ask for row F backwards — you just give them F10, F9, F8, etc. If they want the four digit numbers backwards also, you can do that too. For example, you know the associated word for F10 (fuse) is blend; instead of giving the number 9521, give it as 1259! F9 is fibbing — backwards the number is 7298, and so on.

If you're asked to give row #6 backwards, simply call off, J6, I6, H6, G6 down, or up, to A6. I know that it is difficult for some people to work backwards with the alphabet I can solve that problem for you, easily. You can learn the representative number of any letter in the alphabet by utilizing the first twenty-six peg words in conjunction with a representative adjective. This is what I mean:

Awful tie	Neat tire
Brave Noah	Old towel
Cute ma	Pleasing dish
Damp rye	Quiet tack
Excellent law	Red dove
Funny shoe	Solid tub
Guernsey cow	Tough nose
Heavy ivy	Ugly net
Idle bee	Virtuous nun
Jagged toes	Wonderful name
Korean tot	X-rayed Nero
Loud tin	Yellow nail
Marble tomb	Zig-zag notch

Notice that the adjective for the peg word for #3 begins with the third letter of the alphabet (c); the 10th adjective begins with the tenth letter J, etc. If you make a quick picture in your mind of each of these, you will know the position, numerically, of all the letters! Of course, you can use any adjective you like, as long as it begins with the proper letter. If you wanted to know the position, say, of the letter "O," just think of the adjective that you used: old towel. You know that "towel" is #15, therefore "O" is the fifteenth letter of the alphabet.

You can use this idea, or, elsewhere in this book (Chapter #12) you will find an idea of how to use the twenty-six letters themselves in order to have a list of twenty-six secondary peg words. You can tie these words to your basic peg words, and you will have accomplished the same thing. You will know the numerical positions of all the letters.

Either one of these methods will enable you to use the letters of the alphabet to a much better advantage. Just thinking backwards from peg word #26 to peg word #1 will make it easy for you to recite the entire alphabet backwards. This in itself is a good stunt, since most people cannot recite the alphabet backwards, without quite a bit of effort. However, the important thing is that this idea will be of use when you're asked to give a numbered row backwards; or diagonally from J10 to A1, or J1 to A10.

After doing this stunt for awhile, you will find that eventually you will not even think of your Key words and associations. As soon as a letter and number is called, the four digit number will pop into your mind.

That is the beauty of mnemonics, it is just an aid to your true memory. It is a means to an end, and once you've reached or acquired that end, you can forget the means!!

CHAPTER TWENTY THREE
It Pays to Remember
Appointments and Schedules

"The man who is always punctual in keeping appointments never loses anything by it."
"No, only about half an hour waiting for the other fellow to show up."

There isn't much I can do about those of you who know that you have an appointment, and get there late, anyway. But I think I can help you if you forget those appointments completely. You've already learned, in a previous chapter, how to remember your errands or appointments for each day. You can still use that idea; but if, in your particular business, or even socially, you find it necessary to keep numerous appointments during the week at certain times of day, you'll be interested in this chapter. The system contained here is one which enables you to make a conscious association as soon as you've made an appointment. By making this association, you can recall all your appointments for each day of the week without bothering with a date or memo book.

For those of you who don't care about remembering weekly appointments or schedules, I would suggest that you learn the idea behind the method anyway. You never know when you might find it useful. Please don't let the length of the explanation frighten you; once you understand and use it, there's nothing to it.

The first thing you must do, is to give a number to each day of the week. Since there are seven days in the week, you'll number them from 1 to 7. According to our calendar, Sunday is the first day of the week; but I have found that many people refer to Monday as the first day. This, I imagine, is because of our work-a-day world, and the first day of work is Monday. I will therefore use Monday as the first day in the following explanation. Remember the days of the week in this manner:

Monday -1	Thursday - 4	
Tuesday -2	Friday - 5	Sunday - 7
Wednesday -3	Saturday - 6	

Once you know the number of each day of the week, you can transpose any day at any hour to one of your peg words. That's right, you will use the peg words which you already know, to help you remember schedules and appointments. Each day at every hour will be represented by a peg word, and you don't have to remember anything to know the words; it works itself.

Any day at any particular hour can be transposed into a two digit number in this way: the number of the day will be the first digit, and the hour itself will be the second digit. For example, if you wanted to remember an appointment for Wednesday at 4:00 o'clock, Wednesday is the third day, so #3 is the first digit. The appointment is for 4:00 o'clock, so #4 is the second digit. You now have a two digit number-#34, and the peg word for #34 is "mower." Therefore, "mower" must represent Wednesday at 4:00 o'clock! Monday at 2:00 o'clock would be "tin." Monday is the first day, and the time is 2:00 o'clock. In the same way, you would arrive at the following:

Thursday	at 1:00 o'clock-rod (41)
Friday	at 8:00 o'clock-lava (58)
Sunday	at 6:00 o'clock-cage (76)
Tuesday	at 9:00 o'clock-knob (29)

Simple, isn't it? Of course, if you can transpose the day and hour to a peg word, it is just as easy to transpose a peg word to the day and hour. "Notch," for example, is your peg word for #26; so it must represent Tuesday (2) at 6:00 o'clock.

There are two hours that cannot be represented by a peg word. That is because they themselves are composed of two digits. I mean, of course, 11:00 and 12:00 o'clock. Ten o'clock can be transposed to a regular peg word, because it is thought of as zero only, instead of one and zero. In other words, Saturday at 10:00 o'clock would be transposed to #60 (cheese), because Saturday is the sixth day and 10:00 o'clock is zero. "Rose" (40) would represent Thursday at 10:00 o'clock; Monday at 10:00 o'clock is "toes," and so on.

I'll give you two methods for handling eleven and twelve o'clock, both of which have been tried and tested. The first method is the obvious one (although not the better one) because it follows the same system as the other hours. Transpose any day at eleven or twelve o'clock to a three digit number by adding the 11 or 12 onto the number of the day, i.e. Tuesday at 11:00 o'clock—211; Thursday at 12:00 o'clock—412; Sunday at 12:00 o'clock—712; Wednesday at 11:00 o'clock—311, etc. Now, you would have to make up a peg word, following the phonetic alphabet, which would fit each day at eleven or twelve o'clock. The words you select would be used all the time for those days and hours. If you want to use this idea (don't make up your mind until you've read the second method) I'll give you some examples of words that can be used. You can pick any of these, or any that you find by yourself.

Monday	11:00-dotted, toted
	12:00-tauten, tootin'
Tuesday	11:00-knotted, knitted
	12:00-Indian, noddin'
Wednesday	11:00-mated, imitate
	12:00-mutton, mitten
Thursday	11:00-raided, radiate
	12:00-rotten, written
Friday	11 :00-lighted, loaded
	12:00-Latin, laden
Saturday	11:00-cheated, jaded
	12:00-jitney, shut in
Sunday	11 00-coated, cadet
	12:00-kitten, cotton

The following method, I think, is the better of the two. First of all, I transpose the day at 11:00 or 12:00 o'clock into a two digit instead of a three digit number. I do this by considering 11:00 o'clock as a one, and 12:00 o'clock as a two. Now, Friday at 11:00 o'clock is thought of as 51; Friday at 12:00 o'clock—52; Sunday at 11:00 o'clock—71; Sunday at 12:00 o'clock—72, etc. Of course, you can't use your regular peg words for these, since they are already being used for one and two o'clock; so use any other word, that fits phonetically, for these numbers.

Let me give you a few examples: for Tuesday at 11:00 o'clock, you could use the word "nut;" later on, when you picture your association (I'll explain the associations in a moment) you will know that "nut" couldn't represent Tuesday at 1:00 o'clock because you would have used your regular peg word, "net" for that. So, "nut" must stand for Tuesday at 11:00 o'clock.

Saturday at 12:00 o'clock could be represented by "chin." Your regular peg word, "chain," represents Saturday at 2:00 o'clock, so you know that "chin" must mean Saturday at 12:00. Do you get it, now? Basically, it's this: for any day at eleven or twelve o'clock use the same sounds that you would use for that day at one or two o'clock, but do not use your regular peg word. That's all there is to that!

If all your appointments are usually made for the exact hour, on the hour, you actually need read no further about memorizing appointments; you have all the information you need right now. Supposing you have an appointment to see your dentist at 9:00 o'clock on Tuesday, and you want to be sure that you won't forget it. Well, transpose Tuesday at 9:00 o'clock, to the peg word, "knob," and associate that to dentist. You might picture a gigantic doorknob as a dentist, or you could see (and feel) your dentist pulling a knob from your mouth, instead of a tooth.

If you had to remember to make a deposit at your bank on Monday at 2:00 o'clock, you would associate "tin" to bank. You have to catch a plane on Friday at 11:00 o'clock, associate "loaded" or "lad" (according to the method you're using for 11:00 and 12:00 o'clock) to airplane. Wednesday at 10:00 o'clock you have to visit a friend, associate "mice" to your friend, etc.

If you usually have appointments with people whom you do not know too well, or if you cannot picture them, use a substitute word for their names in your associations.

That's all you have to do. If you have made an association for all your appointments for an entire week, and you want to remember what you have scheduled for, say, Tuesday, simply go over the peg words for that particular day: Tuesday—nose, net, nun, name, Nero, nail, notch, neck, knife, knob, knitted or knot, and Indian or neon. As soon as you reach a peg word that has been associated, you'll know it! You might reach "neck," and know immediately that you've made a picture of neck, and say, hospital. This will remind you that you have to visit a sick friend at the hospital at 7:00 o'clock on Tuesday! That's all! Again, you need only try it to be convinced that it works.

As far as I personally am concerned, this is all I use to remember my weekly schedule. Some of my appointments may be arranged for the hour exactly, and others for say, 3:15, 3:30 or 3:45, but I find that it does not matter. If I associate the day of the appointment at 3:00 o'clock, on the hour, true memory tells me that the date is for fifteen, thirty or forty-five minutes past the hour. However, there may be some of you who must remember the exact time, to the minute, for some appointments, such as catching trains, etc. In order to do this, you must add only one word to your mental picture. You would actually be remembering a four digit instead of a two digit number.

The second pair of digits will represent minutes, while the first two digits represent the day and the hour. For example, if your appointment with the dentist was on Tuesday at 9:42 o'clock, transpose the day and hour to "knob" (29), and get "rain" into the association to represent 42. You realize, of course, that in this case you are faced with the same problem as you were when learning to memorize the four trunk line digits of a telephone number.

In the above example, how will you be sure that your dental appointment is for Tuesday at 9:42, and not for Thursday at 2:29? This could happen if you weren't sure as to which peg word belongs first, and which belongs last. Well, the problem is solved in the same manner as it was solved for telephone numbers. The best solution is to make a "logical-illogical" association, so that, even though it is a ridiculous picture, one peg must logically follow another.

If you made a picture of your dentist pulling a "knob" from your mouth, instead of a tooth, and doing it in the pouring "rain," you would know that knob came first, followed by rain. Any of the other suggestions that I gave you for telephone numbers will apply for appointments, too. If you used the Link for your picture, you would associate dentist to knob, and then knob to rain. The idea of using a word other than the regular peg word, for the last two digits (in this case, the digits representing the minutes) is just as applicable here. That would help for any day at any time, except 11:00 or 12:00 o'clock, where it wouldn't be necessary, since you are not using a regular peg for the day and time, anyway.

You are the best judge as to just which ideas to use. I would suggest trying them all; the one that comes easiest to you, of course, is the right one for you. Although, as I told you, I don't think it necessary to bother with the minutes of an appointment. If I did want to remember the minutes, I would do it this way: on Monday at 3:25, I must remember to pick up a television set — I would picture a television set acting as a "tomb" stone, while "nails" perform on the screen.

You see, I use the logical-illogical picture idea. The association above will leave no doubt that "tomb" (Monday at 3:00 o'clock) comes first, followed by "nail" (25 minutes). One other example: on Wednesday at 12:10, I have a date to go swimming, so I would make a picture of myself swimming; I hit a "mine" which injures my "toes." Now, when I go over my pegs for Wednesday of that week: mice, mat, moon, mummy, mower, mule, match, mug, movie, map, mitt and mine (I always use "mitt" to represent Wednesday at 11:00, and "mine" for Wednesday at 12:00) I will be reminded of this ridiculous picture. I know that "mine" is not one of my regular pegs, so it must represent 12:00, not 2:00 o'clock. "Toes" (10), being the last part of the association, represents the minutes; so I know that my swimming date is for Wednesday at 12:10.

These are the ideas that I use; but again let me stress that what is best for me, is not necessarily best for you. This must be left to your own discretion; which I'm sure you will use, once you understand the basic principles involved.

You might be wondering about one little thing at this point, and that is, "How do I differentiate between say, 7:00 A.M. and 7:00 P.M.?" Well, that is a good theoretical question, but if you stop to think for a moment, you will realize that there can hardly be any conflict, if you use this system for practical purposes. The appointments that you make for the evening are usually so vastly different than those made for the morning, that they couldn't possibly become confused. You will certainly know, for example, whether you usually see your dentist in the morning or in the evening. You also would know that your dinner date is for 7:00 P.M. and not 7:00 A.M. And, if you had an appointment to meet a friend for lunch in front of the Public library, and got there at 1:00 A.M., you'd be awfully hungry by the time you had lunch.

So you see, there's really no problem there. Of course, if you had to, you could put a word into your ridiculous association to tell you whether it was A.M. or P.M. You could use "aim" for A.M. and "poem" for P.M., or any other words that use those letters. You might even use white and black; get black into your mental picture to stand for P.M., and white for A.M. But, believe me, all this is hardly necessary; I only mention it to show that you can remember anything with the use of a conscious association.

Now you can discard your note and memo pads, if you use the systems explained in this chapter. Remember, only if you use it, will it help you.

Here are the bare bones of the system:

• When you make an appointment, transpose the day and hour (and/or minutes) to peg words.

• Associate the appointment itself to these peg words.

• When you arise on the morning of each day (or, if you like, the evening before) go over all your pegs for that day.

• When you come to a peg that has been used in an association, you'll know it—this will remind you of what you have to do at that particular hour.

• As the day goes on, you might make it a habit to check your peg words for the day, periodically. This is in case one appointment has slipped your mind, even though you were reminded of it in the morning.

In the next chapter, I will show you how to remember important dates throughout the year, such as, anniversaries, birthdays, etc., but for the time being, you should never forget any weekly appointments, if you follow these rules.

The information you've been taught here can be practiced, or used as a memory stunt in the following manner:

Have a friend call out certain errands for different hours of different days of the week. They needn't be called in order, since appointments are never made in any particular order, anyway. Have him write these down as he calls them off to you. After he has called about twenty of them, simply go over your peg words for Monday (toes, tot, tin, tomb, etc.) and call back all the Monday appointments. Do the same for each day of the entire week. Or, he can give you the time of day, and the day, and you give him the errand, and so on.

Then give your friend a half hour to remember the same list. The odds are he will fail miserably!

CHAPTER TWENTY FOUR
It Pays to Remember Anniversaries, Birthdays and Other Important Dates

"Does your husband forget your anniversaries?"
"Never. I remind him of it in June, and again in January; and I always get two presents!"

If a man's memory is so poor that he can be led to believe that he has an anniversary every six months, then he deserves to have to buy two presents.

Seriously though, the Peg system can be applied to remembering not only important anniversaries, but also important dates in history. It is also helpful for memorizing addresses, prices or style numbers.

As far as dates are concerned, if you want to remember people's anniversaries or birthdays, just associate the people, or substitute words for their names, to the date. Suppose Mr. Gordon's birthday is April 3rd. If you associate Mr. Gordon, or the word, "garden" to "ram," you would remember it. "Ram" represents 43, and Mr. Gordon's birthday falls in the 4th month, on the 3rd day!

Of course every date will not be able to be transposed into a basic peg word. You can do that only with those that fall within the first nine months, and for the first nine days of those months. All other dates will be a three digit number, so a different idea must be used. I could tell you to make up a word which would represent the three digit number, and I will tell you to do that in most cases. But, if done all the time, it may confuse you.

If the word in your association was "tighten" (112), how would you know whether it meant the first month, 12th day, or the 11th month, 2nd day? You wouldn't, and your birthday card would be a bit late if you sent it on November 2nd to someone whose birthday is January 12th. It would be late, or about two months too early.

So, you must have a definite distinction to avoid this. I would suggest that the easiest way to do it is to use one word for the three digits, only for the first nine months. For October, November and December, use two words, your peg word to represent the month, and another word to represent the day. If you feel that you wouldn't know which word came first, then always use a word that is not a basic peg word for your day. That way you'll know that the regular peg always represents the month.

Actually this isn't necessary if you're going to use one word to represent the month and day for the first nine months. If you do, you will know that wherever you have two words in your association, the one that denotes two digits must represent the month, and the other, the day.

If you have two words in your association, both of which denote two digits, then naturally the one over twelve would have to stand for the day. Only in the few cases where the day is either the 10th, 11th or 12th in the 10th, 11th or 12th month will you have to use the ideas suggested in the chapter on telephone numbers. You would have to use a "logical-illogical" picture to know which word comes first, or, always use the basic peg word for the month, and make up a word that fits phonetically, but is not a regular peg word, for the day.

If, as in school work, it is necessary for you to remember the year as well as the month and day, simply get a word to represent the year into your association. For instance, although everybody knows the date of the signing of the Declaration of Independence, I can use that as an example. If you associated the Declaration, or a substitute word, to "car cash," you would know that it was signed on July 4th (74-car) in the year 1776 (76-cash). It is almost never necessary to bother with the first two digits of the year, because you would usually know the century in which an event occurred. If not, get a word for those digits into your picture, too.

School students usually have to remember only the year of an historical event. This is a cinch, because all you need in your association, besides the event itself, is one word to represent the year. Napoleon was crowned emperor in the year 1804. If you made a ridiculous picture of Napoleon being crowned, and the crown hurting his head, or making it sore (04), you would remember it.

The Chicago fire was in 1871; just associate fire to "cot" (71). If you made a ridiculous picture of a giant ocean liner sinking because it is made of "tin," you would remember that the Titanic went down in 1912.

Sometimes it is necessary to remember the year of birth and the year of the death of important people. Just as an example, if you made an association of a stevedore dressed as a lass, fighting a bear, you would recall that Robert Louis Stevenson (stevedore) was born in 1850 (lass) and died in 1894 (bear).

Now you won't be like the little boy, who when asked how he was doing in school, complained that the teacher expected him to know about things that happened before he was born!

Talking about school work, in geography it is often important to know the products that a country exports. So, why not use the Link method to remember them. Also, if you want to remember the general outline of the map or any country or state, you can always use the idea that is usually used to remember the shape of Italy.

Italy is shaped like a boot, which makes it easy to recall. If you look at the map outline of any country, with a little imagination you can make it look like something that can be pictured. Just associate that to the name of the country, and you'll always have a general idea of its shape.

Now, if you fellows want to be able to throw away those little black books full of addresses, you can. Just remember the addresses of the young ladies by using associations. The same methods apply to this. Simply transpose all the numbers into sounds, the sounds into words, and associate the words to the person living at that address. If you made a picture in your mind of yourself flying a rope, and landing it on a carpet (landed rope), it would help in remembering that Mr. Karpel lives at 5211(landed) 49th Street (rope).

The same ideas, of course, apply to style numbers and prices. If you happen to work in the clothing line, and wish to remember the style numbers of, say, dresses, associate the number to an outstanding feature of the dress. If style #351 is a dress with a back panel, you might "see" that panel melting; melt-351. The dress with puffed sleeves is style #3410; associate "mattress" to the puffed sleeves, etc.

The prices of the dresses can be included in the same association. I'm giving you only one or two examples for each idea, because it is always best for you to use your own imagination. It is entirely up to you as to which method you will use for remembering dates and how you will associate style numbers and prices, etc. The ideas, however, can be applied in any business.

Prices can be memorized just as anything else that has to do with numbers. Just associate the price to the item. To avoid confusion, you might decide to always use the basic peg words for dollars, and any other word that fits phonetically, for cents. The same methods have to be used here, as for telephone numbers and dates. You can use one word to represent three or four digits because you'll usually know if an item is priced in the hundreds of dollars, or not.

If you had associated "maple" with book, you'd know that the price of the book is probably $3.95, and not $395.00. On the other hand, if you had associated "maple" to television set, it would be $395.00, not $3.95, or I would buy a couple of dozen.

Well, there you are. After this you should never forget any dates, prices, style numbers, addresses, and so on. I must repeat that it might seem easier, at first, to write down this type of information, but after awhile you will be able to associate faster than you can write.

Most important, don't worry about cluttering your mind with all these associations. Again, I want to remind you that once you have memorized the information through associations and you use this particular information, well, you've etched it into your mind. The associations have served their purpose and you can forget about them.

CHAPTER TWENTY FIVE
Memory Demonstrations

A few theatrical agents were gathered together at a carnival, to see an act that everyone was raving about. As everybody watched in awed silence, Bosco the Great, climbed up a ladder to a tiny pedestal, four hundred feet in the air. On the pedestal, he took a deep breath, and then started to pump his arms to and fro. The drums rolled until they reached a noisy crescendo, and at this precise second, Bosco the Great, actually left the pedestal and flew!
His arms pumping madly, he flew around the entire arena, up and down, back and forth. Just then one of the agents turned to another, and asked, "Is that all he does, bird imitations?"

I suppose that some of you are wondering why I am teaching, or have taught, all the memory feats in this book. You think that since I am a performer, and my performance does consist of memory stunts, I am creating competition for myself! Well, perhaps I am, but it doesn't bother me too much. I know that if any of you do want to perform in front of an audience, you will have the ingenuity to put together your own stunts and plan your own routine. And, most important, you will realize that you have to sell yourself, not your memory feats.

Most of the people in show business are aware of the fact that it's not what you do that makes you a good entertainer, but the way that you do it. The specialties that performers do, are simply means to an end. Whether you tell jokes, dance, sing, do memory feats, acrobatics or bird imitations is unimportant, as long as you entertain your audience.

Although my main reason for teaching you the memory stunts is that the ideas used in them can be applied for practical purposes in many ways, I also feel that the best way to learn the systems, is to give you an incentive by giving you something with which to show off for your friends. So, if you want to use the stunts to entertain at your lodge meeting or church affairs, feel free to do so. However, be sure that you know them well enough so that you do credit to yourself and my system.

There are unscrupulous characters in show business as well as in other fields, who would do anything they feel will further their careers. There is one "culprit" who steals a new act every year or so. Last year, he did me the "honor" of stealing my entire act, leaving out only the difficult demonstrations.

People who "steal" material are common in show business, but to take someone's entire act is almost unheard of. However, this fellow did it, but what annoys me, is not so much that he is doing my act, but that he does not do it well. This is to be expected because if he was a good entertainer, he would never have to resort to using an act or idea that someone else has already built up.

No, I don't mind creating competition for myself by exposing these memory feats — as long as the competition is good. As a matter of fact, the rest of this chapter consists of stunts that I have used, and some that I still use occasionally.

One of the stunts you can use, is remembering objects and initials. First have your friends call any object and any two initials. Do this with as many as you feel you can handle. Then you have the audience call any object and you give them the initials, or vice versa.

This stunt is not only impressive, but easy to do. Just make up a word that starts with the first initial and ends with the last, and associate that word to the object called.

For example: if the initials are R.T., and the object is "chandelier," you might associate rat to chandelier. The initials B. D. and bottle—associate bed to bottle. The initials P.S. and fan—associate puss to fan, etc.

Here is another example of how the systems can be twisted and manipulated. You can do the "missing card" stunt with numbers if you want to. Have someone number a sheet of paper from 1 to 52, or up to any number you like. Have them call numbers haphazardly and cross out the numbers as they call them. They can stop calling them any time they like, and you can tell them which numbers are not crossed out!

Do exactly as you do for the "missing cards." Just mutilate the peg words which represent the numbers called. Then go over your words mentally from "tie" to the peg word of the last number listed on the paper. When you come to one that is not mutilated, that is one of the "missing" numbers.

One very impressive card demonstration is the "hidden card" feat. This is most effective when you are working for a group of at least fifty-two people. (For less people, use less cards.) Hand the deck to the audience and let everyone take one card. Now, have each person call the name of his card and also give you a hiding place for it.

What you do, is associate the card word for the card called to the hiding place. If someone called the Jack of Spades hidden in a typewriter, you would perhaps, see yourself shoveling typewriters (with a spade).

After all the cards have been "hidden," you can hear the name of a card and immediately give the hiding place. Or, you are given the hiding place, and you name the card hidden there!

Do you want to impress your friends with your ability to remember numbers? Well, if you've learned another peg list up to 16 or 20, as I've taught you, you can do this:

Have your challenger number a piece of paper from 1 to 16 or 20. Then have him call any of these numbers and write a two digit number alongside. When all the numbers have been called, you can go from one to the end telling him the two digit numbers, or have him call any two digit number and you tell him what number it is at, or vice versa.

Just use your other list to remember the sequence, and use your basic pegs for the two digit numbers, i.e., #3 is called, and the two digit number to remember is 34. Well, if you're using the alphabet list, you would associate "sea" (3) to "mower" (34). The #14 is called and the number to remember is 89 — associate "hen" (14) to "fob" (89).

If you feel confident, you can have your friends call an object and a two digit number for each number listed. You can memorize both, by making one ridiculous picture for all three. The number called could be #9, the object is a toaster, and the two digit number is 24. Any combination of associations is possible here; you could see Nero (24) popping out of a toaster, playing on an eye (9) instead of a fiddle! I have been using the alphabet list idea in these examples. Of course, you could use the other idea wherein the pegs look like the numbers they represent. In that case, 9 would be "tape measure," 3 would be "clover," 14 would be "farm," etc.

Any one of the systems in this book can be used for a stunt of some sort, just as the ideas for all the stunts can be used for practical purposes in some way. If you want to apply substitute words to a stunt, you can memorize names and playing cards, names and objects, and so on. You can utilize the system for remembering long digit numbers, by having people call their names and the serial number on a dollar bill, or their social security number. Then you should be able to give the number when you hear the name, and give the name if you hear the number. To do this you simply make up a substitute word for the name, if necessary; associate that to the peg word for the first two digits of the number, and make a link to the end of the number.

Although the following is not actually a stunt, the idea grew from the initial and object feat that I mentioned earlier. The Morse code is a very difficult thing to remember because it is almost completely abstract and intangible. The dots and dashes are meaningless and cannot be pictured. I don't suppose that too many of you will ever find it necessary to have to remember the Morse code. However, I do want you to see that there is no limit to what you can do with conscious associations, and the knowledge that anything meaningless is easy to remember if it is made meaningful. Your only limitation is your own imagination.

Since dots and dashes have no meaning, I decided to give them meaning by making the letter R stand for dot, and the letter T, or D represent the dash. With this in mind, you can make up a word or phrase for each letter, which can be pictured and that will tell you the code signal for that letter

A . -	rat		N - .	tier
B -. . .	terror		O - - -	touted
C - . - .	torture		P . - - .	rotator
D - . .	tearer		Q - - . -	tethered
E .	air		R . - .	writer
F . . - .	rear tire		S . . .	roarer
G - - .	tighter		T -	toe
H . . .	rarer rye		U . . -	rarity
I . .	rower		V . . . -	re-arrest
J . - - -	ratted		W . - -	retied
K - . -	trout		X - . . -	turret
L . - . .	retire her		Y - . - -	treated
M - -	toad		Z - - . .	teeterer

All that remains to be done, is to associate the word to the letter itself, so that one will remind you of the other. You could use the peg words that sound like the letters—associate ape to rat, bean to terror, sea to torture, dean to tearer, eel to air, effort to rear tire, and so on to zebra to teeterer.

Or, you could use the adjective idea by associating an adjective that begins with the proper letter, to the word—awful rat, big terror, crazy torture, dreamy tearer, excellent air, flat rear tire, and so on to zigzag teeterer. If you know the position of all the letters, then you could just use your regular peg words, by associating them to the signal word.

The way you associate them is up to you. The idea is that now the dots and dashes are no longer unintelligible. It shouldn't take you more than half an hour to memorize the Morse code with this system. Of course, this doesn't mean that you will be a telegrapher. Speed in sending code comes only with lots of practice and experience, but the system does make it easier at the beginning, when you have to memorize the signals.

So, you see how the systems can be twisted and manipulated to help you with most any memory problem. I've tried to teach you many stunts in this chapter and throughout the book, and I'm sure you'll be able to think of many more.

. . . And then there was this theatrical agent who was watching an act with a friend. The act was on a high wire, hundreds of feet above the ground. There was no net to catch him if he fell.

He balanced a golf ball on the wire, and balanced a chair, upside down, on the golf ball. He then proceeded to stand on his head on one of the upturned chair legs. In this precarious position, he began to play a violin with his feet!

The theatrical agent turned to his associate, and sneered, "Aah, a Jascha Heifetz he'll never be!"

CHAPTER TWENTY SIX
Use The Systems

A violin virtuoso living in America truly believed that he could play so well that he could actually charm a savage beast. Despite the warnings and pleas of his friends, he decided he would go to darkest Africa, unarmed, with only his violin. He stood in a clearing in the dense jungle and began to play. An elephant received his scent, and came charging towards him; but, when he came within hearing distance, he sat down to listen to the beautiful music. A panther sprang from a tree with fangs bared, but also succumbed to the music. Soon a lion appeared to join the others. Before long, many wild animals were seated near the virtuoso; he played on, unharmed. Just then a leopard leaped from a nearby tree, onto the violinist, and devoured him! As he stood licking his chops, the other animals approached, and asked, "Why did you do that? The man was playing such lovely music!" The leopard, cupping his ear, said, "Eh, what did you say?"

So you see, no matter how beautiful music is, unfortunately, if you can't hear it, it doesn't mean a thing. Similarly, no matter how useful and helpful the systems in this book are, they won't do you a bit of good if you don't use them.

I do hope that most of you have given some time and thought to them. If you have, you should be pleased with the progress you've made. The flexibility of the systems, I believe, is their greatest asset. I, personally, have yet to come across anything, pertaining to memory, to which the Systems were not applicable.

Take the time necessary to learn how to make conscious associations and once you've mastered it, it will take care of itself. Every once in awhile you may come across some piece of information that you want to remember, that is made to order for an association. If you wanted to remember that a certain item sold for $17.76, you could, of course, use peg words as you've been taught. However, you have all heard of the "Spirit of '76." That phrase will create a picture for most of us of the famous portrayal of the "Spirit of '76"; a man with a drum, a man with a fife, and the third holding our flag. If you were to associate the item in question, with this picture, you would recall that $17.76 was the price.

The Japanese volcano, Fujiyama, is 12,365 feet high. Again, you could use peg words to remember this, or you could associate Fujiyama to "calendar." The reason for "calendar" is that the number of feet is the amount of months in a year (12), and the amount of days in a year (365). You would associate calendar either to volcano, or a substitute word for Fujiyama.

I'm not suggesting that you do this with all numbers; the Peg system is the only infallible one. However, looking for numbers that fall into this category, is good for your imagination and observation, and it helps create an interest in numbers.

In an early chapter I told you that you could remember the names of the Dionne quintuplets by remembering the word "macey." Now you know that in order to remember the word, you would have to associate the quints to "macey." You might "see" Macy's Department Store completely packed with quints, etc. If you want to know the names of the four living quints, drop the odd e, for Emilie and you'll remember, Marie, Annette, Cecile and Yvonne.

This idea would aid you in recalling the names of the five Great Lakes. If you made a picture in your mind of a lot of "homes" on a great lake, you would always remember that the Lakes are Lake Huron, Ontario, Michigan, Erie and Superior!

If you've learned to make up substitute words quickly and easily, this will become your greatest move towards a better memory. Actually, I should say substitute thoughts or pictures; you know by now that it is the picture created in your mind that's important, not the word itself.

Did you know that the capital of New Mexico is Santa Fe? Well, just make a picture of Santa Claus wearing a Mexican sombrero, and you'll probably never forget it.

If you "see" yourself throwing little rocks at an ark, you'll have no trouble recalling that Little Rock is the capital city of Arkansas. Do you know a girl whose name is Helen or Helena? Picture her climbing a mountain, to help you remember that Helena is the capital of Montana. If you picture boys eating raw potatoes, you'll remember that Boise is the capital of Idaho (Idaho potatoes). Of course, you could picture Ida hoeing boys, and get the same result. You can easily memorize the capitals of all the fifty states with this idea.

You understand, I'm sure, that it would have been impossible for me to give direct examples of how my systems are applicable to all businesses. Be assured that they are applicable to just about anything where memory is involved. Your own particular problem may require a certain twist or change of one of the Systems, but you would know that better than I.

Nowadays, most of us are diet conscious, and I've noticed people carrying around little calorie counters to tell them what not to eat. Well, this is fine, but you could use the Peg system to help you memorize the amount of calories contained in the foods you usually eat. If you made a ridiculous picture between a fried egg and "disease," you'd know that a fried egg contained 100 calories. Did you know that one tablespoon of mayonnaise contained 92 calories? Well, if you associate it to "bone," you won't forget it. If you keep gaining weight, and you drink lots of bock beer, you ought to associate "tackle" to the beer, and you'll remember that an 8 ounce glass contains 175 calories.

If any of you still feel that it is too much trouble to use my methods, let me repeat that I call this the "lazy man's" way of remembering. It is the so-called "natural" or rote method of memory that is difficult. Not only is it difficult, but not as efficient, not as retentive, not as rewarding, and not as much fun. Most important, my methods are unlimited. At the risk of seeming repetitious — "you are limited only by your own imagination."

I just used the word "repetitious," which reminded me to mention the fact that many students have trouble remembering that this word is spelled with an e, not an i. If you would print the word on a piece of paper, making that e extra large, make it stand out (repEtitious) and look at it for awhile, you won't misspell it again. If you want to catch your friends, ask them to spell the word, "liquefy." I think nine out of ten people will put an i before the f, instead of an e. Print the word like this: liqu-E-fy; look at it and concentrate on it for a moment, and the chances are you'll spell it correctly from here on in. Try this with any word that you are not sure of, and you'll certainly improve your spelling.

Many of the ideas that were taught to you, were taught as memory feats. I've done this for a variety of reasons. First, I believe that it makes it much easier to learn, because you can actually see your goal. I've seen too many people start to try to learn something, and then give it up midway because they couldn't see the use or benefit of it right in front of their eyes. Seeing the goal gives you an added incentive to learn. The fact that you can use the feats to entertain your friends, is an extra added incentive.

When you can do or understand the stunts, you've grasped the idea, and that's all I care about. Once you've got the idea, you will be able to apply it when you need it. This is where you must put your imagination to work. Any memory problem that may present itself, can be solved by using one or more of the methods and systems; whether they were taught to you in the form of a memory demonstration or otherwise.

My purpose in writing this book has been to give you the basis and groundwork of a trained memory. The Systems are more far-reaching and more applicable than the space allowed me could possibly show. I do hope, however, that I have given you an inkling of what can be done with my systems. The rest is up to you!

NOTES

....
....
....
....
....
....
....
....
....
....
....
....
....
....
....
....
....
....
....

SECRETS OF
MIND POWER

In Memory
of
Mike Estrin

"We are born unarmed.
Our mind is our only weapon."

Ayn Rand, THE FOUNTAINHEAD

CONTENTS

Foreword

Since I originally wrote *Secrets of Mind Power*, back in 1961, my books on memory training have become bestsellers; they have been translated into as many as eighteen languages. My first book on the subject,
How To Develop A Super-Power Memory, first appeared in 1957 and is still selling—along with some of my later books on the subject. *Secrets of Mind Power* was my second book. I'm leaving most of it exactly as originally written. I've updated it a bit, and added some material. It's interesting that the thoughts I had and recorded those forty years ago still hold up today.

The fact that my memory books continue to sell proves something I've always known—that people from all walks of life, in every field of endeavor, are interested in improving themselves and organizing their minds.

In my opinion and, admittedly, I'm a bit biased, a trained memory is one of the most important factors in mental organization. There are, of course, many other factors involved.

It is mostly with these other factors that this book is concerned, although the subject of memory has not been ignored.

There is no doubt in my mind that the person with a well-trained and organized mind is the happy and successful person.

Abraham Lincoln once said, "Most folks are about as happy as they make up their minds to be." It's difficult to argue with that. The search for happiness need not be a long or difficult one—you can find happiness within yourself.

Yes—you can be a better and happier person than you are now! Yes—you can use your mind much more efficiently and effectively.

There's no doubt about it. Just make up your mind that this is true and you will be able to use the brain power you have to much better advantage.
Samuel Johnson wrote:

> "The fountain of content must spring
> up in the mind, and he who has so little
> knowledge of human nature as to seek
> happiness by changing anything but his
> own disposition will waste his life in
> fruitless efforts and multiply the griefs
> which he purposes to remove."

CHAPTER ONE |
Organize Your Mind for Full Efficiency

Mind is the great lever of all things; human thought is the process by which human ends are ultimately answered.

—Daniel Webster

There is only one thing that can help you avoid chaos in business—in social dealings—in life itself; and that thing is organization. Without it everything would fall apart; there would be no learning, no science, no knowledge, no writing, no creative thinking, no competitive business—nothing!

This should be obvious to you. One's entire life is built around organization from the moment of birth—even from the moment of conception. The world we live in, the universe, everything about us is organized. All our activities, whether they be directed toward making a living, or enjoying ourselves, or both, are planned and organized.

An expectant mother follows a definite regimen suggested by her obstetrician. After the baby is born, he is fed, bathed and made to rest according to a definite system. Even his food consists of a formula of planned ingredients.

When the child starts school, he is faced with more order, planning and organization. And so it goes, until he becomes the reluctant participant in a carefully organized funeral. So, from conception to death, we must organize our pursuits, our activities, even our joys and our sorrows. Above all, we should and must organize our thinking.

I don't mean that you should organize your thinking just to aid you in business or in your job; although that is quite an important part of the entire picture. I mean you should organize your mind in general for all things, throughout the rest of your life. If you look at life with an organized mind instead of through the proverbial rose-colored glasses (although they have their place, too), you will surely see success and happiness from a much better vantage point.

If you manage to organize your mind, you will organize and manage your life, and it is to this end that this book is dedicated.

Be Your Own Efficiency Expert

To organize your mind is to control it, and according to Charles Darwin, "The highest possible stage in moral culture is when we recognize that we ought to control our thoughts."

Business, of course, recognized the importance of organization long ago. That is why the business world uses so many "efficiency experts" — another name for one who is an expert in organization. Just as it is another name for "efficiency engineer" and "efficiency consultant."

Basically, organization is simply a question of systemization. Have you ever watched a good short-order cook at work during a busy lunch hour? Well, when you get the chance, observe one carefully. Almost every move he makes is done for a definite purpose. All the ingredients that he may have to use are within easy reach; the most used, closest to him. He is so familiar with the positions of these ingredients that he can reach for any one of them almost without looking.

One of the countermen may order a "B and T down" — bacon and tomato on toast. The short-order man immediately puts two pieces of bread into the toaster and places the bacon on the griddle, and takes out a couple of slices of tomato, almost in one continuous movement.

If eggs are ordered, he stops whatever he's doing for just enough time to put out two eggs. The fact that the eggs are out is enough to remind him of that standing order. If he were to try to remember every order as it was called, he'd be in a mess in no time at all. Any competent short-order cook has at least one key ingredient for every order, which he immediately places on his working surface the moment the order is called.

That is the organized or systematic way of being a short-order cook. The same idea can be, and certainly should be, applied to any other activity. The fastest, most efficient, easiest and best way of doing anything, including thinking, is the organized way. The short-order cook example is a good instance of advance preparation, which is one of the first steps in organization. Preparation, planning ahead, anticipating and getting ready for minor difficulties or obstacles are all part of, or synonymous with, organization.

Remember: This book is an effort on my part to aid you in systematizing your thinking. I'm taking quite a chance, too, because it has been said (by Don Marquis) that, "If you make people think they're thinking, they'll love you. If you really make them think, they'll hate you." Well, I'm willing to take that chance, even though I know that most of us tend to be lazy and become quite annoyed at having to make the effort necessary to think clearly and in an organized manner.

In this day and age, when efficiency and organization are virtually essentials for success, I see no reason for anybody to tolerate inefficiency. Particularly when something can be done about it! Fundamentally, there is only one person responsible for how you think, for what goes on in your mind, and that person is—You!

The fact that you're reading this book right now is your first step toward the goal of an organized mind. You're interested and interest is an essential element for learning anything. Another essential for learning is to do something about it and when you picked up this book, at least you did something!

Unfortunately, too many people in this world are talkers and wishers instead of doers. And—sad but true—those who need help most are the ones who rarely will make the effort to procure that help. People who have a perfect set of teeth will visit the dentist twice a year. The ones who should see their dentist rarely do.

Going to a psychiatrist has become the thing to do in certain circles, but again, many of those who really need psychiatric help never admit it and, therefore, never get it. Since my main business is memory, I meet the "talkers" and "wishers" almost constantly. After one of my keynote talks, most of those who already have pretty good memories will be the ones most anxious to go out and pick up one of my books on memory training.

Then I always get a few who say, "I have the worst memory in the world, nothing can ever help me!" Well, nothing ever will so long as they feel that way about it; and they're the ones who need it most. Then I get those whose attitude is "Boy, I'd give a million dollars for a memory like that!" But will they walk into a bookstore and spend only thirteen to twenty dollars for a book that would give them a memory like that? Very seldom.

I mention all this, not because I'm trying to sell any of my books on memory—they do quite well, thank you—but because I have the feeling that most of the "how to" books written today rarely get into the hands of those who need to learn "how to" most desperately. As for those who won't make the effort to get help—well, as the song says, "That's their Red Wagon" and they have to keep draggin' it around. I guess Benedict Spinoza had people like that in mind when he said:

"So long as a man imagines that he cannot do this or that, so long is he determined not to do it; and consequently, so long is it impossible to him that he should do it."

You Live the Way You Think

Organized thinking really means controlling thought reactions properly, and solving problems in the most efficient manner possible at the time. As you will see further on in this book, it is my contention that most of our thinking is directed toward solving some problem or another.

The way we react mentally to anything that happens to us, that we see, hear, touch or experience — and the way we go about solving the problems it poses — is what occupies our minds all the time. This being so, it is an obvious conclusion that you might as well react and solve your problems in an organized way as in any other way.

There are examples of this throughout the book, but I feel that it is necessary to give you one or two right now. One example of proper reaction is described in something I read recently. It is an instance of reaction to an insult, and it was written by Russell Lyons. He wrote:

"The only graceful way to accept an insult is to ignore it; if you can't ignore it, top it; if you can't top it, laugh at it; if you can't laugh at it, it's probably deserved."

Now, I admit that this is not a cataclysmic event — being insulted, that is. But if you're going to have your mind react properly, you might as well do so with small events as with large ones.

The way you think is the way you live. Think properly, clearly and effectively, and success and happiness must come to you. This is true regardless of the obstacles, disabilities, irritations and annoyances that must inevitably face all of us.

Pry open that closed mind, and imagination, organization and creativeness will be sucked into it as air into a vacuum. When Sir Isaac Newton was asked how he went about discovering the law of gravity, he answered, "By thinking about it." This, of course, was a true answer, but obviously not quite so simple as it appeared.

Many men had witnessed an apple falling to the ground, just as Newton did. However, Newton "thought" about it; he reacted to it properly. His mind asked questions: "Why did the apple fall down? Why didn't it fall up?" His thoughts did not stay in one groove. They covered and worried the subject from all possible angles, trying to solve the problem, or answer the questions.

It is not my intention to teach you to discover great natural laws; but perhaps you will learn the importance of seeing things clearly, and thinking of these things properly and effectively, after you've read what I have to say. You may be of the opinion that you do think clearly about things. Well, maybe you do—but since early Greek civilization, philosophers have been suggesting that before everything else we should "know ourselves." We all spend more time thinking about ourselves than about any other subject, yet isn't it amazing how little we do know about ourselves?

When thinking about a problem, you must learn to get out of the well-worn grooves. Think or observe from every possible angle. For example: here is the Roman numeral IX. Now for a little problem—or riddle, if you will. Can you add just one mark or symbol to this Roman numeral, and change it into the number 6?

You should be able to work it out in just a few moments. The reason you won't solve it immediately is because your thinking has been "misdirected" — it has been steered along a groove; the wrong groove, of course.

Misdirection is the greatest weapon of our professional magicians. If they fool you, it is not because the hand is quicker than the eye, but because they make you think along the wrong lines. They throw in a few "red herrings" to keep your mind occupied, while the important machinations that make the trick come off go unnoticed.

In this particular case, I've led you to think along the lines of Roman numerals. If you persist in thinking that way, you'll never solve this simple problem. Eventually, of course, you'll get out of that mental groove, and the answer will all but hit you between the eyes.

If you haven't solved it yet—well, simply place an "s" in front of the letters IX, and you've formed the word "SIX." People who are accustomed to thinking about things from many angles will solve a riddle like this almost instantly.

Do You Think or Merely Daydream?

Organizing your mind also implies heading toward a definite goal. If your thinking is just daydreaming, in most cases you're heading nowhere. Don't misunderstand—if daydreams are constructive, if they act as inspiration, if they lead to action, then they are productive. But if they take the place of action, that's bad! Too many of us learn to become satisfied by daydreams; they become substitutes for the real thing, and we may find ourselves refusing to make the effort or working toward reality.

The late Richard Himber (musician/magician) was a good friend, and a successful man. When I asked him to give me one sentence on how to become successful, he said:

"Hard work applied properly and intelligently, and thinking in an organized manner, must lead to success."

Well, it's difficult to argue with that. Hard work is an asset, if it's applied properly; and the ability to think is our most useful asset if it is organized thinking!
Professor William James said that:

"Compared to what we ought to be, we are only half awake. We are making use of only a small part of our mental resources."

Well, I doubt if, in our lifetime, we will ever learn to use all our knowledge and mental resources — but let us at least try to make the best use of what we have! Attempt to organize and discipline those resources, and you are on your way to a more successful, happy and creative life.
here is only one thing that can help you avoid chaos in business — in social dealings — in life itself; and that thing is organization. Without it everything would fall apart; there would be no learning,
no science, no knowledge, no writing, no creative thinking, no competitive business — nothing!
It is the mind that maketh good or ill, that maketh wretched or happy, rich or poor, yet we spend more time on inconsequential things than we do on organizing our minds. Time is more important than money; it's the most valuable commodity we can spend; so if you're looking for a bargain, spend some on your thinking powers. Just make up your mind that there is much room for improvement, and you'll make some improvement.
Remember: There is no limit to how much we can learn, you know, if we will only acquire that most important single piece of knowledge, and that is the knowledge of how little we know!

"Follow the Girls" to Success

In this chapter I've attempted to tell you a little bit of what this book is to be about. An organized mind will help to get rid of fears, worries, doubts, indecision — uncertainties, in general. It will help you to react properly, to solve problems effectively. It will help you to replace bad habits with good ones, to plan ahead, to make life easier — and, above all, to live a happy and successful life.
An organized mind encompasses a myriad of subjects, many of which

I have no space to write about. I've selected the ones that I feel are most essential.

One of our cliches is: "Live for today only." Well, I agree with that, except that I would like to change it to "Live for today and tomorrow only!" I believe in looking ahead, at least until tomorrow; the day after tomorrow can be planned for, and thought about—tomorrow.

Just recently, at a resort hotel where I appeared for a corporate convention, I marveled at the thinking ahead of the proprietor. There was a sign at the entrance to the dining room which said, "To avoid the carrying of fruit out of the dining room, there will be no fruit served in the dining room!"

I was quite favorably impressed one day as I waited for a friend on New York's Madison Avenue. Some of the most beautiful women in the world can be seen strolling on Madison Avenue. I watched some of the men watching the girls. One man in particular liked to follow them (with his eyes) as they passed.

I guess he didn't want this to be obvious, so he planned ahead. When he saw a particularly attractive female approaching from the direction he was facing, he turned to face in the opposite direction before the girl passed. In this way, he was able to "follow the girls" without a breach of manners, and without making it obvious. Now there was an organized mind!

CHAPTER TWO
Cultivate Your Interest to the Pitch of Success

Art thou lonely, O my brother? Share thy little with another! Stretch a hand to one unfriended, And the loneliness is ended.

—William Arthur Dunkerley

We are all, each and every one of us, completely and irrevocably alone. No matter how many friends a person may have, nor how close those friends may be, it does not change this thought—or fact, if you will—that we are each an entity unto ourselves.

I'm sure that many, if not all, of you have experienced the dismal feeling of being more alone in a crowded room than when you were actually physically alone.

I've mentioned close friends, but the same goes for relatives; even someone as close to you as your husband or wife. There is always something that just cannot be communicated to anyone—something that cannot be put into words, or just too personal to confide in others.

Probably a thousand people have greeted you this last year with the question, "How are you?" Have you ever answered that question literally? In other words, really told these people how you are? Told them about your personal aches and pains, about the trouble at your job or at home? If you have, you may have noticed a subtle glazing of your acquaintance's eyes after a few moments. Perhaps they got a bit fidgety, and probably left you talking to yourself after a while. Because, don't you see, people aren't really interested.

Your troubles and problems are yours, my friend, and nobody else really cares. You know why, don't you? Because they all have problems of their own. Certainly theirs are more important to them than yours. And, conversely, nobody's problems are quite so important or imperative to you as are your own.

Curing the Private "I" Complex

This is all leading up to a very helpful point. I've told you, and I'm sure you agree, that we are all completely alone. But there is a way, a comparatively simple way to relieve that loneliness just a bit.

And that is to overcome the overpowering dictates of the great "private I." Most of us are so firmly imprisoned in that seemingly escape-proof cell of ego, that dark, despairing dungeon of self, that we tend to believe that the entire world revolves around "me." This is an all-too-common ailment, this "private I" complex, but it can be, shall we say, arrested, if not completely cured! How? Simply by being interested in others.

Now is that such a difficult pill to swallow in order to alleviate such a painful disease? Of course not—although it's not quite so easy as it sounds. At first you will probably have to force yourself to be interested in others. Pulling your interest away from yourself, your problems, your cares, is like pulling two powerful magnets apart, but you can do it! Force it for a while, and I think you'll be surprised to find that in a short time you actually will be interested in others.

It may help you to do this if you make a habit of trying to think of the other person as another "I," instead of "he," or "she," or "they." I know that this is a large dose to swallow; it's a concept that almost goes against nature, but try it. You needn't be afraid, you'll never really be able to completely stop thinking of yourself; and I doubt if it would be a wise thing even if you could. Selfishness used intelligently can be a good force. But identifying yourself with others will tend to relieve that momentous loneliness.

Yes, this does involve doing things for others, too. If you are really interested in others' welfare, you will want to do things for them. Tolstoy said:

"We love people not for what they can do for us, but for what we can do for them."

Tolstoy knew what he was talking about. Many others, all certainly more knowledgeable than I, have said repeatedly that the only way to be happy is to try to make others happy. Dr. Albert Schweitzer said that in so doing we find "our secret source of true peace and lifelong satisfaction." To my mind, it all boils down to doing something about that ever-present individual loneliness. You'll never be so close to anyone as when you are doing something for them with no other motive than their happiness or welfare.

Please don't delude yourself into thinking that you're doing something selfless when you have some ulterior motive in mind. You may actually be helping someone, or doing something for them—but if you do it with a secret, selfish motive, it isn't the same thing. You may fool everyone else, but you'll find it almost impossible to fool yourself.

Oh, there are many people who put up a great front of total altruism. Virtually everything they do is to help others, or so they would have you believe. But down deep they know that they choose the people for whom they wish to do things for purposes of their own. Either that or they have a martyr complex which they have to satisfy— which is just as selfish a reason for helping others as any other.

Be honest now—would you go as far out of your way for someone who meant absolutely nothing to you as you would for a person who might throw some business your way, or who might return the favor in one fashion or another? I think not. Don't get me wrong, I'm not suggesting that every time you do something for someone it has to be completely unselfish and altruistic. As I said before, not only is this impossible, but not too desirable either.

Breaking Out of the Box of Loneliness

On the other hand, if you never help anyone without a selfish motive in mind (and too many of us go through life behaving this way), you will have a tough time relieving that loneliness.

Forget what you want for a moment, and think of what the other person wants. If you will only realize that everyone has basically the same desires and hopes that you do, you may find this easier to do. I don't wish to go into a lot of examples of how certain people attain their own desires while earnestly striving for others. You can find such examples in the biography of any successful person; in any book which teaches you how to attain success.

You'll discover the truth of this once you really and earnestly try doing for others as you would for yourself. No—I don't mean "Do unto others, etc." I mean do for others. I've always been a little careful about following the "golden rule" too literally, because it does not take into consideration the completely different tastes and preferences of different people.

Doing unto others as you would have them do unto you is fine when you know that the others in question like the same things that you do. As an extreme example, I certainly wouldn't be too happy about a masochist applying the golden rule to me! What he would have others do unto him, I can live without!

To get back on track, I think you'll find that showing an honest interest, and having an honest interest, in others will cause others to be more interested in you. This will create just a little nick in that iron constitution of the "private I"— but enough to make it just a bit less private.

Instead of always thinking of yourself, or of what you're going to say next, when someone talks to you, LISTEN!

I have never yet met anybody, from any walk of life, from whom I haven't learned something. Some part of their experience, some thought or idea, no matter how minute, was passed over from them to me. If such a thought or idea did not get across, I would work to make it happen. I feel a sense of personal loss if I don't learn something from each and every individual I meet.

This could not happen if I weren't listening —I mean really listening— to them. And, as has been said before, your education doesn't really begin until you start to listen.

Of course, one activity blends into another. It is almost impossible to separate attentive listening and interest. If you have trouble listening to people, get interested in them. If you are finding it difficult to get interested in people, start listening to them attentively. One helps you accomplish the other.

Now then, as I've explained, you will not relieve that relentless loneliness until you can be interested in, or do things for, others unselfishly. If the thought is with you that you are doing all this for that very reason, it is no longer unselfish. Stop thinking about it —just do it. Although, if you start following these instructions right now, you'll do so for a basically selfish reason, I think you'll forget that reason in a short time. Because, you see, you'll become genuinely interested in the people you're doing things for.

If You Dislike People, You Become Dislikable

The loneliest people in the world, of course, are those who dislike other people. If you dislike someone, it's a bit difficult to be interested in him. Well, there's only one solution, you know, and that is to stop disliking people. I know we can't love everyone we come in contact with, but if you dislike most people, I'm afraid there's something wrong with you!

A group of college students was asked to list, as quickly as possible, names of people they disliked. When the time allotted had elapsed, every student had listed a different number of names. It was discovered (not to my surprise) that those who disliked the most people were themselves the most disliked.

I have some more thoughts on the subject of disliking people, and how to go about avoiding it, which I'll discuss later on. I will only repeat now what Benjamin Disraeli once said:what Benjamin Disraeli once said:

"Life is too short to be little!"

Perhaps you are wondering what all this has to do with organizing your mind. If you are, then I haven't as yet emphasized strongly enough the far-reaching power of the mind. Everything, every ability or talent for which you have been given credit, is really due to mind power. Of course, I'm not including physical strength, or the ability to wiggle your ears—although it can be argued, convincingly, that these things, too, are really a part of mental organization.

The degree of interest that you show toward anyone or anything can be controlled. The way your mind controls that interest can change your entire life for the better. It's up to you—there is no way that anyone can help you other than what I'm doing right now: trying to impress upon you the importance of controlling your interest.

You may think that I'm giving far too much space to the subject, but I must disagree. As a matter of fact, I'm not through with it yet. Most of the following chapter is devoted to it; and you'll find the subject of "interest" mentioned throughout the book.

Don't sell it short, please. To be blase may be chic, but it certainly won't help you toward an organized mind. Anyway, to sum it up, when you become genuinely interested in others, you'll definitely be helping yourself. That's the important thing! I'm only interested in you right now.

One thing that I must keep repeating "ad boredom" is the fact that some people will agree with all these things, but never apply them. Please remember that applying them is the only way in which they can help you. Lots of people read books, and then complain that they didn't benefit from them. Well, they must blame themselves, not the authors. If you have just read through this chapter and it has left you with only a vague feeling about trying to be interested in others someday, forget it!

Remember: If you're looking for help—if you want to work toward organizing your mind and, therefore, your life—work at it!

For your own sake stop being vague about it; stop agreeing with me if you don't intend doing what I suggest. I'd rather that you actively disagreed than passively agreed. If you believe that being interested in others will help you—if you believe there's a chance that it might help you—then you must start being genuinely interested in others right NOW! You'll eventually have to agree that the end justifies the means; and the means may even become more important to you than the end.

CHAPTER THREE

Awaken Your Enthusiasms -
Increase Your Incentive

Psychiatrist: Well, I think I know how to solve your problem. You've got to be more enthusiastic; you need more get up and go; more gumption. You must throw yourself completely into your work. Incidently, what sort of work do you do?
Patient: I'm a gravedigger!

I am sure you realize that the above is just a gag and should not be taken too literally. There are limits to everything, of course. Very few things can be safely carried to extremes. However, Ralph Waldo Emerson once said that:

"Nothing great was ever achieved without enthusiasm."

Now I am usually not inclined to accept a blanket statement as definite as this one. But with this I go along all the way. I know of no exceptions to it and, frankly, I don't think that one exists. Nothing great was ever achieved without enthusiasm—adequate or pretty good achievements, maybe, but not great ones.

No individual has ever accomplished a great feat without being enthusiastic about it while he or she was accomplishing it. I don't think that any bridge or building, or anything of outstanding merit, has ever been created without enthusiasm. No person has ever acquired an amazing fund of knowledge without being enthusiastic about doing so. All great salespeople have one thing in common—enthusiasm for their product.

To acquire any skill at all; to become proficient in any art; to do anything worthwhile—one must be enthusiastic. Of course, since all of us can't be fortunate enough to be instrumental in causing great things to come about, you may well wonder why I'm raving so about it. Well, on a more ordinary level, enthusiasm makes anything and everything easier to accomplish. The ancient philosopher Terence said:

"There is nothing so easy but that it becomes difficult when you do it with reluctance."

Have you ever had to write an essay? If you approached it as a chore, or with distaste, you don't need me to remind you how difficult it was. If you were able to generate some enthusiasm about it, it was not only a better essay, but it probably didn't resemble work at all. You found that it could even be enjoyable.

If you are the kind of person who simply abhors writing letters, stop considering it a chore. Approach it with enthusiasm and you will start looking forward to letter writing.

In the preceding chapter, I stressed the importance of interest in others. I also advised you that merely nodding assent and promising that you'd be interested in others someday won't do much good. You've got to start now, or you won't start at all. To start now, your interest must be aroused; and the only way to arouse interest is via enthusiasm.

If I had to choose two words that would help more people than any other words in this book, I would choose "enthusiastic interest." A lethargic interest in anything is akin to no interest at all.

All I'm trying to bring out here is that you can't really be interested in others if you're not enthusiastic about them. I know that I have acquired the friendship of many people simply by being enthusiastically interested in their interests and/or problems. It's repetitious, I know, to remind you again to listen to people when they speak to you, but I think it's important enough to warrant repetition. Wilson Mizner once said:

"A good listener is not only popular everywhere, but after a while he knows something!"

Are You Doing Only "The Best You Can?"

Now then, one's incentive in everyday living—the goals one sets for himself or herself—is closely related to enthusiasm. All the things that have been said, and can be said, about enthusiasm are usually also true of incentive.

I am not a psychologist or psychiatrist, so I won't give you scientific explanations of what enthusiasm and incentive are; or how to go about acquiring them. But I can stress my firm belief that these things are self-controlled and must originate in the mind.

Anyway, I'm sure you realize as well as I do that without incentive there isn't much success. The trouble is that too many people set up goals for themselves which are not in keeping with their latent abilities. Either that or they set up no goals at all. There are far too many "almost successes," who are what they are only because they have made themselves believe that they're doing the best they can.

Well, I feel that this has become a time-honored and inept excuse — "I'm doing the best I can." Everyone is given the same piece of advice: "That's the best you can do, so forget about it." Perhaps in some cases this is so, but more often than not, this attitude helps in setting up a mental barrier which gets more difficult to penetrate as time goes on.

Instead of always believing that you're doing the best you can, and setting up these mental barriers, why not try to break through them by setting your goals just a bit higher than what you believe to be your best? Believe that you can do it and you probably will!

Contractions are often distractions. Forget the can'ts, won'ts, wouldn'ts and shouldn'ts, and you'll reach some of those goals. No, I'm not preaching moral looseness or bucking convention when I tell you to forget the can'ts and shouldn'ts. I'm merely trying to impress upon you that many people keep themselves from success by their own short-sightedness, their easy-to-attain goals, and their attitudes of "I can't" do this or that.

You Can Handle Anything That Comes Up

Wouldn't it be a wonderful feeling to know that you could handle any situation or problem that would ever confront you? Well, you can! If you make yourself sincerely believe that, you'll be a much happier person. It's true, of course. You can handle any situation that comes up. According to J. A. Hadfield, "Common experience teaches that, when great demands are made upon us, if only we fearlessly accept the challenge and confidently expend our strength, every danger or difficulty brings its own strength."

I'm sure that you've heard stories about people suddenly attaining superhuman strength in emergencies — people who lifted automobiles when loved ones were pinned beneath them, or accomplished other unbelievable feats because they "had" to. Some of these tales may be a bit apocryphal, but many of them are completely true accounts. Circumstances may back you up against a wall and all seems lost — but it may be the best thing that ever happened to you.

When put in a position of having to do something, one usually does, either physically or mentally.

I'm reminded of the story that the late humorist Sam Levenson told of the poor family that had been trying to marry off its only daughter for years. Finally, a very wealthy young man became interested in her. The girl's mother, being an excellent cook, decided to deliver the coup de grace by inviting the boy and his parents to a home-cooked dinner. They were, of course, led to believe that the young lady was doing the cooking. The mother strained the budget and purchased a beautiful turkey with all the trimmings. She outdid herself in preparing the bird. It looked almost too good to eat.

The big event arrived, and it was time for the turkey. One could almost hear a drum roll as the daughter made her entrance from the kitchen into the dining room, carrying the beautiful and succulent turkey on a tray.

As she stepped from the kitchen, her heel caught, she tripped, and the turkey flew off the tray skidding and rolling across the dining room floor into a corner of the room. There was an explosion of embarrassed silence. The girl's mother saw the ruination of all their plans right then and there. She was backed into a corner just as the turkey was.

She looked up at the ceiling for a moment, as if praying for assistance from the Almighty. She must have gotten it, for her face lit up as she turned to her stunned offspring and said, "That's all right, my dear, just take that bird back to the kitchen and bring out the other one!"

I had something similar (being backed into a corner, I mean) happen to me some forty years ago. At the time I was doing a lecture demonstration of memory with a male partner. We used to split up the memory chores. While on stage, he would remember half, and I, the more difficult half.

Well, my partner decided to go into another business. I was left in a spot, because I had some lecture dates to fill—and no partner. I called the lecture bureaus who had booked me and told them I couldn't possibly fulfill the commitments. Fortunately for me, some of the bureaus told me that it was too late, they couldn't get anyone to replace me, and I had to go on.

I was in a predicament. I didn't think I could do it alone; there was too much for one person to remember. Also, the physical staging of the performance would be difficult for one person to handle. One agent said that he had booked the act as a double—that is, two people—so why didn't I use my wife Renee to help me out?

Well, Renee had never spoken in front of an audience before, although she had been a professional model. Since I really had no way out, I cajoled and coaxed her until she finally agreed to help me just to fulfill the commitments.

We were two frightened people when we appeared in front of our first audience together. She didn't think she'd be able to get a word out, and I wasn't sure I could remember what I was supposed to remember and entertain the audience at the same time. Since I can't sing or dance or do bird imitations, I was expecting calamity.

We had been backed into a corner by circumstances, however, and the emergency brought its own strength. Our program went over much better than it ever had. You see, it was much more impressive to the audience to see only one man, instead of two, memorizing all that I did memorize. Renee added the glamour that had been lacking to make this a "class" performance, and we were on our way.

That "do or die" effort, from necessity, was the best thing that ever happened to me. After that, my wife and I performed for audiences throughout the country. I have had the honor of writing bestsellers on the subject of memory. I'm now a high priced after dinner speaker and (memory) seminar conductor. I've appeared on every national television show — here and abroad. None of this would have happened, if circumstances hadn't forced me to use abilities I didn't realize I had.

So, although I'm not suggesting that you manipulate things to bring about situations that back you into a corner, I am suggesting that you make enthusiasm, incentive and initiative bring about the same results. These three will give you the same impetus that being cornered will, without the desperate feeling of impending defeat. Most of our lives are made up of little "cornerings," so to speak — problems that must be solved in one way or another. All right, then — once you've acquired the habit of enthusiasm and incentive, they'll be solved faster, easier and usually with less awareness that you even had a problem.

Remember: Once you've acquired the habit, stop worrying and fretting about your problems; believe instead that you can handle any setback, and you will handle it, more often than not.

How to Make Self-Hypnosis Work for You

Believing that you can do something is almost tantamount to accomplishing it. No, I'm not talking about moving mountains or anything like that (although, according to James Barrie, "Most of us are confident we could move mountains, if others would move the hills out of the way"), but anything within reason, and sometimes things a bit unreasonable.

Hypnosis is a good example of this. Hypnotic suggestion is merely making the subject believe implicitly that he or she is something he or she isn't; or that he or she can do something of which they ordinarily wouldn't be capable.

A person under hypnosis can be made to believe, thoroughly and without doubt, that a fountain pen is too heavy to lift. Once completely convinced of this, he or she will not be able to lift the pen. I'm sure you've all seen hypnotists demonstrate this or similar experiments. I'm also sure that most of you know that hypnosis is nothing more than suggestion.

Self-hypnosis, or auto-suggestion, works with each and every one of us very often. We are easily swayed by suggestion, either from ourselves or from others. You know how you get the urge to yawn when you see someone else yawn, or how your eyes start to tear when you see someone else's eyes tear? If I were to talk about minor itches right now, you'd probably have to scratch your arm, leg or face in a moment. You're probably scratching right now, aren't you?

Do you remember the Ouija Board craze of many years ago? Do you recall how people marveled at the fact that the gimmick moved, and spelled out answers to all kinds of questions? I hope I'm not shattering too many beliefs when I tell you that this was all suggestion. Subtle self-suggestion, perhaps — but suggestion, nonetheless. Do you want to prove it to yourself? Try this:

1. Tie a small object, like a ring, to the end of a piece of string, about nine or ten inches long.
2. Lay out, face up, perhaps five playing cards.
3. Hold the string at one end with the ring about an inch or so over one card at a time.
4. Give the ring a bit of a swing, starting at the first one. You'll find that the ring will always swing back and forth over the black cards; and it will always swing
   in circles over the red ones.
5. Get the sequence in your mind, definitely and strongly, before you try it. Back and forth over the black cards and in circles over the red ones. Try it now, or have a friend do it and you'll see that I'm right. Give the ring a moment or two over each card to make sure it has time to do one or the other. This, of course, is just an example of auto-suggestion; an example of how your mind controls physical actions, so subtly at times that you may not notice it yourself.

So you see, making yourself believe that you can do certain things, being enthusiastic about them, can, and will, actually help to accomplish them. This is well demonstrated in the story of the salesman who always referred to himself as a "$25,000-a-year man." He always managed to earn just about $25,000 in commissions each year.

His territory was cut down by 80 percent one year, but he still earned

$25,000. The following year, his territory was again cut down; but he still managed to earn his $25,000. The next year he was sent to virgin territory—an area that had never been sold his particular product before. He still earned only $25,000!

You see, his mind was made up that he just wasn't capable of earning more than that. He had suggested it to himself for years, and he believed it. So he simply never tried to earn more. If he was in a territory where it was difficult to make $25,000, why, he worked that much harder to make sure he did earn it. But if he was placed where it was easy to earn that much, he worked accordingly, he took it easy—he knew he wouldn't earn any more than $25,000 anyway, so why work so hard!

This may seem silly to you, but we all do it. Why? Search me—I don't know. We form opinions about ourselves, classify ourselves, and set quotas, perhaps subconsciously, which we rarely try to overcome. There's a simple solution for our $25,000-a-year salesman—he just has to convince himself that he is a $50,000-a-year man!

The same solution holds true for all of us. Stop being so terribly afraid of failure that you set your sights on a goal you know you can easily reach. Set them higher; if they're really a bit beyond you, you'll find out soon enough—but you'll probably have gone way past the goal you set for yourself originally. Go about trying to reach that goal with enthusiasm, and mistakes will not deter you. Just remember that every mistake you make is one that you won't make the next time you try!

Make up your mind to win; work toward winning with enthusiasm, and the odds are with you. If you're the kind of person whose goal is merely to avoid failure instead of to attain success, you're looking at the pits instead of the peaches. You are one of those "almost successes" I wrote about, who could be much more successful if you saw the peach first. You're the salesman who is afraid to try for more than $25,000 because he doesn't believe he can do it. You're the wishful-thinking writer who never writes anything because you don't want to fail at it. You're always leaving an "out" for yourself. Your attitude is: "I'll try this but if I can't accomplish it, I can always get out of it this way—or do so and so instead."

If you leave yourself an out, too often the out is uppermost in your mind instead of the goal you wish to achieve. William the Conqueror decided to back himself into a corner when he successfully invaded England. He burned his boats on the beaches as soon as he landed, leaving his armies no escape. Then he had to win; and he didn't have time to think of a way out if he lost—there was no way out!

The Only Selfishness That Pays Off

Without some selfishness there would be no incentive. I've written about selfishness in different parts of this book, and I've mentioned that some types of selfishness are good for you. The bad kind is the petty kind and the kind that hurts others.

But I realize that selfishness is what gives each individual whatever drive, incentive or initiative he has. I've appeared for many sales groups and organizations, where awards and trophies were given to the top men. I've always noticed that these men were egotistical and selfish enough to want to be tops in their fields, and I think that's good.

These same men were capable of generating enthusiastic interest in others, in their customers particularly. Read any book on salesmanship and you'll learn that in order to get anywhere near selling tough customers, you've got to be interested in them, not in yourself and how much money you can make by selling them. Be interested in their business problems and you'll know how your product can help them.

I use salespeople as examples only because we are all salespeople. We may not be going out on the road to sell a particular product, but we're all always trying to sell ourselves, our ideas, thoughts and personalities to others. It makes no difference what you do for a living, you are a salesperson.

So then, let's get back to our original premise about being interested in others. Since it is impossible for the mind to think of two things simultaneously, thinking of others will stop you from worrying and thinking too much about yourself.

It has been said that no man is an island, yet many of us go through life just like that—an island. If you have no interest whatsoever in the problems of others, they in turn will have no interest in you.

You've got an imaginary wall surrounding you at all times. You can't get out, and no one else can get in. Well, you can get over that wall only by showing some interest in others. If, at first you seem to be getting nowhere, you've got to make that interest in others, and in whatever you're doing, more dramatic—or, in short, enthusiastic. Try it and see!

Thinking of Others Instead of Yourself

Many years ago, I asked a man who earned millions of dollars per year to tell me, succinctly, the secret of his success. Without hesitation, he said, "Thinking of my clients rather than of myself." He was in the management business, managing people, their finances, taxes, and so on. And he was absolutely right, because helping to make his clients successful automatically also made him successful.

As I thought about it I realized that it's a philosophy I've lived by and adhered to throughout my career. I still do. When I'm contracted to write a book, I set my mind to think about the publisher—I'd like to do a book that the publisher can "run" with, can have a large success with. I think of my literary agent—it would be a great help to the agency if my book is a successful one. I also think of the consumer—the person who will walk into a bookstore and buy the book. I want to give that person more than his or her money's worth.

Well, obviously, if I can do that, if I can give my publisher a book that will sell, and if I can make the consumer happy—then I, too, must be successful.

That kind of thinking has been, and is, a great help to me. I use it for most professional circumstances. When I'm being interviewed by a newspaper reporter, I click my mind onto that track —"I want to help this person do a good strong newspaper piece. I'd like him or her to be congratulated by his or her editor. So, I'll be really good, I'll give this person the best interview I possibly can" —and so forth. It's an almost no-fail attitude. It helps to take your mind off yourself, it enables you to be at your best because you're thinking of the other person.

When I'm appearing as the keynote speaker at a corporate affair, I think of the person within that corporation, or at the advertising agency, who was directly responsible for hiring me. I want that person to get kudos, be congratulated for being astute enough to "get" Harry Lorayne. The truth is if that person hired bad speakers two or three times, he'd be in trouble; the advertising agency could lose the account. So, I do a terrific job for that person. That doesn't hurt me at all! I act exactly the same way when doing a television appearance—I think of the producer and/or the talent coordinator. I make myself think that I want to help them out, make them look good.

When I'm conducting a memory-training seminar I want those people to learn to do something with their minds, their memories, that they never could do before, never dreamed possible. I want to see eyes light up! Of course, it's definitely not entirely altruistic. Because I'm thinking that way, I teach my subject better than anyone; I make sure my people learn. I make sure they're happy—and then they talk about me and my systems and my teaching for years to come. Again, that can't hurt me.

The philosophy works in any area. The best salespeople are those who really want to service their clients; want their clients — the buyer — to look good in the eyes of the buyer's employer. When insurance agents and real estate agents really want to do the best for their clients, and they stop thinking about their commissions for the moment, they're bound to instill confidence and trust, and continue their business relationships with their clients.

I know a man who runs a recording studio where be makes "demo" tapes for aspiring recording artists, both instrumental and vocal. He always thinks of the client first, that's his first priority. "How can I make him or her sound better?" And he makes the person sound better even when he has to put in extra time and expense. But, he's always fully booked; people fight for his time because he thinks and works that way.

There's no way you can lose if you apply this concept. Even if it doesn't work for you, which I find difficult to believe, you'll be no worse off than when you didn't apply it. I can't conceive of it not making you better in every way.

Remember: The nitty-gritty, and part of the whole... do you want others to be interested in you? Easy—be interested in them and show it.

CHAPTER FOUR
Think Effectively to Get Results

Thinking is the hardest work there is, which is the probable reason why so few engage in it.

—Henry Ford

What is thinking? Well, offhand I'd say that the term "to think" is not easy to define. One dictionary I looked at had about thirty different definitions or categories for the word "think."
From all these, the following three seemed most applicable:

- to turn over in the mind; meditate; ponder; reason; to give continued thought to, as in order to reach a decision; to understand or solve
- to bear in mind, recollect or remember
- to anticipate or expect.

These three definitions give us a pretty comprehensive picture of what thinking is. Thinking in the present is mainly problem solving; thinking in the past is remembering; and thinking in the future is anticipating.

All three activities, of course, are immensely important. Our lives are continually affected by the way we solve our problems, small and large. Remembering is essential for problem solving; our remembrances are our experiences and knowledge, and I needn't remind you that it is much easier to solve a problem if you've had some experience pertaining to it. Anticipation is looking or planning ahead. In order to solve problems or make decisions, we must think of the results. Thinking of results is anticipating.

Without getting into the inevitable discussion about whether a person who is perfectly satisfied is happy, I'd like to point out that we think in order to satisfy a need. A completely satisfied person has no need to, and doesn't, think. Because we all have our own personal definition as to the meaning of happiness, this is a blind alley debate. But in my opinion, a non-thinking person cannot really be happy—satisfied, perhaps, but not happy. A. B. Alcott said:

"Thought means life, since those who do not think do not live in any high or real sense. Thinking makes the man."

Thinking clearly and effectively is the greatest asset of any human being. We are constantly reminded that the one superiority that man has over other animals is the ability to think. Most animals can take care of themselves much more efficiently; can move faster and better on land, in the sea or in the air; some of them live longer and are stronger than human beings. It is primarily our ability to think that sets us apart from other animals.

Too many people, however, take this ability too much for granted. They assume, perhaps, that thinking is something that just happens; they give no time or practice to it. Unfortunately, this tends to form one of those vicious circles we're always hearing about. You see, if you neglect your practice of thinking, if you do not think properly or clearly, the chances are you don't know it, because you never think about it. And if you don't think about the fact that you aren't thinking effectively, you'll never realize that something should be done about it. You see what I mean about that vicious circle?

The Art of Effective Thinking

Effective thinking is an art, and an art must be kept alive by constant practice and use, like painting and music. George Bernard Shaw once said of himself, "Few people think more than two or three times a year. I have made an international reputation for myself by thinking once or twice a week." I can't help but agree with him. Not so much about his thinking once or twice a week — I never had the pleasure of knowing the man personally, so I don't know — but one must agree that few people think clearly or effectively very often.

Too often our thinking is cloudy and fallacious. This may not be as bad as not thinking at all — but it isn't good either. Just knowing the reasons, sources and causes of incorrect thinking is a definite aid to avoiding these sources. You'll find a few of them — those that I feel are important — mentioned in this and the following chapter.

One reason is the hectic era in which we live. Many people spend at least a third of each day at a plodding, boring type of employment where there is no need for thinking — or, more usually, they don't think there is. Another part of their waking hours is probably spent sitting in front of their television sets. Here, again, there is no need or urge for thinking involved, usually. Or they spend a few of their leisure hours at a movie, watching a horror show, leaving, perhaps, time for the newspaper — the sports page for men, fashion page or fashion advertisements for women — and the comics, and so on till bedtime.

Well, what can we do about it? No, I'm not going to suggest that we outlaw television, movies or newspapers. I don't think we would get along as well without any of them. I'm just trying to stress the importance of taking some time for thinking. Yes, I said take the time for thinking. Don't you think that the ability to think effectively deserves at least as much time as reading your daily paper?

I do — particularly for people like those involved in the following news item. It seems that the U.S. Secret Service in St. Louis was receiving queries from people who wanted to know if two-dollar bills had become surplus. The story goes that these people had been given the opportunity to buy a package of twenty-five, two-dollar bills for $95! The package of bills had been marked "surplus." These people were told to practice their multiplication tables.

Remember: No more energy is consumed in using your brain than in just keeping it alive, so you needn't be afraid of using it. It's apparently true that life, at times, is a battle of wits; so why fight the battle unarmed? Learn to make use of the most fantastic mechanism in existence—your brain.

Making Use of Your "Intelligent Ignorance"

Actually, besides the God-given natural ability to think, two more things are necessary in order to think effectively. These are knowledge and organization. The reason you can't think clearly about certain problems is that you do not have enough relevant knowledge or experience pertaining to them. If you have no knowledge of a subject, you have no starting point for thoughts; or you will think from a wrong premise and, of course, think incorrectly. Since thought is the "go" sign for action, it seems likely that you will act incorrectly and do the wrong thing.

Obviously, the next thing to worry about is how to go about obtaining this relevant knowledge. Again, you must take the time to go out and search for it, if it pertains to some particular problem you must solve. Aside from definite and particular problems, your relevant knowledge can only be acquired through experience, from society in general, from listening to others and from reading.

Don't think because you converse with other people almost constantly, and read quite a bit, that you are necessarily acquiring all the knowledge you are exposed to. One important ingredient may be missing — interest. You must have a spontaneous and genuine interest and/or curiosity about a subject in order to gain much knowledge about it. One good way, incidentally, of being interested in others is to stop thinking of yourself so much. Listen a little more than you talk and you may learn something. Another way of acquiring knowledge is to read with your mind instead of only with your eyes.

The salesperson who wants to have a ready answer for any argument must know his product inside out. He makes it his business to learn all he can about it. The executive who has a reputation for always coming up with good practical ideas at the conference table may appear to be pulling these ideas out of the air, but nothing could be further from the truth. She usually has spent a good deal of time studying all the problems that may come up. She is not the type who shuts off her thinking ability the moment she leaves her office. She does research into her business; she is genuinely interested in it. There you have some work cut for you. If you want to think clearly and effectively about your own line of endeavor (or anything else), learn all you can about it!

After you have obtained relevant knowledge of a subject—and you never can stop learning, you know—you must be able to organize your thoughts. Organization is as essential for clear thinking as it is for anything else. Assume you have some knowledge of how a radio set is put together, and how it works. One day you find that yours is on the blink, and you are overcome with the sudden urge to fix it yourself. Well, of course, if you were experienced at the job, you wouldn't have to worry too much about organizing your thoughts; they would already be pretty well organized. However, it has been assumed that you have only some knowledge of what it's all about.

What many do in this situation is the perfect example of ineffective thinking. They'll touch a resistor here, push a condenser there, loosen a few wires and wiggle a few tubes. The knowledge they do have on the subject lies dormant through disorganization. An organized thinker will first try to see through to the core of the problem. What's wrong with the radio: what is the symptom and what, from the little I know, causes this particular symptom? Ah, yes, the condenser. Well, check it; but check it properly, or have someone do it for you. You don't know how to test a condenser? Well, find out how! Once you find out, you've added another chunk of experience, another slice of knowledge, with which to think. Next time, you won't have to have someone else do it for you.

If you know that you haven't the proper know-how to do a certain thing, you're on the way to learning it. Charles Kettering put it this way:

"A man must have a certain amount of intelligent ignorance to get anywhere."

There is no excuse today for anyone to be merely ignorant, but without intelligent ignorance we would rarely have anything to think about.

As far as organization is concerned, all the knowledge you may have pertaining to any particular thing won't help you much if you don't organize your thoughts, or use that knowledge properly. If you've ever tried to force one wire hanger out of a bunch, without success, you know what I mean. You knew that metal wouldn't go through metal, yet you tried to produce just such a phenomenon, in vain. If you had organized your thoughts, as you probably did eventually, you could have disentangled the hangers without too much trouble.

Agreed that it is difficult to have no thoughts whatever in your mind, you're always thinking, you say. Yes, we're always thinking perhaps, but those thoughts are not organized unless they are directed toward some definite goal. Don't mistake daydreaming for thinking!

If you haven't spent a lot of time and effort practicing how to concentrate, it is very easy to fall into the habit of daydreaming. This is simply because it takes concentration to keep your thoughts heading straight for a goal. A thought must lead to some action, and daydreaming rarely does.

You won't have to do concentration exercises for years before you can crystallize your thinking (although you'll find some of those exercises on concentration in Chapter 8). There is a way out—and that is, writing while thinking! This sounds like a simple idea, I know—but don't sell it short. The next time you are trying to reach some sort of solution, or round out an idea, or create or invent something, and you haven't gotten very far just thinking about it—try writing your thoughts.

The action has started once you begin to write. You'll make progress because once a particular thought is written, you must go on to the next one, and so steadily on toward your goal. Thinking without serious concentration or writing is too ephemeral and too vague to do much good. So, to paraphrase G. D. Boardman: "In order to reap an act, sow a thought."

Prejudice: Believing What You Want to Believe

Of course, it is important to realize that man has been a victim of his emotions since long before he was able to think. These emotions, of anger, frustration, pleasure and fear, are too deep-seated to be pushed aside completely or easily. But you must try to think with your mind and not with your emotions. Our emotions are what cause us to be suggestible; they make us prisoners of prejudice and habit. We are all prejudiced in many ways, and our prejudices must inevitably lead, mold and distort our thinking.

"Prejudice" means what it sounds like—to "pre-judge" someone or something unfavorably. Nowadays, the word "prejudice" is frequently used as a synonym for "intolerance," whereas, "intolerant" is often used as another way of saying that someone is "bigoted," usually in a religious or racial sense. No matter which word is used, it still means that he who thinks along those lines is thinking ineffectively.

However, I have used "prejudice" here in its dictionary meaning. Don't prejudge anything (it's tough enough to judge correctly when you have all the facts) if you wish to keep moving toward the goal of an organized mind.

I am not suggesting that we get rid of our emotions entirely. Not only is that impossible; it is undesirable. If we had no emotions, we would resemble the characters you read about in science fiction stories—just thinking machines.

No, we cannot get rid of our emotions, but we can learn to master them or hold them in check. Stop thinking emotionally, and you may stop thinking in extremes. If you should meet one foolish woman, and think, "What fools women are," you're thinking in extremes. If you say of an acquaintance, "He's the worst card player in the world," you're thinking in extremes. If you fail with something on the first try, and say, "I'll never be able to accomplish that"—well, besides being negative thinking, it's also extreme. Thinking in extremes is, in most cases, emotional and prejudiced thinking.

While on the subject of prejudices and emotions in thinking, we cannot possibly go on without mentioning rationalization. We all rationalize, and always will, probably, but if we realize that we are doing it, that may help to lessen it.

If you've ever heard a man speak of golf as a "silly game, where grown men waste their time knocking about a silly little white ball," then you can be sure that he is not a good golfer. If he is bald, and sensitive about it, he may rationalize by believing fictions such as: the higher the forehead, the more intelligent the person (How intelligent can you get?)—or that if one thinks a lot the brain enlarges and forces out the hair (Albert Einstein had a full head of hair when he died), and other ridiculous theories. (Back in 1961,when I originally wrote this book, I said, "You probably realize by now that I'm doing a bit of rationalizing myself—I have a full head of hair; at this moment anyway." That, unfortunately, has changed.)

On the other hand, if a woman says she thinks bald-headed men are better lovers, or kinder or more considerate, you have a safe bet that she's married to a bald-headed man, and wishes he still had his hair.

Most of us will not stand for any criticism directed at our relations or close friends. We will give all kinds of reasons to justify their improper actions. Now I'm not implying that this is wrong; just that such thinking is not particularly conducive to seeing or believing the truth.

Of course, we always recognize when others ascribe false motives to their actions or beliefs more readily than when we do it ourselves. Rationalization is really just a way of feeding our egos, and a little bit of it can't do any great harm.

Now, the realization that we are prejudiced and suggestible and tend to rationalize our motives should, and will, lead to clearer and more effective thinking. One leads to the other. Your efforts toward clearer thinking will help to do away with some of your prejudices; and realizing you have prejudices will lead toward clearer thinking.

It is inevitable that most of us have a tendency to believe what we desire to believe. If you always keep in mind that prejudice is really just wanting something to be true whether it is or not, you're well on your way to breaking its bonds.

Breaking Bad Thought Habit Patterns

The next thing you've got to consider is getting rid of some of your lifelong thinking habits. Many of your thoughts fall into certain patterns only because you've allowed them to do so most of your life. Just because you have thought for years that some facts are true does not make them necessarily so. Being naturally lazy and always looking for the easy way, many of us believe too many things without ever really thinking about them, or checking them. Robert Leavitt said:

"People don't ask for facts in making up their minds. They would rather have one good, soul-satisfying emotion than a dozen facts."

One of the standard cliches is, if an eating place advertises "home cooking" then it must serve good food, but it stands to reason that the chef in any first-class restaurant (that does not serve home cooking) certainly should be a better cook than most wives (my wife, anyway).

After some of the home cooking I've had to eat in various restaurants, I am no longer lured by such a sign. I may decide to try it, and if it's good, why, fine — then I'm a customer. If it's no good — well, that's what I mean: a "home cooking" sign is no criterion.

As long as I'm on the subject of food, will someone please tell me why everyone has decided that all truck drivers must be gourmets and fine judges of food? How many times have you heard someone say, "Oh, the food must be good, all the truck drivers stop there!"

There's a paradox for you, if ever I heard one. I'm too small to arouse the ire of the kind of men who drive trucks, but I think they'll agree with me that some of the places at which they stop to eat serve lousy food! They stop at such places because they're probably the only places open at that particular time on their particular routes. Such a place is either the only place, or it's the least of several evils.

The point I'm striving to make here is that we must question things almost constantly in order to think effectively. There's no need to be a chronic disbeliever; but stop going along with the crowd. Take the time and effort to examine some of those "thinking cliches" every so often, and you'll relieve yourself of some bad thinking habits.

We form habits in thinking as in anything else, and they are not always good habits. Sticking to your guns, or having the "courage of your convictions" is fine at times—but remember that Adolf Hitler had the courage of his convictions, to cite just one example, and that surely didn't make him right.

No, it would seem to me that often it is more praiseworthy to check into those convictions, and have the courage to admit that they are incorrect, if and when you find them to be incorrect. There is no shame involved in admitting that something you've always believed to be true is not. On the contrary, it's the first sign that you're starting to make the effort to think for yourself; and to think clearly—and that's a step forward to be proud of.

It's Not Wrong to Admit You're Wrong!

When Michael, the son of a close friend, was perhaps seven or eight years old, he had a problem at school. He was being teased by other children. It seems this school (an expensive private school) couldn't control it or handle it. Well, they handled it—by allowing it. Michael perpetuated the problem by the way he reacted to it, making it obvious that the teasing affected him. We all know how cruel children can be. The more he cried or showed he was upset or tried to argue or tease back, the more he was teased. It got to the point where he didn't want to go to school.

I finally helped him solve the problem by telling him how I solved it when I was a schoolboy. If, when playing ball for example, I'd make a silly mistake, the teasing would start immediately. I would, just as immediately, agree. More important, I'd make it worse than it really was!

When another boy said in a teasing tone, "Yeah, yeah you dropped the ball, butterfingers, butterfingers," I'd answer, "Yeah, I can't believe I was that clumsy; that had to be the worst error in the history of baseball!" I agreed with the teaser(s) and exaggerated the thing I was being teased about. "Boy, did you ever see a sillier error than that?! And I thought I could play baseball—I sure thought I could catch a ball." I topped the teasers! And most of the time, the teasers would stop teasing and try to make me feel better. "Oh, come on; it wasn't that bad. I guess I could've made the same error." And so on. We became friends.

Michael had the tendency to freeze when he was called to the front of the room and asked questions by his teacher. He'd stammer, hesitate, answer incorrectly, or simply remain silent. The teasing would start as he returned to his seat. It took the form of "Dummy, dummy; Michael is a dummy." I suggested to him that he agree and make it worse than it was. "Boy, I sure am dumb; that had to be the stupidest thing I ever did." And/or: "I feel like the dumbest person in the world—I just stood there." And/or: "How could I be so stupid?" I told him to do just that, exaggerate it, put himself down, whenever anyone started to tease. It worked; the teasing stopped. I knew it would; it had worked for me.

Why am I telling you this? Well, if you're the parent or relative of a child who's having a problem with teasing, you might teach him or her the idea. But, the main reason is that the concept stayed with me as I grew older—it simply evolved to learning to admit I was wrong! I've found that to be very important to me both in my personal and business life.

Part of today's inefficiency and what tends to make it even worse, is that the person who makes the mistake, who is completely wrong, rarely admits it. Worse—he or she will blame you for it; act as if you were wrong. That is not the way to build good will, nor is it the way to attract and keep customers.

And—years ago when I did an "act"—it consisted of performing feats of memory entertainingly—I thought I had to be perfect, never "forget" anything. When I did "forget" something, it upset me, threw off my timing, and so forth. It showed. I finally grew up. If I didn't remember something (I probably remember more during one appearance than most people remember in years), I simply said so, usually laughing at myself. (Now I tell the people that they're in at the birth of a legend—the world-renowned memory expert "forgot!") Audiences laughed with me; my timing wasn't affected and I realized that, in most cases, the people in my audiences enjoyed themselves more than usual, and—they thought I was kidding!

It's almost a cliche — laugh at yourself before others laugh at you then they'll laugh with you, if they laugh at all.

CHAPTER FIVE |
Think Logically and No One Can Stop You

"I don't know enough to go out into the world on my own."

"Don't worry too much about the things you don't know. What gets you into trouble are the things you know for sure that ain't so."

It is not my idea to discuss logic in detail in this book. I don't want to get into a technical treatise which would necessitate using and explaining words and phrases like complex dilemmas, indirect reduction, subaltern proposition, division and definition.

However, I do want to touch lightly upon one aspect of the subject. Practical philosophy consists of two branches: ethics and logic. Each of these is a full college course, which is why I couldn't possibly go into complete detail on either of them.

There are also two branches of logic: **epistemology** — which discusses the nature of truth and certain knowledge of truth; and **dialectic** — which is more to my purpose because it consists of treating the correct ways of thinking in order that we may reach truth.

Dialectics consists of three main operations of the intellect: Simple Apprehension means the grasping or seizing by the mind of an object or thing; just being aware of it and going no further. On the other hand, if you were to think, "This is a round fruit," you would be going into Judgment. Simple Apprehension would be merely: "This is a fruit." If you became aware of a girl walking toward you, and you thought, "This is a girl" that too would be Simple Apprehension.

Now, in order to reach a Judgment, two Simple Apprehensions pertaining to the same subject are necessary. Using the fruit as an example, one Simple Apprehension is the fact that the object is a fruit. The second Simple Apprehension is that it is round. This leads you to the Judgment: "This is a round fruit." Your first Simple Apprehension was: "This is a girl." If you think, "This is a gorgeous girl," you've made a Judgment.

A few more examples:

- "This is grass," is Simple Apprehension.
- "This grass is green," is Judgment.
- "This is a book," is Simple Apprehension.
- "This is a good book," is Judgment.
- "Here is a man," is Simple Apprehension.
- "Here is an intelligent man," is Judgment.

Now then, just as Judgment needs two Simple Apprehensions, similarly, two Judgments are necessary to become Reasoning. If your two Judgments lead you to a third Judgment, or a Conclusion, that is Reasoning.

As a simple example:

- This is a good book. (First Judgment)
- I liked reading this book. (Second Judgment)
- Therefore I like good books. (Conclusion)

Correct Thinking Will Never Fail You

Although there are two kinds of Reasoning , Induction and Deduction, for our purposes here, we will discuss only Deduction. For that matter, only a small part of Deduction. Logic is an art and a science, and if you're interested in going into it more deeply, there are many good books on the subject, as I'm sure you already know. The part of Deduction I want to discuss is the Syllogism. The syllogism is the expression of the act of deductive reasoning. It is an inference by which we derive a new judgment or conclusion from two other judgments from which it necessarily follows, as explained above.

It is also a form of thinking and reasoning that all of us use constantly in everyday living; most of us without realizing that we are doing so. It is a form of thinking that can, and, very often does, lead us astray.

First, let me give you an example of just what a syllogism is:

This seems to be the standard example used in most books on logic.

1. All men are mortal.
2. Socrates is a man.
3. Therefore Socrates is mortal

Basically, it's a matter of thinking that because this and this is true, so and so is also true (the two judgments leading to a conclusion). They are always formed of three separate steps, although we usually tend to think of the first two steps as one; and sometimes of all three as one.

Even though we don't realize we're using them, we do so constantly, and if not utilized properly, they can lead to fallacious thinking or reasoning. They can be the harbingers of false premise; the mistake of using an instance to prove a generalization, and the most common error of substituting all for some. With a little thought, you can think of an example of each of these. Your reasoning and thinking ability may be quite correct, but will still lead you to a false conclusion. To give an example:

1.   Soups are always served hot.
2.   Vichysoisse is a soup.
3.   Therefore vichysoisse is always
       served hot.

The reasoning in this example is fine, yet the conclusion is incorrect, simply because the original premise, the starting point of the thinking, is false. Soups are not always served hot and, as a matter of fact, vichysoisse is served cold. Of course, this type of syllogism brings us back to a form of prejudging; making up our minds about a class of things from one instance.

You can also reach an incorrect conclusion even if your original premise is correct. In this case, we illogically substitute "all" for "some" or "one":

1.   Joe Jones is a liar. (True)
2.   Joe Jones is a politician. (True)
3.   Therefore all politicians are liars. (False)

Then, the word "all" itself can start the premise off incorrectly:

1.   All women are bad drivers.
2.   Jane Jones is a woman.
3.   Therefore Jane Jones is a bad driver.

Well, she may be; on the other hand, she may be an expert driver.

How Straight Is Your Thinking?

Don't say that you never think in any of these grooves. Most of us do.

The "home cooking" and "truck driver stops" mentioned in the preceding chapter are good examples of it. And, how many times have you seen a red glow in the sky at twilight time, and said, "Oh, look at the sky; it's going to be a lovely day tomorrow." See what I mean? The false premise is that every time there's a red sky at sunset a lovely day must follow. The same goes for cloudy skies—they do not necessarily bring rain.

Even if your syllogistic thinking brings you to a correct conclusion, your reasoning may still be undependable. For example, if you reasoned:

1.   All animals are carnivorous.
2.   Dogs are animals.
3.   Therefore dogs are carnivorous.

You would have arrived at a true fact—dogs are carnivorous. But your thinking would have been cloudy, since the premise is incorrect. All animals are not carnivorous, as you well know.

That's one of the problems inherent in organized thinking. When you're thinking of facts that you know definitely, it's difficult to fall into a syllogistic trap, so to speak. When the bits and ideas of your thinking are fairly new things, not so familiar to you—that's when you've got to keep your guard up. As an example of what I mean, look at the following two syllogisms—and answer these questions: Which of these two is obviously incorrect thinking? Are they both incorrect? If so, which one did you realize was incorrect immediately?

1.   All X's are Y's.
2.   All Z's are Y's.
3.   Therefore some X's are Z's.

1.   All dogs are animals.
2.   All cats are animals.
3.   Therefore some dogs are cats.

If you haven't already realized it, both these syllogisms are exactly the same. Of course, you knew that the second one was incorrect as soon as you read the third part of it. But didn't it take just a little more time to decide about the first syllogism? If it did, you understand the point I'm trying to make.

Dogs and cats are familiar to you; you know what they are. The letters represented things that you weren't sure of; they could stand for anything actually, even things that would make the conclusion of the syllogism correct—but the thinking would still be faulty.

So, if you are using syllogistic thinking or reasoning, try to check the facts and information, and make an effort to understand the component parts of the syllogism.

Again, you may feel that these are trivial examples, and I agree. Yet I have no choice but to use them. I have no way of looking into your mind and knowing your particular problems or thoughts, so that I may use them as examples. My desire is to show you a process simply. Once you understand it, it's up to you to apply it to your way of thinking and to your individual problems.

Are You Swayed By Mass Advertising?

A chapter ago, I expressed the thought that it's a good idea to question things almost constantly. Don't take things for granted, or as truism, just because you hear them proclaimed loudly, repetitiously, and from people or sources that you've been made to believe are incapable of stating anything but facts. Robert Lynd has said:

"It is easier to believe a lie that one has heard a thousand times than to believe a fact that one has never heard before."

Also, if the lie that is heard so often is big enough, the tendency to believe it is even stronger. This is exemplified by our modern advertising trends. Some beer companies are the biggest offenders; they use all three techniques—repetition, loudness and seemingly unimpeachable sources. Perhaps it's my imagination, but I'm almost certain that the volume of my television or radio goes higher each time a beer (or any other) commercial comes on.

Certainly there is no need to prove the repetition to you. The fact that many of the phrases and tunes in commercials become part of our language—and are hummed constantly by people on the street—is proof enough.

Using a "big name" source has long been a standby of some advertising companies. Millions of dollars are spent to pay famous personalities to allow themselves to be connected with various products. The syllogistic way of thinking brings people illogically to the conclusion hoped for by the advertisers:

1.   Joe Jones is a famous movie star.
2.   Joe Jones smokes Brand X cigarettes.
3.   Therefore Brand X must be a very good cigarette.

Why? Why do people allow themselves to think this way when obviously the only part of the syllogism that they know is true is the first part of it?
Certainly we are not naive enough to believe that Joe Jones really uses every product he lends his name to. And if he did, what in the world makes Mr. Jones a criterion? He may be an excellent actor, but for all we know, he may be a terrible judge of cigarettes.

Well, the answer is that we all like to be led along that easy-to-travel path of least resistance. I have no bones to pick with the advertising companies. They are doing their job, and doing it well. Also, I have no quarrel with the manufacturers of the products. They want to sell as much of their products as they can—and if the type of commercials mentioned here didn't sell them, they wouldn't be on the air.

So don't misconstrue me. The commercials are okay with me—but don't let them fog your thinking. You've heard or seen commercials for perhaps ten different beers that claim to be the largest seller in the country. Now it shouldn't take too much reasoning to realize that this is impossible. Only one brand can be the largest-selling brand.

Some of the toothpaste commercials involve a man in a white jacket, which suggests that he is a doctor or dentist. He has tested them all, mind you, and Brand X is best. Do you honestly believe that all these men are dentists or doctors? If they are, would they spend all their time testing toothpaste? And if they do, shouldn't they get together and check their testing methods and equipment, since they all come up with different results?

One "recent" advertising brainstorm has been to hammer home the idea that such and such a product is the only one to contain the new chemical XYZ. (It was "recent" in 1961, when I first wrote this—it still prevails.) This chemical makes this product the outstanding one in its group. Of course, many advertised products have one secret chemical or other. Don't you think that if these chemicals or secret ingredients really were so advantageous, the competitors would get it into their products, too? As far as I know, chemicals are in the public domain, and any manufacturer can use them. And, every manufacturer has qualified chemists who can surely smoke out that secret ingredient.

Years ago, some toothpaste companies were screaming that their pastes did not contain any abrasives whatsoever. I remember my dentist laughing about this and telling me that if your toothpaste contains no abrasives at all, you may as well brush your teeth with sour cream. It's the abrasives that clean the teeth, removing the foreign matter and stains.

A man in the suburbs drinks such and such brand of beer. If you live in the suburbs, you must drink it, too. If you commute, I guess you must have two favorite beers

Enough of this diatribe against commercials; I only want to stress the point that it is essential for clear thinking to question constantly, and to be on guard against fallacious syllogisms. Most of our advertised products are good products, but learn to think about them for yourself — look into things before taking them for granted. I've selected commercials as an example to bring out this point, which holds true for reasoning about anything.

Increased Vocabulary Means Greater Mind Power

When we think, we are actually talking to ourselves. That's right — we conjure up pictures of the things we're thinking about in our minds; and we discuss them with, and to, ourselves. Scientists have proven this by applying sensitive instruments to the lips and larynxes of people while they were thinking. They showed that these organs moved in time with thinking.

The more words you are familiar with, the easier it will be for you to think accurately. So make it a practice to work at enlarging your vocabulary. This is a simple thing to do, yet many of us are just too lazy to bother. If you would make it a habit to look up any word you hear or read that you never heard before, or whose meaning is not clear to you, your vocabulary would show immediate improvement.

If you can't get to a dictionary right away, jot the word down on a small pad, which you should always carry with you. When you're reading at home the best thing to do is look up an unfamiliar word then and there.   If you don't, you'll either forget the word or forget to look it up. Not only that, it's always better to know exactly what the word means while you can still see it in its proper place and context.

A while ago I mentioned that it's a good idea to read with your mind occasionally, instead of just with your eyes. You'd be surprised how possible it is to enjoy reading and learning at the same time. Learn to be selective in your reading material — read some biographies, for example; learn about great people and how they think. You can always find time for good reading, just as you manage to find time for anything you're interested in. What the heck, if you're going to talk to yourself, you might as well make it an intelligent conversation!

Exercises to Enlarge Your Mind Power

You want some thinking exercises? Well, reading good books is one of them. Another is to solve problems that have nothing to do with you. Try finishing the next crossword puzzle you attempt. If you've never attempted one, why haven't you? Afraid you won't get far with it? Possibly — but you'll get better as you go along. You know why? Because your vocabulary will grow with each one you try, if you look up the words you missed. If you've never had any interest in crossword puzzles, try challenging yourself. Challenge yourself at least to almost complete one.

If you play charades when you're with friends, you're exercising your thinking powers. If you want something less violent, less physical, try the little game, which for lack of a better name, I've called "solvems." They're really only riddles with a twist. The idea is this: One person sets up a scene or some sort of action, and the rest of the group must come up with a logical answer as to "why." The method used to arrive at this logical answer is for the group to ask the person questions that can be answered with "Yes," "No," or "Immaterial." The person posing the problem must give one of these three answers to each question asked.

Let me give you one or two examples. The problem might be this: John is lying in bed and he is having difficulty falling asleep. He goes to the phone, gets a number, and says, "Hello, Joe," hangs up, and then goes back to bed, where he now falls asleep without any difficulty. The questions asked, and the answers to them, might go something like so:

- Was Joe a friend of John's? No (or Immaterial).
- Was John calling for sleeping pills? No.
- Did he need a doctor? No.
- Was he worried about something? No (or Immaterial).
- Was he married? Immaterial.
- Is it important to find out why John couldn't sleep? Yes.
- Was he in pain? No.
- Did he call to see if someone was home? No.
- Did he know that Joe was definitely home? Yes.
- Was Joe the reason John couldn't sleep? Yes.

If you were thinking, the last question and answer should give you a clue to the whole thing. John is in a hotel room, and can't sleep because the fellow in the next room is snoring too loudly! He picks up the phone and asks to be connected to the room next door. This stops the snoring because Joe has to wake up and answer the phone. John says, "Hello, Joe," just to say something—he doesn't know the man at all.

Now, there's a logical and seemingly obvious answer to the problem posed; yet it will take people who don't know it some time to work it out. If you like the idea, here's another:

• Mr. Jones is going to business this morning. He kisses his wife goodbye, gets into his car and takes off. He drives about six or seven blocks, then turns around, drives back to his house and kills his wife! Why?

Of course, the first thing your detective friends will have to find out is what made him turn around so suddenly. If the questions are well thought out, it shouldn't take long to find out that it was something he heard on his car radio.

The complete solution is that he tuned in on a giveaway program, one which called people at home. Mr. Jones heard them call his own home number, and a man answered the phone!

Try to make up your own "solvems," and see if your friends can work them out. It's a good thinking exercise for all of you. They're easy to make up. Here's just one more to make sure you have the idea:

• Cleo is lying dead on the living room carpet. She is surrounded by broken glass and water. Tom is asleep in the bedroom. Why?

The answer to this one is kind of silly, but it still takes some thinking to latch on to it. Cleo is a goldfish; the broken glass and water are her former home—the fish tank. Tom is a cat who knocked the whole thing over! That's all.

Have you ever tried to solve cryptograms? I never did until just recently, and I found them to be a wonderful thinking stimulant. In order to solve one, it is necessary to keep your mind on it without wavering. Once you waver, you're lost. If you can learn to keep at it, you'll find they're not too difficult at all.

All that takes place in a cryptogram is that certain letters or numbers are substituted for the letters in the message. Each one follows a definite pattern. Once you find that pattern, you can go ahead and figure it out. Whether you solve it or not is unimportant, the fact that close attention and clear reasoning is necessary to try is important.

The simplest form of cryptogram would be to substitute the number of a letter in the alphabet, for the letter. A is 1, B is 2, and so on. The word "what" would be coded 23-8-1-20. Now here's one a bit more difficult, but a moment of study should give you the key to it.

USBHFEZ BOE DPNFEZ
(TRAGEDY AND COMEDY)

Try finding the key to it yourself before reading on.

Simple, isn't it? All I did was to use the letter which follows in the alphabet for each letter of the phrase: U represents T, S represents R, B represents A, and so on to Z, which represents Y.

Remember that usually in solving cryptograms you are not told what is being coded. You just have the coded message itself, and you have to break it down, so that you will know what it says. Here I'm telling you what the cryptogram represents, so it should be fairly easy for you.

Here is my name, Harry Lorayne, coded in a different way. Try decoding it before you read the solution.

GIZBQSQSXZ KMNPQSZBXZMODF

It shouldn't take you too long to work this out. The letter that appears in my name most often is the letter R. If you study the cryptogram, you'll notice that the pair of letters, QS, appears three times. If you assume the QS represents R you've got it.

What I did was to use the letters on either side of the letter to be coded. Therefore, H is represented by the letters GI, A is coded by using ZB, and so on to DF, which represents the letter E.

Do you have the idea? If you have, try rendering your own name in the same way.

Here is my name again, coded differently. I'm not going to break this down for you, but you should figure it out in a jiffy.

EXOOV ILOXVKB

Of course, they get quite a bit more tricky than that, but solving, or trying to solve, them is great exercise for those gray cells. If you're interested in going into it a bit further, there are cryptogram puzzle books sold on most newsstands. Pick one up, and see what you can do with the puzzles inside.

Brain Twisters to Set Your Thinking Straight

Attempting to solve good logic riddles also makes a good exercise. Here's one for you: You're lost in a forest which is inhabited by Red men and Green men only. The Red men always tell the truth; the Green men always lie. You come to a fork in the road; you have to get to a town called "Umgowa," but you don't know whether to take the right or left road. There is a man standing at the fork, but it is too dark to see if he's Red or Green. The problem is this: Can you ask just one question of this man, which calls for a "yes" or "no" answer, and find out which is the correct road to take?

This is not so easy as it may seem on the first reading. Remember that you do not know whether the man is Red or Green; therefore you have no way of telling if he'll tell the truth or not. Even if two questions were allowed you'd be in trouble. You couldn't ask, "Are you a Red man?" because you would get a "yes" from either one. A Red man would tell the truth and say, "yes"; a Green man would have to lie and also say "yes."

However there is a way of asking just one question and finding out which road to take toward Umgowa. The answer follows, but use a little willpower and try to solve it yourself before you look at it. Get a piece of paper, and go to work. You see, I think I know the capacity of your brain power better than you do—I know you can solve this if you try hard enough. Use elimination—write out different ways of stating questions, and see if they apply. If you don't write them, you'll forget which you've tried, and you'll go around in circles.

I'll give you one hint: A little thought will make you realize that the question must be worded in such a way as to make it immaterial whether the man is Red or Green! To avoid getting a glimpse of the answer to this before you really want to; I'll print it upside down.

The question you would put to the Red or Green man is this: You would point to either road, and say, "If I had asked you before, would you have said that this was the correct road to take toward Umgowa?"

Putting the question in the past tense is what does it. If you were pointing to the correct road and asked the question of either a Red or Green man, he would have had to answer "Yes." If you were pointing to the wrong road, either one of the men would have to give you a "no" answer.

Let me break that down for you; I know it's confusing at first. We'll assume you happened to have been pointing to the correct road. A Red man would have said "yes" before, therefore his answer is "yes" now. The green man, who must lie, is a bit more complicated. If you had pointed to the correct road originally, he would have lied, and said "no." You're asking him if he would have said it was the correct road; well, he wouldn't have, so he must lie again and say "yes," he would have. Therefore you would get a "yes" answer from either man, and naturally take the road you were pointing to.

Now assuming you were pointing to the wrong road: A Red man would have answered in the negative before, so he must do it again. The Green man would have lied before; he would have said, "yes" when you pointed to the wrong road. Since he would have said "yes" before, and you're asking him if he would have said "yes"—he must lie, and answer "no." You'll get a "no" answer from either mae so you take the other road and you'll get to Umgowa!

Try that one on your friends; see how long it takes them to solve it, if at all. Here's one that's much easier, but will still exercise your thinking ability: You're to fill in the three blank spaces in the following sentence, using the same seven letters, in the same order and make it a logical sentence.

THE_____ SURGEON WAS _____
TO OPERATE, BECAUSE HE HAD _____.

If you look at the answer, of course, you're defeating the purpose Try to reason it out. The letters used must be exactly the same, and in the same order. I've given you a hint again by the size of the blanks. Here's the solution, upside down.

The letters are N O T A B L E. "The notable surgeon was not able to operate, because he had no table.

And If You're Really Smart...

Simple, eh? Well, if you're so smart, solve this final one: You have twelve pennies. One of them is a bad penny, and is either heavier or lighter than the others — you don't know which. You have a jeweler's balancing scale — no pennies will be weighed; there are just two sides that will either balance or not, according to which pennies you put on each side.

The problem: Within three, and only three, weighings or balancings, you must find out which of the twelve is the bad penny, and whether it is heavier or lighter than the others!

Again, this is not easy. Your solution must take in all contingencies. In other words, no matter how you break down the weighings, you must have a solution if the scales balance or if they don't balance.

For example: If you started by putting two pennies on each side, for your first weighing (this is not the right way to start, incidentally), there are three possibilities: (1) The scales will balance. (2) The left side will go down, while the right side goes up. (3) The left side will go up, while the right side goes down.

Why not spring this on your friends and let them help you work it out? That will be more fun and better exercise than just reading the answer.

The solution does not appear in this chapter because I don't want you to strain your willpower. It's somewhere in this book, but I'm not going to tell you where. You'll come to it eventually... Come on, now — no flipping through to find it! Try working it out by yourself or with friends to help you, even if it takes a few days. You can check the answer afterward. As a matter of fact, understanding the answer is almost as difficult as working out the problem itself, and you'll be able to grasp it better if you've tried to solve it, and are more familiar with it.

So there are a few ideas to help you exercise your thinking ability and reasoning powers. If you do exercise it, either via the methods I've suggested here or otherwise, you may find that when it's important to think clearly about urgent problems, socially or in business, you'll be better equipped to do so!

CHAPTER SIX
Think Creatively and Climb Out of All Your Ruts

> The sorcery and charm of imagination, and the power it gives to the individual to transform his world into a new world of order and delight, makes it one of the most treasured of all human capacities.
>
> —Frank Barron

Imagination or creative thinking is one ingredient success cannot do without. It is difficult to write about imagination in a concrete and definite manner—and yet it is a specific and definite activity.

How can I teach you to be more imaginative, to think creatively? Well, the only way I know is by forcing you to go ahead and do it!

You've got to practice creative thinking just as you do anything else. If you practice kindness, you'll become kinder; if you practice courage, you'll become more courageous. If you practice creative thinking, I assure you, you'll find yourself using your imagination more and more.

Unfortunately, most of us nowadays have fallen into mental ruts that are difficult to climb out of. Years ago people had to practice creativity in order to live. Too little imaginative exercise is necessary in today's way of life.

Except for those in creative fields, like the arts, most of us would much rather exert ourselves physically than mentally. Of course. It's really much simpler to grab a shovel and clear the snow from the driveway, or wash floors, or polish the car, than it is to create the idea for a novel, or poem or to invent something—to think!

And yet although physical labor was necessary, I agree with Henry J. Taylor that, "Imagination lit every lamp in this country, produced every article we use, built every church, made every discovery, performed every act of kindness and progress, created more and better things for more people. It is the priceless ingredient for a better day."

You Have to Be Born Creative—and You Were

I think you agree that creative imagination is of cardinal importance. And I'm sure you'd like to be able to think creatively. I also realize that most people think that the ability to use imagination creatively is something you have to be born with.

You're right! You do have to be born with it—and most of us were. Children have the most vivid imaginations. But as we grow older we tend to let those imaginative powers grow dormant. Some of us go through life without ever reawakening them. What a terrible loss! Your own personal loss, and perhaps a loss to mankind—who knows?

Who knows what wonderful things and ideas your imagination might have created if only you had used it? Or, do you think that only a privileged few can come up with new ideas? Well, maybe so, but with a little effort and exercise on your part, you may become one of those privileged few.

No, I just don't believe that imagination is a special gift. We all have it, if we want to work at it, and for it. It's really nothing more than a habitual way of thinking.

Then how do we acquire that habit? Well, some of the things I've already written about are necessary here. Enthusiasm, curiosity, interest —all are part of the habit. A man who writes short stories may take a walk through the city streets and come back with numerous ideas or plots for his stories. His interest and curiosity are geared to be on the alert for such ideas. He is always looking for them.

Almost forty years ago, I was watching one of the late, unlamented televised quiz shows. I watched one man win an unbelievable sum of money, and I remarked off-handedly to my wife that soon the only people with real money in this country would be those who appeared on quiz shows—and won. Quiz show winners would start looking down their noses at losers, and even at those who never appeared on a quiz show.

Well, from that simple starting point, a little imagination helped me write a short story, called "The Poors" (the "Poors" being those who never won), which sold immediately.

I mention this only to show you how any chance remark, any observation, with a bit of thought and exaggeration, can be turned into a story plot.

Exaggeration is a necessary ingredient in creative imagination. All I did in writing "The Poors" was to exaggerate that one thought. This idea works for inventions and other creative ideas as well. The steam engine, after all, is basically an exaggeration of the tea kettle!

Let me give you some concrete rules on how to strengthen your creative powers. First of all, stop thinking that there is "nothing new under the sun"—that everything has already been invented, and that all ideas have already been explored.

You know this isn't so. As a matter of fact, although I wrote a while ago that imaginative exercise isn't necessary in today's way of life

—conversely, it's about the only way to really get ahead.

The people who become large successes are those who create new ideas. I'm talking about using your imagination in whatever it is you do.

Large and small companies try to stimulate their employees to use their creative powers by utilizing suggestion boxes. They give prizes and bonuses as incentives. These companies realize that good suggestions or ideas can improve their industries and their products.

I'm sure that you're familiar with the story, perhaps apocryphal, about the man who was paid a small fortune for two words. He approached the Coca-Cola people, who were then in the business of manufacturing Coca-Cola syrup. The two words they purchased were: "Bottle it!" They did —and the rest is history.

You see, you need no bonus or prize for putting a suggestion in the box. The incentive is there without it: more money; easier and better working conditions; most important, the knowledge that you have created a working idea, the feeling of fulfillment, is incentive enough.

Imagination is what creates more efficient filing systems, better book-keeping systems, and easier working conditions in general. And there is room for these in any business, and in any walk of life.

Strengthening Your Creative Powers

Now, then, for that concrete suggestion on exercising your creative ability. It is my contention that creative imagination is based on correlations. Correlating one thing or thought to or with another is the basic beginning of all new ideas. Also, it is a good exercise.

In order to correlate one object with another, you must use words which either sound alike, mean the same, are exact opposites, or are brought to mind by some association or other. For example: to correlate pencil to light bulb, you might think this way:

Pencil—lead—heavy—light—bulb.

Do you see? Pencil logically brings you to lead. Lead (the mineral) is heavy. Light is the opposite of heavy and light leads you to bulb.

How would you correlate stamp with fish? Well, let's see:

Stamp—lick—lack—lake—fish.

Diamond to cigarette:

Diamond—ring—smoke ring—smoke—cigarette.

Book to dance:

Book—read—reed—musical instrument—band—dance.

You'll find that you can correlate even the most unlikely things with each other using just a bit of imagination. Why not make a party game out of it? You'll find it's a lot of fun, besides being a good exercise in thinking. The idea should be to try to correlate two objects with each other in as few words as possible. For example, you could correlate car to dog this long way:

Car—wheel—circle—round—square—box—boxer—dog.

A shorter way is:

car—ride—walk—dog.

See what you can do with:

—thread to paper
—book to scale
—suitcase to playing card
—ashtray to television
—chair to gun
—lamppost to bus

Yes, you'll have to think a little, and use your imagination even more, to work these out, but that's the idea, isn't it?

Now, as I've already stated, most any new idea or thought must begin basically with a correlation. If you've practiced the simple ones I've listed above, you will at least have become familiar with the idea.

You can now stimulate your creative ability by questioning or correlating and exaggerating anything. In writing my story, "The Poors," I correlated the original thought of the quiz show winners to a story plot. I exaggerated the original thought, and came up with a story.

Many years ago I learned a system which enabled me to memorize a deck of playing cards. I utilized this system for some time, until I thought to myself; "why not use similar systems to help me remember names and faces, speeches, numbers, appointments—for that matter, anything?"

There was my correlation: from a system for memorizing cards to a system for memorizing anything else. It became a question of exaggerating the card system. Of course, it was not so easy as it sounds. It took a lot of thought and work, but I finally got it.

Creative Activity Increases Creative Ability

If you ask questions about any definite thing—questions like: "Would this be more practical if it were larger?" "Smaller?" "Rounder?" "Perhaps upside down?" You'll be surprised to find ideas coming to you faster than ever before.

Asking yourself a question about anything, and then searching for the answer, will start your creative imagination working. And don't be ashamed because you think some of the questions are silly; it doesn't matter. The silliest question put to yourself or someone else may lead to the brightest ideas. "He who asks a question is a fool for five minutes; he who does not ask a question remains a fool forever."

Even if some of your questions are not very practical, even if you don't come up with any answers at all at times, you'll still be better off than if you hadn't tried. Quantity, sooner or later, will breed quality!

Don't allow yourself to be disappointed. Many people whom you have envied because their work or contributions seemed to have the inspiration of genius will tell you that it was really the product of long, patient and dull hours of work.

They had the stamina and tenacity to finish what they started, and that's quite important. As a matter of fact, here's a good rule to follow: Any time you start out on some creative effort, finish it.

Even if it's unsuccessful, bring it to some sort of culmination. If you start to write a story, finish it. If you have some kind of plan for your office, get it down on paper, even if you tear it up when you're through.

Many times, something you've created that seems worthless to you may turn out to have merit. Most important, you'll get into the habit of finishing whatever you start. And your failures will be stepping stones to your future successes.

So don't be afraid to use your imagination. The more you use it, the better it will become. Nobody becomes proficient in any endeavor until he or she has been "through the mill" a bit. The greater your creative activity the greater will become your creative ability!

I have found that many people are afraid or embarrassed even to try to create new ideas. And if they do, they don't have enough confidence to deliver them. Well, it's the usual story—don't worry about what others think; just go by what you think.

Incidentally, another interesting exercise to stimulate your creative processes is to try to make up figures of speech, such as: "as superficial as a bikini," "as noiseless as a thought," etc.

Instead of fretting over business setbacks, why not use your brain like the man who owned a clothing store, with a competitor on each side of him. The store on his left had a large sign that read, "Closing Out Sale." The one on his right had a sign saying, "Big Fire Sale." So our man in the middle put up his own sign, which read simply: "Main Entrance!"

Remember: You are limited only by your own imagination.

CHAPTER SEVEN
You Can Find Time for Everything

Dost thou love life? Then do not squander time, for that is the stuff life is made of.

—Benjamin Franklin

Here is one respect in which we are all definitely born equal. Nobody has more time than you have, and nobody has less. No one can inherit time—or keep it in a bank to gather interest.
An hour contains sixty minutes no matter who is using it. And even knowing the "right" people cannot get you more than twenty-four hours per day.

As far as I can see, the only way to save time is to spend it wisely, which really means investing it properly. Invest your time in bettering yourself mentally and physically, in making yourself more skillful, in duties and in pleasures—and you're investing it the way you should.

Everybody is constantly complaining, "I just haven't got the time." Of course you have, if you know how to use it. Goethe once said:

"We always have time enough, if we will but use it right."

It's true, you know. For some strange reason, the busiest people have time for anything. There's an old saying that tells us, "If you want something done quickly, give it to a man who is too busy to do it. He'll find time for it."

I guess the reason is that a busy person can't afford to let the chores mount up. If you accomplish one thing at a time, all the chores are usually taken care of. The busy man has to learn to organize and economize his time. To him, time is too valuable a commodity to handle wastefully.

Now I think everyone will agree that organization is certainly essential in order to use time properly. Those who have no time for anything are just not organizing well.

Beat Indecision and You Beat the Clock

The first thing that has to be looked squarely in the face is procrastination. And, procrastination is half-brother to indecision. I think that more time is wasted, more headaches caused, and more opportunities missed by indecision than by any other time-consuming habit.

There's an anecdote about the farmer who hired a man to sort his potato crop. The job was to place the large potatoes in one pile, medium in another, and the small in a third. After some hours, the hired man decided to quit the job. He looked as if he had lost weight in that short time, and was as perspiring and disheveled as if he'd been digging ditches.

The farmer asked if the work was too hard for him. The hired man's answer was, "No. But the decisions are killing me!"

I'll assure you of this—you're far better off making mistakes than not making decisions. I believe that most procrastinations are due to the fear of making a decision. You've got two courses to take; you're not sure which is the better one, so you put off the decision.

The thing to do is to take either one, but take it now. Take the first step in any direction. Once you're involved or in motion, you travel on momentum—you'll get something done. Remember that the longer you take to make a decision, the closer you get to making no decision at all. You're avoiding one. And even if your decision is the wrong one, you can correct it. If your choice was wrong, well, you'll know it, and then take the remaining choice. At least you won't have to decide any more.

I know that I used to spend a lot of valuable time trying to make inconsequential decisions. Of course, important things may, and do, require thought before being decided

But it's the little ones that we spend too much time on, such as: Should I take a cab or walk? Should I take the plane or train? Should I buy this one or one that's a couple of dollars more? Should I take a bus from the airport or the limousine? And soon, ad infinitum.

Well, I've come across a little trick that has saved me countless minutes. First off, if it doesn't involve money, I do the thing that is easiest for me. It's as simple as that. Why bother about making a momentous decision over small things? Do the one that requires less effort on your part, and then forget it.

Where money is involved, if it's a large sum, you may probably want to think about it. But when it's an amount that isn't too important to you, and when your decision revolves around that amount or less, why not make up your mind, again, to choose the way that's easiest for you?

The amount, of course, is up to you and your financial situation. For example, say you choose five dollars. You must set your mind, once and for all, that you will look upon any amount up to five dollars with indifference.

Now, if you can't make up your mind whether to buy an item that costs eleven dollars or one that sells for fourteen dollars, stop wasting time and buy the better one. The difference falls within your five dollar range.

If the difference between the bus and the limousine is five dollars or less, take the limousine! Do you get the idea? Once you can make yourself believe that the amount (whatever it is) is inconsequential, there is no longer any need to take time deciding. Use that time for more important things.

Don't be like the fellow who was asked if he was good at making decisions, and answered, "Well, er— yes and no!"

Most people who procrastinate over things that should be done, or decisions that should be made, will spend large chunks of time on projects that are unproductive. We must learn to invest our time in things that are really important.

It's like the story of the animal trainer who had heard that nobody had ever seen a camel walk backward. Camels only walk forward, never backward.

Well, the animal trainer decided he would accomplish the impossible. He would train a camel to walk backward! He worked for years until he did it.

The next scene is at the circus. People have turned out in droves because the publicity and advertising promised something never seen before.

There in the center ring, our friend, the animal trainer, is demonstrating the phenomenon of a camel walking backward. Thousands of people turned to look at each other in bewilderment. The attitude of everyone in the place (except the trainer) was: "So what?"

That's a good example of time wasted on a project that just didn't matter to anyone. Of course, this is an individual thing—it's up to you to decide on what to spend your time. No one can decide it for you.

If what you're doing is particularly enjoyable to you, even though it is of no special interest to anyone else—why, go ahead and do it. I guess it's better to occupy yourself that way than to do nothing at all. Time can be your enemy if it isn't used!

Use it correctly, and you're on your way to success. "Wishing will make it so," says an old song lyric. Don't you believe it! Alexander

Woollcott once said:

"Many of us spend half our time wishing for things we could have if we didn't spend our time wishing."

If you have a goal in mind, do something about it. Don't wait too long for the "right" time, either, because that rarely comes. In most cases, the time is now. Instead of taking valuable time to fret about whether you should do something, worry about how to do it—but do it. If it doesn't work out right—well, at least it's off your mind, and you can give your attention to something else. If you keep procrastinating, to paraphrase Cervantes, you're traveling the streets of "by and by," which only lead to the house of never.

So, here's a thought for you: If you find yourself wasting time, debating whether you should perform some duty, or if you're thinking of one idea, and can't get it out of your mind, get the duty over with—write down your idea.

Remember: You must make room for other thoughts and ideas, and you must make time for other duties.

Organize Your Time and Do Everything You Want

Let's get down to some definite rules. Are you always way behind in your duties or chores? Well, either you're attempting to do too much or you are not organizing your time properly. It's obvious that you must either take less upon yourself or organize your time more efficiently.

Deciding to take on less work is your problem. I can't help you there. However, if you have a lot of work and you don't know what to do first, I would suggest that first you do the things that can wait; then do the urgent ones.

In this way, you're backing yourself into a corner. You've got to take care of the urgent things—they will get done anyway. It's those items that can wait—that do wait and wait, and sometimes are never off your mind—which aggravate your indecision and hold up your work.

So do those first. You'll be amazed at how much more you'll get done. When you know there are urgent duties awaiting you, the minor ones will get done faster. Otherwise, they take too much of your valuable time.

It's always that way. Parkinson's Law, you know: "Work expands so as to fill the time available for its completion." If you were doing only minor chores without the urgent ones there waiting to be done, you'd take that much more time to do the minor ones. More time would be available for their completion.

The importance of interest has been gone into elsewhere in this book. I just want to mention that interest is also important when it comes to organizing or utilizing time. Although you may constantly complain that you have no time, you always find time for the things you're really interested in, the things you want to do.

So, get yourself interested in the things you feel you should do, and you'll do 'em. Stop trying to "find" time for things—you very rarely will. You've got to make time for them.

Another essential is to endeavor to make routine chores—things you must do all the time—habitual or even automatic. Of course, you've already done so in many instances. I'm sure you don't think about it too much when you're brushing your teeth, or shaving, or setting the alarm clock at night. You've time to think of other things while doing those.

This may seem petty to you, I know. But it's amazing how much time you'll save if you can do that with all small and repetitive chores. Try putting things in the same place all the time. Make it a habit, and you'll save hours because you won't have to search for things too often.

An excellent time-saving habit to get into is to start things on time. A little procrastination, in this instance, goes a long way. As someone once said, "Lose an hour in the morning and you will be all day seeking it." It's when your chores or duties start to overlap that you get into trouble. It's just as easy to get out of bed the first time the alarm rings as it is to set it for another five or ten minutes.

The Busier You Are, the More Time You'll Have

Once you're in the habit of starting things on time, you should make it a practice to allow a little more time for any particular thing than you think necessary. The television industry, where time is of utmost importance, has been using this idea since its inception (when most shows were live shows).

They always leave a "cushion" of time for every program. This is to allow for any accidents, or for any part of a show that takes a little longer than originally planned.

So, why not give yourself a "cushion" whenever you have a chore to do? If you think it will take an hour, allow yourself one hour and fifteen minutes, at least. Then, if the chore really takes only an hour, you can start your next one earlier, and have your "cushion" at the beginning of the next job.

I know that I used to give myself just the exact amount of time traveling to my lecture dates. We never took into consideration the fact that we didn't know the area, and would probably get lost. We didn't leave any leeway for traffic jams, or bad weather, or unforeseen mechanical failures in our transportation.

More often than not, I'd have my heart in my mouth during the last part of the trip, because I was sure I'd be late. I learned, years ago, to use that "cushion" I'm referring to now.

For the last few years, when a committee, or program chairman, tells me it takes an hour to drive to his club, I know that it takes him an hour because he knows just how to get there, I give myself an hour and a half. I'd rather be early than late, anyway. (I do only corporate appearances now, and most of my traveling is by air—but I still use the "cushion of time" idea.)

Plan your day with "cushions" of time, and you'll very rarely have to suffer that breathless, rushed feeling. Also, you'll probably wind up saving an hour or so most days — and you'll be able to use that for those things you "never have time for."

Stop restricting yourself to exact amounts of time. The penalty for going over the limit is too great. Tenseness, lateness and disappointments can easily be avoided if you use the "cushion" idea. Start off in the morning by getting up a few minutes earlier, and that breathless rush to the office can turn into a more leisurely pace.

Utilize all the time you have up until bedtime. Whether it be work, hobbies, recreation or what have you. If you find yourself waiting for bedtime, or thinking about going to sleep, you're bored, and more important, you're wasting time.

A well-planned day should bring you to bedtime without having to "kill time" waiting for it. Incidentally, don't overlook recreation. John Winemaker once said:

"People who cannot find time for recreation are obliged sooner or later to find time for illness."

I hope you haven't misconstrued me. I'm not attempting to instruct you to overlook or shirk responsibilities, or to take a lot of extra time to do any particular chore. Just plan and organize your time to meet the requirements of any given activity, that's all.

Keep busy, of course. I'm a strong believer in work, or rather, activity. I think that any activity is a better recreation than just loafing. And although it sounds contrary, you'll find that the busier you are, the more leisure you'll have!

Knowing that procrastination and indecision can almost put you in a state of suspended animation — and that "cushions" can make things easier for you — should all be helpful toward organizing your time.

One final word: Don't waste too much time worrying or fretting about past mistakes. Once you've made a decision, forget it. Start each day afresh. Use today's allotment of time for today or for planning for tomorrow — yesterday had its chance. As Plutarch said many years ago:

"The greatest of all sacrifices is the sacrifice of time!"

CHAPTER EIGHT

Multiply Your Output with the Habit of Concentration

> Success in life is a matter not so much of talent and opportunity as of concentration and perseverance.
>
> —C.W. Wendte

Just as automobile manufacturers have learned they must streamline their cars so that they can cut through air with less resistance, so should you streamline your mind. Learn to cut through to the heart of a problem without placing all kinds of resistance in your path. In other words, learn to concentrate.

The art of concentration can be learned just like any other skill. Have you a bad habit you'd like to get rid of? Well, why not substitute the habit of concentration? Yes, like most good qualities, concentration is a habit.

We've all heard that most people use only eight to ten percent of their brain power (which is probably giving most of us the benefit of the doubt). Well, get into the habit of concentrating and you may start using some of the remaining 90 percent.

How do you learn to concentrate? It isn't easy, I assure you. The dictionary says that concentration is "exclusive attention on one object." Have you ever tried to give your entire and exclusive attention to one object? Again, it isn't a simple matter. But practicing to do it is, I think, worthwhile.

But first, let me give you my definition of "exclusive attention." This means that no other thought, no matter how trivial, can be allowed to enter your mind. You must be thinking of concentrating on, and visualizing nothing but that pencil. The moment any other thought flits across your mind, stop trying! Your attention is no longer exclusive. You must strive to fix your mind on the pencil, or your problem, or whatever it is you're doing, and hang on.

Not as easy as you thought, is it? Of course not. People who know anything about, or who practice, Yoga know how difficult it is. A true Yogi must continually practice concentrating on a truth or concept, and push all external things from his mind. He sometimes practices an entire lifetime before he is satisfied with his results.

How Hard Can You Concentrate?

Here is an exercise in concentration to practice without staring at a particular object. Simply try counting without allowing anything but the numbers themselves to occupy your mind. This is even more difficult, in my opinion, than concentrating on an object. There isn't really much to latch on to. But it's good practice, and a good exercise. I frankly doubt if you can get up to five the first time you try it. That is, if you're honest with yourself. You must stop the second any other thought presents itself — your mind may turn to some sound for just an instant, in which case you must stop and start again.

After some time, and much practice, you may get up to ten. If you ever manage to get up to one hundred without any outside or external thoughts interfering, you're approaching the genius class!

You are probably wondering why I'm making such an issue over this. You want to know how being able to concentrate on an object, or to count with exclusive attention, can help you in everyday living. Well, I'll tell you. The object and the counting, of course, are merely means to an end. They're not important, but the ability to keep your mind on a problem or goal is.

How often has this happened to you? You leave your home in the morning; you're going to work, heading toward the subway or bus. You have a problem you'd like to solve before you arrive at the office. It's on your mind as you leave your doorway, but within no more than half a block, usually, your mind has wandered over perhaps a hundred different unimportant things. Things which have no relation at all to the problem that must be solved.

So — you arrive at the office no closer to a solution than when you started out. You'll solve it eventually, of course, but that's not the point. The point is that if you could have kept your mind on the problem, it would have saved you time and, perhaps, money. So you see, you just have to practice dragging your mind back to the subject whenever it strays.

The ability to concentrate also enables you to see a problem clearly. I feel that many of the problems that are plaguing you could not be clearly defined if you tried to do so right now. If you stop to think for a moment, you'll realize that most of the things that are annoying you cannot be pictured in their entirety. The problem is usually quite vague in your mind; you see the tentacle of the octopus, but not the octopus itself. You can do this or that and get rid of one of those tentacles; do that or this and get rid of another one. But the body, the cause, the nucleus of your problem is still with you.

I think this is why many of our problems stay with us as long as they do, sapping our energy, causing mental fatigue, and making us more tense and neurotic than we already are.

Nowadays when a person has a nervous breakdown, people say, "Well, he was working so hard and trying to do so much."

I can't agree with that. I am more inclined to agree with the saying, "Hard work never killed anybody." I believe that most nervous breakdowns are caused by the fact that the victim was getting nowhere solving his or her personal problems. If he or she was working hard and doing so much and solving all problems, he or she would most probably be a happy person.

Practical Problem Solving

So practice concentration, which in turn should help solve some of your problems. Concentration will enable you to look directly at the heart of a problem so that you can decide the exact steps to take to overcome it.

Take a piece of paper and start writing out one particular problem that's been annoying you. I think you'll agree with me—you'll discover that it was quite vague in your mind. Now as you write it out, you'll find many of the incidentals surrounding the problem can be put aside; they have no vital connection, anyway. Probably they were merely anticipations. They were the "might be's" and the "what will happens." They should not concern you now.

Finally, you get down to business; you get to the heart of the problem in all its ugly nakedness. You're giving your conscientious and exclusive attention to that problem only, at that moment. Okay, now that you've gotten rid of the fog surrounding it, you can start doing something about the problem itself.

Remember: Most problems well organized and defined are already partially solved.

List all the obstacles standing in the way of solution. Beside each obstacle list any and all solutions that come to mind. Don't worry if some seem ridiculous or far-fetched, at first. Get them down on paper. Before you know it, you'll be much closer to a solution than you've ever been before. At least, you'll know just what steps to take to alleviate the problem—which is just as important.

Do that with most of the things that are bothering you, and before you know it, you'll have much more time for enjoying life, instead of fretting about problems.

I'm not trying to make it appear oversimple. Problem solving is a lifetime's work; you're engaged in it all the time. I'm just suggesting that you make it as easy as possible. I know full well that there are many things that are too big to solve by simply writing them out.

But the ability to concentrate, which is aided by the writing, will be your springboard to action. As Benjamin Disreali once said:

"Action may not always bring happiness; but there is no happiness without action."

Once you're doing something about your problems, in a direct and intelligent manner, there's much more chance of getting them solved.

CHAPTER NINE

You Can Solve Your Problems
Once You Know What They Are

Patient to Psychiatrist: Well, doctor, my wife has a mink coat and a sable coat. We live in a duplex penthouse apartment. We own a yacht, and a summer home, and we drive around in a chauffeur-driven Cadillac limousine.
Psychiatrist: My dear man, what is your problem?
Patient: My problem? Doctor, I only make $200 a week!

In the preceding chapter I said little about what some of you may consider the really big problems of life. Of course, many small ones, as in the above anecdote, can blend together and form some of those really big ones. But no matter how big they are, the same principles hold true: Try to see clearly to the heart of the problem. Many times, those small annoyances keep us from getting to the more important ones. We can even lose sight of which are important and which aren't. So why not take care of the one that happens to be occupying your mind now? Your mind is incapable of thinking of more than one problem at a time, anyway, so take care of the present occupant, and make room for the next one. Unfortunately, there's always another tenant to take over the lease, but in this way you'll make some headway.

This applies to anything, of course. Take care of one thing at a time, instead of worrying about everything. If you've got a tremendous job staring you in the face, it always looks bigger if you picture all its parts simultaneously.

I do suggest that you picture it in its entirety at first, just so that you'll know what you're dealing with and where you're heading. After the first visualization, take it a step at a time, and you'll wear it down before you know it. But, start someplace. Don't allow it to hang over you, making you wonder how it will come out. The uncertainty can drive you insane. Uncertainty, doubt and indecision are a few of the habits we want to kill or replace, not nourish.

If you're thinking at all, allow that thinking to bring about action. Start with the first thing in sight, and you're advancing; anything else is just standing still. Goethe put it this way: "Do the duty that lies nearest thee; thy next duty will then become clearer."

What About the Really Big Problems?

Now, I know that you may be thinking, "Well, what about things like lack of money, poor health, physical handicaps? You can't just brush those problems off so easily." No, you can't brush them off easily, that's true. But you can make them easier for yourself, or try to.

People afflicted with serious problems like those mentioned have been offered all kinds of methods to make themselves feel better. "This too shall pass" and "I cried because I had no shoes, until I saw a man who had no feet" are some of the cliches suggested. Well, these points of view do come in handy at times, I guess, if you can really make yourself believe them; but I don't go along with them for real problem solving.

Thinking about how much worse off someone else is can be a temporary relief. But, unfortunately, the way most of us are built makes us more interested in a small wound on our bodies than a war on another continent. So, to me, that's the easy, and not too helpful, way out—if it is a way out.

Sure, it's true that somewhere someone is suffering more than you are, but that isn't relieving your situation any. Thinking about someone who is poorer than you are may make you feel rich compared to him, but let's stop kidding ourselves. That's not really helping you—it's making things worse. It may stop you from doing something about it!

What can you do about those troubles or problems? Well, the first thing, perhaps, is to remember that one way to make ends meet is to get off your own! Few of us are fortunate enough to have someone to take care of our obligations. Since you've got to take care of yourself, what are you waiting for?

No matter how well off or how poor the other guy is, or no matter what problems we have and he doesn't, if all the troubles in the world were gathered together and auctioned off to the highest bidder, most of us would buy back our own rather than the other guy's.

Not enough money to get by on? Well, there aren't many people who don't have that problem. I guess this is the era of living up to every penny we earn. And because it's also the era of no down payment, or very little down payment, too many people live way over their heads.

There are too many consumers who often feel that charging something is like getting it for nothing. Then it's a constant struggle to keep their heads above water.

There are only two solutions to this problem. One, of course, is to earn more money. To that you're likely to say, "that's a big help; wouldn't I earn more if I could?" Yes and no. There are many people who are earning top money according to their skills — but just as many who aren't.

Some of the reasons for this are laziness, fear of changing to a new job or new location, and lack of confidence. One of the saddest types of business failure is the person who has remained in the same place for years — afraid to make a change. This person also firmly believes he or she just didn't have the right opportunities. Well friend, opportunity is a state of mind — plus action!

Then, too, there is no crime in trying to make money in your spare time. You'll be surprised at the many ways there are to do this, if you'll just take the time to look into it that you usually take to feel sorry for yourself.

That's one solution. The other, and probably more to the point, is to manage what you do earn more efficiently. Start a savings plan; don't buy anything you can't pay for — no matter how much time you have to pay for it. Understand that these things must be paid for eventually. Buy only what you need and what you can definitely afford; at least until you feel a bit less hemmed in.

Problems We Own and Problems that Own Us

One important question to keep uppermost in your mind is: are you contributing toward the solution of a problem, or are you becoming a part or cause of that problem? If you're a bloody spendthrift you certainly have no cause to complain about lack of money. You are the problem. So do something about that.

Of course, health is very often something that is entirely out of our hands. But in many cases it's something we can control. For example, we can make it our business to have a complete physical checkup at least once a year. I'm not suggesting that you become a hypochondriac, but if you feel that something is wrong, why worry about it? See a doctor and find out if it is something to worry about.

I knew one fellow who suffered from terribly painful boils. He suffered and suffered for months, until the pain finally all but carried him to a doctor. I never could understand people like that. Don't they realize that the awful pain, the sleepless nights it causes, and so on, are far worse than the pain (if any) involved in having a doctor take care of it?

Quite some time after the Salk polio vaccine was available to the public, there were articles in all the newspapers urging all adults under forty years of age to get their polio injections. There seemed to be vast numbers of people who hadn't done so, and probably didn't intend to. Well, again, I cannot, for the life of me, understand such things. Are these people martyr types who want to become ill? I don't know, but it sure seems that way. Lack of money can't be the reason, either. The injections were offered free of charge, but people still stayed away in droves.

Stop procrastinating. One who procrastinates will gain more weight. If you feel it's necessary to go on a diet, stop talking about next week or tomorrow — start now or you probably won't start at all. Keep in mind that most of the time, in almost every type of problem, it's not what you do that tires or hurts you in any way; it's what you don't do that causes the trouble!Dr. John Donnelly wrote:

"Every problem of frustration which is faced realistically and dealt with in an organized way adds to the strength of the personality. Every failure from which a lesson has been learned provides both an experience and an asset which increases our capacity to meet new problems."

It's Your Ability that Counts—Not Your Disability

If you have a physical disability of some kind, I will not try to make you feel better about it by telling you that there are people worse off than you are. I might, however, suggest that you stop worrying, or even thinking about your disability. Replace those thoughts with the truth that it's your ability that counts, not your disability.

Your mental attitude is more important than your physical disability. There may be nothing you can do about the latter, but you can, and must, do something about the former. Martha Washington once wrote in a letter to a friend: "I have...learned from experience that the greater part of our happiness or misery depends on our disposition and not on our circumstances."
Sir Roger L'Estrange said:

"It is not the place, nor the condition, but the mind alone that can make any-one happy or miserable."

So act accordingly.

Some forty years ago, I did my memory demonstration/lecture for the students and alumni of the Bulova Watch Repair Training School. My audience consisted mainly of paraplegics, and people with false limbs, or people who were badly maimed in one way or another.

These people are perfect examples of what I'm discussing. I spoke to them before and after my performance and as far as I could see, they were all happy, well-adjusted human beings. They were active in their communities, and most of them were members of baseball or basketball teams. They kidded about their disabilities, and one of them, who had a false leg, jokingly challenged me to a race around the block.

All these men and women, most of whom had the use of only their arms, and in some cases only one arm, had come to this school in order to learn something with which they could earn a living. They were all expert mechanics, and could repair any watch. Most important, they had acquired an ability to overcome their disabilities.

Perhaps one of the best-known handicapped people in America was Helen Keller, and she must have believed Emerson's statement:

"No man had ever a defect that was not somewhere made useful to him. I thank God for my handicaps for without them I could not have succeeded."

Whether you agree with her statement or not, you must agree with her attitude. There is no other good way of looking at it. Your mind can conquer all. What has happened to you is not half so important as how you reacted to it. Stop concerning yourself with what might or should have been, be concerned rather with things as they are.

So I hope you'll agree that there is something you can do about the big problems, even if it's just a matter of attitude. Let's face it: "What cannot be cured must be endured" — but we should make it as pleasant for others and ourselves as we possibly can. Where there is something, anything, tangible that can be done, by all means do it. If not, make the best of it anyway.

I saved myself much aggravation once I had made up my mind never to argue with the "authorities" when I knew it was to no avail. I gave up that kind of crusading when I realized that you only score your point perhaps once out of hundreds of times — and ulcers are too high a price to pay for one small victory. No, in most cases it's best to be like the individual who knew that his package would be roughly handled, so he said to the post office clerk, "It's very fragile, so would you kindly throw it underhand!"

It's amazing what we can learn to live with once we make up our minds to do so, or once we have to do so. Somewhere I read or heard the story about the gardener who wrote to the Department of Agriculture saying, "I've tried everything you told me to in all your booklets and in all your instructions on how to get rid of dandelions, but I've still got them."

In the next mail, the gardener received a wise piece of advice. It was: "Dear Sir, if you have tried everything we've told you to, and you still have dandelions, there is only one thing left to do—learn to love them!"

CHAPTER TEN

Strengthening Good Habits - Discarding Bad Ones

Habit is either the best of servants, or worst of masters.
—Nathaniel Emmons

I feel that a discussion of habits, both good and bad, is essential in a book such as this. However, many of the things I would like to write about, pertaining to habit, really belong within the realm of psychology and psychiatry.

I am neither a psychiatrist nor a psychologist, so I don't think it would be wise to get into those areas. However, for what it's worth, here are my thoughts on the subject of habits.

First of all, as the quote at the head of this page says, habit can be a wonderful servant. It can save you much time and effort, and make things in general much easier for you.

There is another saying that goes, "A man's fortune has its form given to it by his habits." And I believe there is a lot of truth in that. If you can train yourself to acquire good habits of health, recreation, prompt decision making, learning and work, you will almost surely form the habit of success and happiness.

On the other hand, the worst and heaviest load you can weigh yourself down with is a bunch of bad habits. These are easy traps to fall into, but quite another matter to get out of. Horace Mann said:

"Habit is a cable. We weave a thread of it every day, and at last we cannot break it."

Do You Want to Break the Habit?

There have been volumes written on methods and procedures for getting rid of, or breaking, bad habits. One authority says that you've got to keep deliberately repeating the bad habit. This, surprisingly enough, does work in many cases. The idea, I assume, is to bring the habit out into the open, force it into consciousness by repeating it intentionally.

For example: A person learning how to type may hit the wrong key each time he wants to type an "e." At first, this may simply be a mistake; but if repeated often enough, it becomes habit. The suggested cure is to hit that wrong key purposely or consciously for a while. In other words, actually practice hitting the wrong key until you can consciously and deliberately hit the right one instead.

This will work in many instances. Some habits are easily broken once they are taken out of the realm of the subconscious. This same method has been used to break such habits as stammering, fingernail biting, and many more. Of course, habits of that sort must be given this treatment by a trained psychologist.

For some bad habits, however, I believe it's pure folly to use this repetitive method. Certainly, if you wish to stop smoking, it would be silly to increase your smoking.

Other authorities suggest simply stopping by an act of will any habit you wish to get rid of. Well, stopping the habit is the end result you desire; it isn't necessarily the road to, or the method of arriving at, that end. It is also easier said than done.

You can tell someone who is a stammerer to stop stammering from now till doomsday, but I doubt if that will stop him or her. Stammering, like many other habits, is psychological in origin, and a psychologist is usually necessary to help put a stop to it.

There has been much talk recently (I wrote in 1961) of hypnosis as a panacea for eliminating bad habits. It has reputedly cured people of the habits of smoking, fingernail biting, overeating and insomnia.

Here, again, if supervised by a doctor, this method may bring results. Usually, however, if hypnotism does help, it is for a short period of time only. The habit manages to return in full force unless you keep submitting to hypnosis. Or, secondly, and more important, another bad habit often takes the place of the one you just got rid of. If you stop smoking via hypnosis, you may find yourself biting your nails, if you stop overeating via hypnosis, you may become a smoker, or smoke more than you did before. I'd like to emphasize that I think the best way to stop petty bad habits is to really want to. People who complain that they can't stop smoking would stop if they truly wanted to. Most of them don't. They enjoy smoking; it's a crutch that they welcome, and so they continue using it.

Aside from tics, stammering— anything psychologically caused—ask yourself if you really want to give up your bad habits. I think you agree that in most cases you enjoy them.

Remember: I can only suggest that you stop complaining, and start working on making yourself want to give up any bad habit you may presently possess.

Make a New One Instead

Try substituting a good habit for every bad one you have, and you'll really make progress. Every time you feel like biting your fingernails, get involved in some piece of work you've been putting off too long. If you really want to stop smoking, when the urge hits you, if you're at home, sit down and write a letter to someone to whom you should have written long ago. Make that phone call you've been putting off, or start reading that book you haven't opened yet. And keep your cigarettes out of reach.

I think that many irritating habits are retained because we don't realize that they're annoying to others, or we don't know how to go about breaking them. Well, take stock of yourself. Just stop and think of all the habitual things you do. How many of them are offensive? If you want to take the chance, ask your friends. However, you'd best be careful there. William James once said:

"We all want our friends to tell us of our bad qualities; it is only the particular ass that does so that we can't tolerate."

No, I think you're much better off if you can spot your own bad habits. As far as knowing how to break them is concerned, make yourself really want to. Try to replace bad habits with good ones.

The challenge idea, mentioned elsewhere, can be a great aid in breaking bad habits. Set up a mental wager with yourself that you won't indulge in a certain habit again. If you really want to defeat the particular habit, tell your close friends about it. Invite them to help you toe the line; to deride you, if necessary, if you digress. In this way, you'll be backing yourself into a corner. You won't indulge in the habit, if for no other reason than to save face before your friends.

You might try the idea used by the 24 Hour Club of Alcoholics Anonymous. (I learned about this after performing for them some years ago.) It's called the 24 Hour Club because they stay away from liquor one day at a time.

They challenge themselves this way: "I won't drink today. I'm certainly man enough to stay away from it just one day. Tomorrow I'll drink to my heart's content — but today, I abstain."

Of course, the next day they do the same thing. You see, if you think about giving something up forever, it can present a frightening picture. But looking at the "sacrifice" a day at a time makes it easier to bear.

After enough time has elapsed, the urge to indulge in the habit is gone, or arrested anyway, and the battle is almost won. Try this method on yourself for any habit you want to break. You'll be amazed at the results you'll achieve.

Don't give in to those little whispers of temptation like, "Why not?" or "Just this once," or "This will be the last time." You might as well make up your mind to the fact that once you do, you're back in the clutches of the habit.

So try these ideas. Challenge yourself; have your friends deride you if you stray. Try the twenty-four-hour method, and don't give in to minor temptations. It will take a little time and hard work, but you'll win out in the end.

After all, something you've been doing for years, and in some cases almost all your life, is not going to be easy to curtail. Don't expect it to be easy. But if you have habits that have been affecting your health, popularity, happiness or chances of success — it's about time you decided you really want to get rid of them. I can't stress that enough — you must really and truly want to. The fact that they're not easy to eliminate will give you a wonderful feeling of achievement when you do eliminate them. Mark Twain said that:

"A habit cannot be tossed out the window; it must be coaxed down the stairs a step at a time."

And you'll be doing just that with these methods.

Concentration Is the Key

Now, I've given a bit of space to getting rid of bad habits. How about acquiring good ones? Well, I would say the first thing to work toward is the habit of doing things habitually. In the chapter on time, I mentioned that habit can be a great time-saving device. And, it can.

I know some people who find it very difficult to do things the same way twice. I believe that lack of concentration is the reason. Learn to do things with attention to how, where and what, and after a while they will become habits. Then you won't have to concentrate on them any longer. They'll practically take care of themselves.

If you have the annoying habit of leaving the toothpaste cap off the tube, force yourself to concentrate on putting it back on. Think about it while brushing. Before you know it, you'll be putting it on, and won't even remember doing it. It will become an automatic action.

Do you always leave the faucet dripping at night — forcing you to get out of bed to stop the annoying drip, drip later? Concentrate on turning the tap until you feel pressure against your hand. This will assure that it's tightly shut. Do this with attention and awareness for a few days, and it will become habit. If the faucet still drips after that, call a plumber.

A little concentration at the beginning will save lots of time and effort later on. Once a thing becomes habit, you need hardly think about it anymore. Those petty worries like, "Did I shut off the water in the bathtub?" or "Did I lock the door?" can be avoided by making these things habitual.

I know that it's no more likely for me to leave my house without checking if the door is locked than it is for me to leave without my clothes on.

So, once more, force yourself to do all these little things with attention for a while. They'll become habit before you know it. I know many successful men who can give most of their time to creative activity because they have trained themselves to run their businesses almost automatically. The small, necessary, repetitive chores and duties have become habit.

Unhappiness, very often, is nothing more than a bad habit! Do you wake up grouchy most mornings? Get in the habit of looking in the mirror and smiling at yourself every morning. Sounds silly, I know — but do it and you'll be surprised at how well it works. Make being happy a habit, and you'll enjoy yourself — it is later than you think.

I cannot stress strongly enough the necessity of the habit of making prompt decisions. Aside from being a terrible waste of time, indecision is a common cause of unhappiness. See Chapter 7 for more on how to avoid this bad habit. According to William James:

"There is no more miserable human being than one in whom nothing is habitual but indecision!"

Get into the habit of trying to make other people comfortable. Think of their petty problems instead of your own, and you'll conquer another cause of unhappiness — shyness.

Being shy is being uncomfortable and uneasy and self-conscious, and it's merely a case of worrying about what others think of you. Once you make it a habit to be interested in others and think of their comfort, you won't have time to think of yourself. Just remember that basically everybody is thinking of how he or she looks to others. Everyone looks for awareness and approval from friends and acquaintances, so you are not alone. Once you realize this, you'll have no reason to be shy — we're all in the same boat.

Well, these have been some of my thoughts and ideas on habits. If you've found a few of them worthwhile and fitting for you personally, I've accomplished something. Try them, use them, and they will work for you.

CHAPTER ELEVEN

You Must Trust Others If You Want to Succeed

> The father had placed his young son on top of the bookcase, and was urging the youngster to jump down into his arms. The boy hesitated; he was frightened.
>
> "Come on, son, jump! I'm here to catch you." Still the boy whimpered and hesitated.
>
> "Now look, I'm your father. I'm telling you to jump. I'll catch you."
>
> Finally, the boy closed his eyes and jumped. The father didn't catch him, and he hit the floor with a thud. He looked up at his father with tears of pain in his eyes. And the father said, "There, that'll teach you never to trust anybody."

Too many books fall into what I call the "blue sky" category. "Blue sky" writing is the kind that's nice and flowery, but doesn't say anything. The worst and most numerous offenders, I believe, are those books that do little but preach, "Have faith;" faith in God or in yourself.

Now please, don't be shocked. One of my maxims is never to argue religion or politics with anyone but very close friends. And even then, I'm quite careful, because after an argument pertaining to one of these subjects, they may be close friends no longer.

I realized a long time ago that it is virtually impossible to make anyone think that my religion, or lack of it, is better or more logical than anyone elses. Or that my political party is better than the one another votes for. So why make enemies? I just very rarely discuss these things.

I mention this to assure you that I am not opening a religious discussion when I say that many of the books that stress faith in God are mostly "blue sky."

Now why write an entire book on the subject when I'm sure at least 90 per cent of the people who will read it, regardless of their individual religions, already know the value of faith? They accept the proposition that faith in God is almost a necessity for a happy life.

But don't you think that perhaps God might prefer you to take care of some of your own problems? I don't think that He wants you to go through life depending on Him always, and doing nothing to help yourself.

After all, we've each been given a brain with which to think for ourselves, and I think that this is a gift with an ulterior motive. He perhaps feels that this relieves His burden a bit.

Let me try to clarify it this way. Having faith in God is both a virtue and, I believe, a necessity. But it can be much more helpful if it is spread around a bit. In other words, I think it is just as important to have faith in others, faith in mankind in general, as it is to have faith in Him. When Andrew Carnegie was asked to explain the secret of his success, his answer was quite succinct.:

"Faith in myself, faith in others and faith in my business."

Those who read "blue sky" books and believe implicitly that faith can solve any and all problems are not being helped, as far as I'm concerned. It was a wise man who first said that "the Lord helps those who help themselves."

It's all right to have faith that what you do will turn out right, because at least you're doing something. It's doing nothing and feeling that "He'll take care of it for me" that I'm definitely against.

What Trust in Others Will Bring You

In this day and age, it is almost impossible not to become at least a little bit cynical. But to be a complete cynic is to be completely unhappy. Having faith when you're ill that you will become well again is fine; but I think you'll agree that you must have faith in your doctor, too.

I know a few people who continually protest that they do not trust in doctors. Well, their views usually change when they get an unexpected pain. It's those who really do not see a doctor when it is necessary that get into difficulties.

Perhaps they had a bad experience once; perhaps a doctor came up with an incorrect diagnosis — so what? Is this adequate reason to mistrust all doctors? Of course not!

Unfortunately, and inevitably, there are bad doctors, just as there are bad lawyers and incompetent dentists — but the competent practitioners in any field surely outnumber the bad ones.

All I'm leading up to is that one good way to solve problems is to take the problem to a competent person in its particular field. That's a good way, and sometimes the only way, to get help.

"Faith in your fellow man" may be a cliche, but I think it's important to have. There are too many people who needlessly worry and fret about a million little things that will never happen, simply because they do not have trust in others.

At one time, circa 1960, in New York City, there was a rumor that garages and parking lots were removing new motors from cars and putting in old ones. Well, maybe one or two places were caught at it, but the odds against it happening to me were pretty high. Yet I couldn't help worrying about it, each time I parked my car in a parking lot. Many an evening at the theater was ruined for me because I was thinking more about the car than the story line of the play.

Well, I certainly couldn't go on mistrusting all parking lots and garages. I simply made up my mind to forget about it. It has been years since I heard that rumor, and I haven't lost any motors yet. President James A. Garfield once said:

"I have had many troubles in my life, but the worst of them never came."

So, why add unnecessary worries to the ones you already have? Give your brain time to work on more important things and stop worrying about being cheated by the butcher, the baker and the parking lot attendant. Most people are reliable and do their jobs as honestly as possible, so have some faith in them.

All this may seem quite trivial to you, but I suggest that you stop distrusting people right now. The time and energy that you can waste during your lifetime worrying because of your lack of faith in others is not trivial. Dr. Frank Crane said:

"You may be deceived if you trust too much, but you will live in torment if you do not trust enough."

But You Think People Take Advantage of You?

This idea, of course, can be carried into any and all aspects of life. Take your job, for instance. I don't have to point out all the petty jealousy and mistrust that goes on in some offices and businesses. Why do so many people always feel as if they're being taken advantage of? It is from lack of faith in their fellow workers and supervisors?

If you are one of those who constantly believes that others are taking advantage of you, or that everyone is against you, look inside yourself, my friend. The odds are there's something wrong with you! You may have some faults of your own to get rid of. Probably, the first feeling you've got to get rid of is that you have no faults. If you feel that way, you'll never get rid of them. If you know you have some faults (and who hasn't?), it's time to stop expecting others to indulge you—try doing something about them.

Worst of all, is to be conscious of none of your own offenses— or an inflated ego makes you imagine your faults are better than anyone else's virtues.

This kind of attitude must make you unhappy at your job, or at anything else for that matter. Perhaps your boss gave that raise or vice presidency to someone else when, after all, you deserved it! Come now, did you really deserve it, or do you just like to think you did? A hundred reasons are running through your mind as to why you didn't get it. Your employer likes the other employee better, plays golf with him or her, goes to his or her home for dinner, and so on, endlessly.

But in most cases, I don't think these things matter very much. Most business people are interested only in who is best qualified for a particular position, promotion or raise. You simply must have faith in your boss, and believe that he or she is interested primarily in bettering the business.

Aside from the fact that your opponent plays golf with the big boss, is he or she also better qualified than you to handle additional responsibility? Does he or she do work more competently? Does he or she do it without grumbling about it? Most importantly, does he or she usually do more than is required?

I think if you answer all these questions truthfully, you will find, more often than not, that you didn't deserve that raise after all.

What can you do about it? Well, first of all, forget about it; stop feeling sorry for yourself. Then ask yourself another question: "Am I happy at what I'm doing?" If the answer is "no," you have two choices: learn to be happy at your work, or if you feel that's impossible, find something else to do!

If you want to put some effort into being happy in your work, try this: Get interested in the business; show a little enthusiasm for it. Find out everything you can about your employer's problems; turn your chores into interesting challenges; keep your mind on what you can give to the business instead of what you can get out of it; don't be afraid of work. It was Arthur Brisbane who described the dictionary as "the only place where success comes before work."

Work never hurt anyone who enjoyed what he or she was doing. Try doing a little more than is required of you. There are many quotes in this book— remarks, writings, thoughts of thinking people. If I were allowed to use only one, I believe it would be the one credited to A.W. Robertson: "If a man does only what is required of him, he is a slave. The moment he does more, he is a free man."

Now, let's get trivial again.

1.   Do you dress neatly?
2.   Are you friendly to your fellow workers?
3.   Are you always showing discontent when you're given what you think is extra work?
4.   Do you always say that you can do everyone's duties better than they can?
5.   Are you a chronic complainer?

If you've had to answer any of these questions contrary to what you know are the right answers, well, stop complaining about not getting that raise or promotion—you're lucky you haven't been fired!

So shape up—make up your mind to have a bit of faith in people, including bosses. And if you're still unhappy about losing out on your raise, remember what Elbert Hubbard said:

"There are two kinds of discontent in this world; the discontent that works. And the discontent that wrings its hands. The first gets what it wants, and the second loses what it had. There is no cure for the first but success, and there is no cure at all for the second."

CHAPTER TWELVE

Curiosity Can Also Lead You to Success

God spare me sclerosis of the curiosity, for the curiosity which craves to keep us informed about the small things no less than the large is the mainspring, the dynamo, the jet propulsion of all complete living.
—John Mason Brown

I have always marveled at people who are not envious about anything; people who just take everything as it comes, and merely shrug off anything they don't understand. I marvel because I can't understand them! How can anyone see or hear something completely new and not at least try to understand the "why" or "how" of it?

I guess many feel that people like that are better off. What they don't know can't hurt them.

Well, perhaps—but I'm afraid I can't agree at all. I'm inclined to think that our greatest asset, next to a sense of humor, is a healthy curiosity. Curiosity may have "killed the cat," but where human beings are concerned, the only thing a healthy curiosity will kill is ignorance.

I once saw, while walking in the city at night, a small sports car parked smack in the middle of the sidewalk. I stood around watching for about ten minutes, and I saw three couples walk around the car, and continue on their way without so much as looking at it! Well, of course, this is no earth-shaking situation. I wasn't curious enough myself to stay all night to find out just why or how it came to be parked in this unusual spot. It may have been someone's idea of a prank. Two or three men could easily have lifted it from the street onto the sidewalk.

But I was amazed at those who walked right by as if the car belonged where it was. I imagine if it had been floating in mid-air without any visible means of support, these people wouldn't have given it a second look either.

Well, I could be wrong, but I think these are the kind of people who are not curious about anything. They go through life, as it were, in a straight line, like a race horse with blinkers on; not caring about or seeing anything but their own little pleasures, frustrations and problems. I simply can't imagine any of these people ever coming up with a worthwhile idea or doing anything interesting unless they developed the habit of curiosity.

People like Edison, Einstein, Pasteur and Fleming couldn't have accomplished a thing had they been willing to leave things as they were. If Edison hadn't been curious about electricity, if Bell hadn't been curious about transporting sound, the world would not have benefited from their inventions. Alexander Graham Bell himself said:

"Leave the beaten track occasionally and dive into the woods. You will be certain to find something you have never seen before."

The All -Time Cure-All for Boredom

Of course, curiosity is the handmaiden of interest. Lack of one automatically kills the other. People who have no curiosity or interest, or very little of either, must be suffering from one of our greatest ills — boredom.

Remember: There is one universal cure-all for boredom, and that is the search for knowledge. Interest and curiosity are the two batteries in your flashlight; without them you cannot search for knowledge.

American educator Nicholas Murray Butler commented that, "The tombstones of a great many people should read: Died at 30, Buried at 60." I think he was talking about the same kind of people that I'm writing about right now: those who have no curiosity or interest whatsoever.

Boredom recognizes no income brackets. A person of great wealth can be as easily bored as one who is poor. We constantly hear of famous and/or wealthy people who have used dope, recklessly dissipated or taken an overdose of sleeping pills. I can't help feeling that in many cases this is caused by boredom.

Sure, many of these people have been everywhere and seen everything, and the danger of growing too blase is ever hovering over them. The trouble is they may have seen everything with their eyes, but not with their minds. An active mind cannot become bored. And your mind is spurred to activity only by a healthy interest and a searching curiosity.

Then, of course, there are the "fence straddlers," people who are not completely bored as yet, but who soon will be, because they seek the path of least resistance away from anything they can't grasp or understand. I'm thinking of the sort of people who will watch a performer at a carnival levitate himself off the ground, or cause an elephant to vanish, and say, "Aah, it's all done with mirrors!" and then forget about it.

Well, again, these are not earth-shaking situations. I'm not suggesting that such people study how to become carnival performers or magicians, but I don't believe that any person with a normal and general interest or curiosity should simply dismiss such events. At least keep them open for discussion. If the magic feats were discussed with an open mind, the spectators would probably come close to reaching the correct modus operandi. Whether they did or not is not important. What is important is that they would be exercising their curiosity and interest, and in so doing, also exercising their imagination and thinking ability.

In my own particular field, I've come across many people who brush things off too lightly. To give you an example, I'll have to risk being called immodest, and tell you a little of what I do during one of my memory lecture demonstrations (as of forty years ago).

For one thing, I meet everybody in my audience once, prior to my performance. Then during my talk, I ask the entire audience to stand. I then call them all by name, pointing to each person as I do so. I memorize objects and hiding places decided upon by individuals; I remember a complete deck of cards in order after shuffling, an entire magazine, the populations of all the states, and many other feats of memory.

Suffice it to say that during one performance I probably remember more than most people do in a year, or perhaps a lifetime. Through the years, I've had people come up with some lulus of explanations as to how I do it. I suppose they just didn't want to believe that I had a trained memory, which is the only and easiest way to do what I do. I've had people accuse me of using Dick Tracy wrist radios, hidden microphones and hidden cameras. One woman even had the idea that my wife, Renee (she doesn't appear with me anymore—hasn't for almost thirty-five years), was coding to me by clicking her fingernails! Of course, this woman didn't bother to explain how my wife could have remembered all the information to transmit to me by code.

Once, after I had finished a demonstration, a gentleman approached me, and said, "Mr. Lorayne, I think I know how you do it." I asked, "How?" and he replied, "You've got a good memory." That was all there was to it, so far as he was concerned. He probably forgot the whole thing immediately.

Well, now, I'm not trying to imply that he should have fawned all over me, or anything like that. It's just that most people, after seeing me work, are curious as to how I obtained my powers of recollection; they've never seen anything like it before, perhaps, and they're interested. Many of them will question me as to how they can go about improving their poor memories.

The point I'd like to stress is that many of those who were interested did eventually better their supposedly bad memories, just because they were interested and curious enough to ask about something they didn't understand. You were curious and interested enough to buy this book, so you'll find that you can better your memory when you read the chapters How to Remember Anything with the Least Effort and How to Remember Names and Faces.

Take Off Those Blinkers and See the World

This perhaps immodest reference to my trained memory and myself demonstrates what I'm trying to impress upon you. For goodness sake, get those blinkers off! Don't take everything you see and hear and feel for granted. Stop every once in awhile along the way—open your mind instead of closing it to something you don't quite understand. Take perhaps only one moment to explore it, out of curiosity, and you may open up completely new interests for yourself.

Almost everyone agrees that children learn everything faster and better than adults. Some argue that it is imitation, and not really learning, others that children learn more easily because they have more room to store away facts. Well, explain it as you will, they certainly pick up languages, for example, very quickly when they're only infants.

Without having made a study of the subject, I would be inclined to think that we learn more from infancy to adolescence than we do during the rest of our lives.

I have rarely met a child who was really bored. They may be for short periods of time, but not long enough to matter. They are fast learners because they are the most curious little rascals in existence. If you're the parent of a young child, I'm sure you know this by now. Curiosity is one of the definite characteristics of a vigorous mind, and children have vigorous, active minds.

Unfortunately, as we grow older and more cynical, we tend to lose that all-important curiosity. If this has happened to you, it's your own fault and you'll have to find it again all by yourself.

Just try it. Awaken your curiosity, spur your interest and you'll push that old "debbil" boredom into the background!

The problem here is a usual one. Those of you who already have an active curiosity and are interested in many things will probably agree with me, and go on being curious and interested. You don't need any help, in this case. But most of you who do need that help, those of you who haven't that active curiosity, will be thinking, "Well, this may be sound advice, but I'm just not, and never have been, a curious person. How can I change now?"

Well, now, cut that out! Replace that negative thought with the positive one: "I haven't been a curious person up to now, but I shall practice being one." And, practice can do it, too. As with anything else, you'll find that after forcing yourself to be curious about things for a while you will be—automatically.

You may be surprised to find that new worlds will be opening for you. New interests can be lasting interests and, as you know, this can lead to the acquisition of valuable knowledge.

Curiosity has led men into hobbies that have lasted a lifetime. Many of these hobbies have turned into well-paying and interesting businesses. Stop belittling those who are interested in stamp collecting, hobby railroading, photography, magic, and other worldwide hobbies. Look into them yourself; a little curiosity will show you why they engage the interest of so many others, and may even lead to your own interest and enjoyment.

Not only will a hobby help alleviate boredom, but it's a wonderful, creative exercise. It will keep your mind sharp and clear. John Mason Brown has suggested that a hobby is an "all-important refueler of the tired mind. It offers rest and stimulation simultaneously." And anyone who has a hobby or two will surely say "amen" to that.

Practical Hints to Waken Anybody's Curiosity

Well, I've tried to convince you of the importance of being curious, and I sincerely hope I've succeeded. But I don't want to close this chapter until I've given you some definite and practical advice about curiosity.

If you are entertaining even a fleeting thought that goes something like this:"Well, now I know it's to my advantage to be curious. But curious about what? Am I to try to develop an interest in every little thing I see or hear? Must I stop to examine everything I ever come across?"—then I haven't quite reached you.

No, of course you needn't stop to examine everything. Selectivity is essential, and before you know it, your mind will seek out only the things that are of importance to you.

One of the largest businesses in New York City is the garment industry. Perhaps 80 percent of the successful operators in this business have come up from the lowest ranks. Many of them have had little formal education or training, but it was their curiosity and interest, urging them toward ambitious goals, that elevated them to their present positions.

To give one concrete example: One man I know spent a few years in the "garment center" pushing and pulling racks of dresses through the crowded streets. Now many of those who push these racks or hand trucks can't see past the front of the truck. They are interested in only one thing—getting the dresses from one place to the next. That's their job, and what else is there to think about?

But the man I'm talking about happened to be of a curious nature. He was interested in the dresses he transported. He learned their prices, and wondered why they were priced so high. During his spare time he went about finding out how much the material per dress was worth. He learned why manufacturing the dresses was so costly; and thought about methods to cut down this cost. In short, he learned all he could about the business from his position behind a hand truck.

I'm not trying to convince you that he did all this in a matter of weeks. It covered some years—but when the opportunity to go into business for himself arrived, he was ready. His ideas on lower manufacturing costs, and therefore lower prices for the same quality merchandise, couldn't help but make him a success. He is now hiring many people to push his hand trucks around; and these people would have the same opportunity he had, if they would just exercise the same curiosity.

The remarks in this chapter have been directed to people of all ages. But the happiest and youngest elderly people I know are those whose curiosity is still sharp and searching. Boredom makes people old before their time; curiosity, you'll find, is the best substitute for the mythical "fountain of youth." Perhaps that was what Harry Emerson Fosdick meant when he said:

"The art of retirement is not to retire from something but to retire to something."

You'll be happier and most likely live longer if you spur your interest and keep your curiosity at a keen edge. To those people whose curiosity has caused them to be interested in many things, the world is full of satisfaction. When you lose interest you begin to grow old instead of older. I really believe that people with a healthy curiosity actually live longer than those whose curiosity has fallen by the wayside.

Perhaps the best thought with which to leave this subject is Rudyard Kipling's:

I had six honest serving men, They taught me all I knew; Their names were Where and What and When and Why and How and Who.

It costs nothing and can do you no harm to utilize the services of these same six honest serving men.

CHAPTER THIRTEEN

You Can Learn What You Really Want To

> It is no great exaggeration to say that living is for the most part learn-
> ing, and that the remainder of life is merely the carrying on in practice
> what has previously been learned. We begin to learn at least as soon as
> we begin to live; very probably the learning process commences some
> time before birth. It does not appear probable that we cease to learn until
> we are in the actual clutches of death.
>
> —Knight Dunlap

The above statement is true, of course. To learn is certainly of great
importance to us as individuals or as members of society. Unfortunately,
many of us reach a certain stage of learning, and go through
the remainder of our lives coasting on the knowledge acquired till then.

Most of the things written in this book are geared toward enabling
you to learn more to pass that point. Curiosity, enthusiasm, interest,
concentration, problem solving, memory and imagination, are all
necessary ingredients.

Curiosity is the starter; interest and enthusiasm are low gears;
concentration and memory are high gears; and accomplishment is the
smooth level ride.

We are all capable of learning, for the simple reason that none of us
know it all—or ever will. I think that when we stop learning we begin to
stagnate—to die. Everybody knows the cliche, "We learn something new
every day." But do we? Can you honestly say that you learn something
new every day? Well, no matter. I'm not suggesting that you do.
However, I am suggesting that there are probably many things you'd like
to learn, but haven't yet—and probably don't ever really intend to.

Where to Begin and How

This brings us to the crux of the matter. That is the difference between
the wish to learn and the will to learn. How many times have you said to
yourself, "I wish I could do that," or "I wish I had the ability for this?"
Well, you can wish and wish but never really learn anything. It's the will
to learn that does wonders. If you've gone through an art museum, or
seen some good paintings anywhere, you may have said in an offhand

manner, "Gee, I wish I understood, or knew, a little bit about art," and that was the end of it.

But if the will to learn is present, you can learn to understand art. I'm sure, if you look around, you'll find many places that teach art appreciation. If there is no such place near you, you can take a correspondence course. And these courses are not expensive; as a matter of fact, if you look hard enough, you'll find that you can even take some of them free of charge.

You may not become a connoisseur of art, but you will have a better understanding of it. And, according to William Allen White:

"A little learning is not a dangerous thing to one who does not mistake it for a great deal."

The important thing here, as I've mentioned before, is to begin. Start learning a subject because you're interested in it, because you want to, and you'll continue to learn.

Do you want to learn how to play golf, or tennis; how to make a speech; write a story; be a better salesman; speak a foreign language or drive a car?

Fine! Stop wishing you could, and start to learn it. If you have the attitude, "Oh, I couldn't do that, I'm not smart enough," that's okay, too—as long as you don't allow it to stop you from trying. Cicero once said, "The first step to knowledgeis to know that we areignorant." If you thought you knew everything, you'd certainly never learn anything!

Of course, some people who are the proud possessors of wealth feel that they do know everything. For those, I've always felt that our modern proverb, "If you're so smart, how come you're not rich?" should be changed to, "If you're so rich, how come you're not smart?"

Anyway, if you want to learn anything, start! I would suggest you start by looking over the entire field of the thing you want to learn. You want to learn to drive a golf ball? Try it once. Get the entire picture of the problem in your mind.

Then go to a good "pro" and have him lead you to your goal, step by step. The same holds true for anything you want to learn. The important thing after you start is to set up a goal. Know just where you're heading. If you have only a vague idea of what you want to accomplish, your accomplishment will be vague at best.

Contrary to popular belief, repetition alone is not a particularly good way to learn anything. To repeat is to do things the same way; and when you first start learning anything, you're apt to make innumerable mistakes. Why repeat mistakes?

If your golf swing is wrong, repetition in this case will only help to ingrain your errors. The wrong method will form in your habit patterns, instead of the proper one.

If your sales approach is wrong, you can see a hundred customers a day, you may even make some sales, but the repetition of the wrong method is not making you a successful salesman.

Any golf or tennis pro will tell you that he would much rather teach a rank beginner than someone who has taught himself a little about the game. Before starting to teach, in the latter case, the pro first has to "unlearn" the pupil to rid him of his mistakes. These mistakes are difficult to get rid of, because they have become habitual through repetition.

So, don't expect repeating something indefinitely will teach you to do it properly. If learning is to advance, you must eliminate errors as you progress. Set up challenges for yourself. This will help immensely. Try to watch others who are more proficient than you are. See what it is they do that you don't do, or what they're doing differently.

I think that perhaps this is one of the best ways to learn anything. If you want to better your sales approach, watch a crack salesman work; if you want to learn public speaking, watch and listen to an established speaker in action.

And, most important, remember that these people were once learners, too—fumbling, trying and eliminating errors. If they could do it, so can you!

When You Are Ready to Give Up

The bugaboo to look out for is discouragement. Allow yourself to become discouraged, or fed up and you forfeit any progress you have made. Success or mastery of any new skill or subject is usually immediately around the corner of discouragement! It's just past that point, so why quit now?

You'll find that once you pass the lowest ebb of that "I give up" feeling, the light dawns, and another step in the right direction has been made.

I don't know why this is so, but it is. Perhaps it's because you are no longer pressing and tense when you're ready to give up. You're probably more relaxed then than at any other time during the learning process. And I'm sure you agree that it is much easier to learn when you're relaxed

You'll also agree, I'm sure, that you drive a car perfectly when you are practicing with your instructor, but when you take the test for your driver's license, you tense up, and probably fail the first time.

When you're on the golf driving range, and nobody's around to see, you're relaxed and drive the ball straight as an arrow, two hundred yards. But once you're on the course with friends, you try too hard, tense up, try to send the ball too far, and usually wind up topping, hooking, slicing—or missing it!

So you've a couple of things to keep in mind while in the process of trying to learn anything. First, try to relax. Second, don't allow yourself to become discouraged.

Remember: Without mistakes there is no learning. Each mistake spotted and eliminated represents another step forward.

One error many people make is to learn something the wrong way and stick to it no matter what. Or they reach an impasse, and try to force their way past it, stubbornly—never admitting that they may be doing something wrong, and starting fresh.

Have you ever kept tropical fish? I have—and if you place a female Siamese Fighting Fish (Betta) in one tank, in sight of a male in another, the male will keep trying to reach her by crashing himself against the inside of his tank.

I've seen one male keep this up for almost an hour, without a sign of stopping, until I took the female away. This is stupid, of course, but fish are stupid.

Please don't allow yourself to fall into the trap of "persistence of error." If you can't get past a certain point in your learning, try a different approach. Try a few different approaches, as many as necessary, until you find the right one—or the right one for you.

This reminds me of the story of the gambler who was being cheated. A friend asked if he didn't realize that he couldn't win. The gambler answered, "Do you think I'm an idiot? Of course I know that he's cheating me. I just want to get even, then I'll quit."

According to some research material I've read, anyone can learn. There is an inborn capacity that makes the difference in degrees of learning. So far, nobody has been able to explain this inborn capacity, but why worry about it? Knowing that you can learn is the important thing. You'll never find out what your capacity is if you don't try to reach it—and I'm sure nobody ever does. Walter Dill Scott said, "It is more than probable that the average man could, with no injury to his health, increase his efficiency fifty percent."

Some of us are more apt to learn mental skills than physical skills, and vice versa, of course. The examples I've used in this chapter apply to either. I also think that people should try to learn more in both areas. Too many of us, as I mentioned in the chapter on curiosity, go through life with blinkers on, never veering from our single path of least resistance.

Knowledge Is Power Only if Put to Use

Don't be a spectator all your life—try to be a doer whenever possible. Ten times to one people are passive spectators instead of active participants. I believe this ratio should be reduced to at least four to one. You'll never learn anything new if you don't participate more often. Why don't you try it? The next time you're asked to participate or join in something new or different (for you), say "yes" instead of "no."

You'll learn more, that's for sure, and you'll open up new vistas for yourself. Even if you think you know something, use it; do it or you might just as well not know it. "Knowledge is power" only when it's put into action. If you don't use it, it remains potential power only. Apropos of that, Jeremiah W. Jenks said:

"The inlet of man's mind is what he learns; the outlet is what he accomplishes. If his mind is not fed by a continued supply of new ideas which he puts to work with purpose, and if there is no outlet in action, his mind becomes stagnant. Such a mind is a danger to the individual who owns it and is useless to the community."

Let's get back to the wish and the will to learn for a moment. The wish is necessary, of course, but as already mentioned, without the will there is little learning. For example, look at these nonsense syllables: brap, pim, mod, baf, nal, lin, rix, sul, pirn, dal, lig, fub.

Can you now, without looking at them again, remember them all? I doubt it. The fact is, you didn't pay much attention to them at all, did you? There was no wish or will to learn them. (Of course, if for any reason you had to remember nonsense syllables often, it would help you to read one of my books on memory training.) However, for our purposes right now, if you look at the syllables again, I'll wager you will remember most of them, for you are looking at them with a different attitude. You would like to remember them. That's the wish. If you really want to (have the will) you can remember them all in a short time.

The will to learn is the main ingredient for learning. Once you have that, proceed systematically, in an organized manner. Don't be slipshod about it, or your work will be many times as hard. Get a definite picture in your mind of what you want to learn, and you'll learn faster and better. A slipshod approach can only give you slipshod results.

Once you've got that picture in your mind of the thing you want to learn, take it step by step. Be sure you understand and can accomplish one step before continuing to the next. Once you've mastered all the steps, you can practice the thing you've learned as a whole.

The same holds true for mental skills, for learning or gathering information. If you want to learn a poem word for word, read it over a few times. Get the meaning, the beat, and feel of it. Then learn it a line or two at a time. Finally, practice reciting the entire poem.

Try to learn things preferably in the environment in which you intend to use them. I know that I never really learned to drive a car until I had battled the New York City traffic a number of times.

If you want to learn how to make a speech, make speeches. Get up in front of an audience whenever you can. You may do a terrible job at first, but you'll learn. Once you get the "feel" of anything you're trying to master, you're almost there. That "feel" will usually come, as I said before, when you're so discouraged you're about to give up.

Keep your goal in mind at all times. "Without motivation, learning is not apparent." Let your interest be your motivation.

For instance, boys learn baseball scores and records much more easily than their schoolwork—because they're generally more interested in baseball. If, when you were studying a foreign language in school, you knew how important it might be to you, you would have learned that language faster and better than you did.

Many adults use the age-old excuse, "I'm too old to learn" or "you can't teach an old dog new tricks." Nonsense! All that is, is a good excuse! They don't really mean they're too old to learn. They mean they're too lazy to learn. Your interest may wane as you grow older, but not your ability to learn. E. L. Thorndike, an authority on adult education, said:

"Age is no handicap to learning a new trade, profession, or anything you want to do at anytime of life."

So, when you feel you would like to learn something, turn that wish into a will to learn. Keep your interest sharp; follow the suggestions outlined here, and you shouldn't have too much difficulty.

And remember that, "Learning is wealth to the poor, an honor to the rich, an aid to the young, and a support and comfort to the aged." (John C. Lavatar).

CHAPTER FOURTEEN

How to Improve Your Powers of Observation

> It is the disease of not listening, the malady of not marking, that I am troubled withal.
>
> —Shakespeare

Although I don't think it necessary or advisable for you to train your observation to the extent that Sherlock Holmes did, I do think most of us could use some sharpening up when it comes to observation.

Too many of us see, but rarely observe. Since the next two chapters pertain to memory, it is advisable to first discuss observation. The reason for this is that you can't very well remember anything if you haven't observed it. The eyes must see in order for the mind to interpret.

For example, look at this box for a moment:

TREES
IN THE
THE
FOREST
x

Now what does it say? Does it say "Trees in the forest"? Look again; I'd like you to be sure before we continue.

All right. Have you checked it out? You can look at it again, if you like. If you still think it says, "Trees in the forest," then you're like most people: You're not observing. I've had people look at it ten times and swear that that's what it read. However, if you read it and point to each word as you do, you'll see that it reads, "Trees in the the forest!" There is an extra "the" in the phrase.

Perhaps you consider this example a bit sneaky. Well, I agree. Our minds tend to jump ahead, or to the end of familiar phrases. But, I still think it proves that most of us just don't observe. Try this on your friends, and you'll concur.

Have you ever come out of a crowded theater or movie house at show break? Did you have to file out slowly because there were so many people trying to get out through one door? This has happened to me quite often. Then when I neared the door, I usually noticed two or three other exits nearby that nobody was using.

Nobody observed or saw those other doors. I'm inclined to think that they weren't observed because we usually do not see the obvious, the familiar or the commonplace.

If you don't agree with that, can you answer these questions? Do you know right now in which direction you turn the key to open your front door? Do you know which light is usually on top of the traffic signal, red or green? Do you know the exact balance in your checkbook? Do you know if the number six on your wristwatch is the Arabic 6 or the Roman numeral VI? Do you know which two letters of the alphabet are not on a dial telephone? Do you know the color of the socks you're wearing right now?

I could go on and on with questions like these, but I don't think it's necessary. I imagine that everyone will agree that his or her capacity for observation can stand some improvement. The first thing you have to learn is to look at things with attention and awareness. The chapter on concentration, elsewhere in the book, goes into some detail on that.

If you want to practice — and observation becomes a habit with practice — you might try this: Get a piece of paper and try to list everything in one of your rooms, without looking at the room, of course. List everything you can think of — pictures, furniture, accessories, everything.

Now, go into the room and check. Notice all the things you didn't list, the things you never really observed. Try listing again. The list will get longer after each inspection of the room. Try the same thing with other rooms. Keep this up for a while, and your observation will improve outside as well as within your home.

Think of a familiar street, one that you've walked on many times. See if you can list all the stores on that street. Try listing them in their correct order. Then check yourself. If you didn't list all of them, try again. Then try it with other streets. Look in the window of one of those stores, then, without looking, see how many of the items you can list.

Try picturing a friend of yours and describing his or her face in minute detail. Then check the next time you see that person. Notice now what you never noticed before. There are many ways in which you can test your observation, and the more you test it, the better it will become. I'll leave you with that. I only want to assure you that if you look and listen with attention and awareness you'll not only save yourself a lot of time and trouble, but you'll improve your memory immediately. Samuel Johnson said:

"The true art of memory is the art of attention."

A Bad Penny Turns Up!

While I'm on the subject of observation and memory, I don't want you to think that I forgot my promise to give you the solution to that "bad penny" problem.

You remember the predicament, don't you? You have twelve pennies, one of which is either lighter or heavier than the other eleven. You have a balancing scale upon which you're allowed only three weighings to tell which is the bad penny, and whether it's lighter or heavier.

I hope you've tried to work it out yourself, mainly because you'll understand this better if you have. At first the solution may sound more complicated than the problem. Take it step by step and you shouldn't have too much trouble. Three of the following paragraphs are lettered A, B, and C, because you are referred back to them once or twice. Now, here's the solution:

First of all, the way to begin is to weigh four against four. Let's take the simplest contingency first. You realize that one of two things can happen: either the scale balances or it doesn't. We'll assume now that it has balanced on your first weighing.

A. Of course, you know now that the bad penny is one of the four that you haven't weighed as yet. For the second weighing, weigh three of these four against three of the known good ones (any three of those you have already weighed). Again, either the scales will balance or they won't.

Assume again that they've balanced. Well, that's your second weighing, and you now know that the remaining penny, the one that has not been weighed at all, is the bad one. You have one weighing left. This one is used to find out if the penny is lighter or heavier. Simply weigh it against any one of the others. The scales cannot balance now. If the side of the remaining penny goes down, the penny is heavier than the other eleven; if it goes up, it's lighter.

That's one possible solution. But lets go back to the second weighing (Paragraph A), where you're balancing three including the possible bad one against three known good ones. What if the scales do not balance? Simple! Keep your eye on the side of the scale that has the probable bad one on it. If that side goes down while the other side goes up, then you know that one of those three is the bad one, and that it is heavier. If it goes up, then the bad penny is lighter.

B. Now, the third weighing: You are down to three possible bad pennies. Simply weigh one of them against another. If they balance, then the third (unweighed) one is the bad one. You already know whether it's lighter or heavier from the second weighing. If the scales don't balance, then knowing whether the bad penny is heavier or lighter tells you which it is. If the second weighing told you that the penny was lighter, then the penny on the side of the scale which is now up, is the bad one. If you knew the bad penny was heavier, then the one which is down is the bad one!

Okay, there you have the complete solution if your first weighing balances. If the first weighing does not balance, it gets even more complicated. Go over this slowly, picturing it all in your mind as you do. At the end, I'll show you an easy way to try it, so that you can understand it more clearly.

If your first weighing is not balanced, the four pennies on the up side can be considered possible "lights," the four on the down side possible "heavies," while the four you haven't weighed are proved to be good ones.

The problem now breaks down to this: You must never leave more than three pennies for the last weighing. Here's how you do it. You are again, for the second weighing, going to weigh four against four, but with this difference — on the left (for description's sake) side of the scale, place one of the possible lights and three of the known good ones. On the right side, place one possible heavy and three remaining possible lights. You will have one known good penny, and three possible heavies left over. Of course, you must keep track of which pennies are where.

C. Now again, the scales may balance or they may not. If they balance, you know that the bad penny is one of the three possible heavies that you did not weigh just now. So end as before (in Paragraph B): weigh one of the possible heavies against another. The one that goes down is the bad, heavier penny. If they should balance, the one remaining is the bad, heavier one.

However, what if the second weighing doesn't balance? Assume the left side goes up and the right side goes down. In this case, the bad penny must be either the one possible "light" on the left side, or the one possible "heavy" on the right. (You see why, don't you? It couldn't be one of the three possible lights on the right, or that side would have gone up. The other three on the left are already known good ones, so it couldn't be one of these.)

Okay, you're left with a possible heavy and a possible light for the last weighing. Simply weigh either one of them against a good one. If the possible heavy is the one you use, and it goes down, that's the bad penny. If they balance, then the possible light isn't "possible" any more — that's it.

Now, if the left side goes down and the right side goes up during the second weighing, the solution is a bit different. You would now know that the bad penny is one of the three possible lights on the right side. (It couldn't be the possible heavy or the right side would have gone down. It couldn't be the possible light on the left side, or that would have gone up.)

So you're left with three possible lights. End as in Paragraphs B and C. Weigh one of the lights against another. If one side goes up, that's your bad, lighter penny. If they balance, the remaining one is it.

That is the complete solution! I know it sounds awfully complicated, but it isn't really. Once you understand it, and learn to keep track of which penny is where, you'll know just how to handle it.

Here's an easy way to practice it. From a deck of cards take eleven black cards and one red card. The one red card will represent the bad penny. Now get a friend who's willing to help you and shuffle the twelve cards. Then place four of them face down, without looking at them, on your left and four on your right, as if you were putting them on a balancing scale. Have your friend decide, individually, whether the red card (bad penny) is to be heavier or lighter.

Now your friend looks at the cards, and indicates with his or her hands how the scale goes — which side is up and which is down or if they balance. You then continue along as per the above instructions. That's all. You'll see that after the third "weighing," you'll be able to tell which is the red card, and whether it was heavier or lighter.

You may even want to go over the solution again, right now, using the card idea to help you follow it, and keep it clear in your mind. Have fun!

Here's one more thing for you to try. Read the following four lines. Count the "F's". Remember your total and check it against the correct answer which, if you keep reading, you'll find in a few pages. Don't look at the answer until you've read the four lines once or twice and arrived at a total number of F's, of course.

FINISHED FILES ARE THE RESULT OF YEARS OF SCIENTIFIC STUDY
COMBINED WITH THE EXPERIENCE OF MANY YEARS.

CHAPTER FIFTEEN

How to Remember Anything
with the Least Effort

> **Patient:** Doctor, you've got to help me. I'm losing my memory. I'm sure I hear a thing one moment and forget it the next. I don't know what to do.
> **Doctor:** When did you first notice this?
> Patient: Notice what?

I think that the one faculty that really exemplifies an organized mind is memory. Perhaps it's because this is closest to me that I feel it's most important. I wrote this, and the following chapter on remembering names and faces, over forty years ago! I'm quite pleased and pleasantly surprised that, aside from a bit of editing, it all holds up quite well. Obviously, I'm only scratching the surface.

Anyone can learn to improve his or her memory. All we wish to remember must be associated in some way with something we already remember. Anything you remember now, you are associating in this way.

How many times have you seen or heard something which made you snap your fingers and exclaim, "Oh, that reminds me!?" The thing that reminded you may have had no obvious connection with the thing it reminded you of. Yet there was an association there someplace. The trouble is that such associations are made subconsciously. If you can learn to make them consciously, you will have a trained memory.

Conscious associations have been used for years to help people remember almost anything. The sentence, "Every Good Boy Does Fine," helped you remember the lines of the staff or treble clef when you went to school. The phrase, "Never believe a lie," helped you remember that "i" comes before "e" in spelling "believe." The word "homes" helps to recall the names of the Great Lakes: Huron, Ontario, Michigan, Erie and Superior.

The Secret of Memory Association

I don't intend to go into a complete memory training course in this book; but I do want to show you how systemization and organization can help you to remember in a way that you've never remembered before.

For example, look at these twelve words: book, flower, cigarette, eyeglasses, shoe, suitcase, car, clock, baseball, pen, necktie, ship.

Now, do you think you could remember all these words in that order, from first to last, after seeing or hearing them only once? I doubt it. I've yet to find anyone with an untrained memory who could do it. Well, I think I can teach you now, in this chapter, how to memorize these twelve (or any twelve, or more) objects, in order, forward and backward.

I've already told you that it's done via association. This simply means that you must connect or tie up two objects at a time — and to make the association stronger, they must be tied up in a ridiculous or illogical manner. We always tend to remember ridiculous, ludicrous and violent things rather than pleasant ones.

Okay, the first object is "book," the next is "flower." Now you must make a picture in your mind of some sort of ridiculous association between these two. For example, you might "see" a flower reading a book — or books growing in a garden instead of flowers. Pick an association that you feel is most ridiculous, and see it in your mind's eye for just a second.

If you don't actually see the picture, you won't remember the objects. Once you've seen it, forget it and go on to the next one.

"Cigarette" is the object we want to remember now. Associate that with "flower." You're smoking a flower, or a flower is smoking a cigarette, or cigarettes (lit) are growing instead of flowers. Pick one, and picture it for a moment.

Eyeglasses. See a large cigarette wearing eyeglasses, or you're smoking a pair of eyeglasses; or you have two cigarettes over your eyes instead of glasses.

Have you got the idea? You always associate the present object with the preceding one, and in so doing, you form a chain which should lead from one object to the next. Each association must be illogical and it must be seen in the mind's eye.

Here are some suggestions for ridiculous associations for the rest of the items. In each case, select the one you feel is most ridiculous and take a second to picture it.

Eyeglasses to shoe:
You're wearing eyeglasses on your feet instead of shoes (the lens break and cut your feet). Or a gigantic shoe is wearing glasses. (See the picture.)

Shoes to suitcase:
You're wearing suitcases instead of shoes. Or you open a suitcase and a million shoes fly out and kick you in the face. (See your association.)

Suitcase to car:

You're driving a large suitcase instead of a car. Or you're carrying a car instead of a suitcase. Or a car is carrying a suitcase. Or a suitcase is driving a car. (Pick one and see it.)

Car to clock:

You're driving a gigantic clock instead of a car. Or a large car is on your table and you look at it to tell time. Or a large clock is your chauffeur and is driving the car. (Be sure to see the picture.)

Clock to baseball:

You're hitting a clock instead of a baseball. Or a large clock (or team of clocks) is playing baseball. (Be sure to see the picture.)

Baseball to pen:

You're hitting the ball with a pen. Or you're writing with a baseball instead of a pen. Or a large pen is playing baseball. (Don't just see the words, see the actual picture.)

Pen to necktie:

You're wearing a pen instead of a necktie. Or a large pen is wearing a necktie. Or you're writing on your tie with a pen. (See the picture.)

Necktie to ship:

You're wearing a ship instead of a necktie. Or you're sailing on a gigantic tie instead of a ship. Or a million ties (instead of people) are sailing on a ship. (Select one and see the picture.)

All right, if you've "seen" each one of these pictures in your mind's eye, you should be able to start with "book," and memorize right down to "ship!" Try it.

When you think of "book" the picture of the flower reading it will come to mind. Then the thought of "flower" will make you think of smoking one instead of a "cigarette." Then you're wearing cigarettes instead of "eyeglasses." Continue down to "ship."

You can go even further. If you've made the associations ridiculous and strong enough, you should be able to start with "ship" and remember back right up to "book." Try it and amaze yourself.

This particular idea can be used to remember anything in sequence. I've mentioned in the chapter on public speaking that the best way to deliver a speech is to try to know it thought for thought. Well, that's a sequence.

If you've got your speech written out, go through it and take one key word from each thought. Your key word must be one that will bring the entire thought to mind. Then simply "link" all these words just as you did with the above objects, and you can throw away your notes!

If you go over your "link" a few times, you'll find that it's easier to remember than to forget them. Try remembering the twelve objects tomorrow, and you'll see that you still can.

As you deliver or finish one thought during your speech, the next one will come to mind almost automatically. And soon, to your conclusion.

How to Remember Things in Any Order

When it comes to remembering things in and out of order, or by number —well, as I said, I don't want to go into a complete memory course here. My books on the subject teach the complete "peg" system for remembering numbers of any length. However, just to illustrate the power of an organized mind plus a little imagination, let me teach you a way, a limited way, to memorize, say, sixteen items, in and out of order. It will also be handy for remembering your daily errands, shopping lists, appointments, and many other things.

Remember: Anything you wish to remember must be associated with something you already remember.

I'll give you sixteen things to memorize once, and that will help you to remember sixteen other things any time you like.

Of course, you could memorize any list of objects as a "peg" list. However, the following one is so simple because each object is selected to represent a number for a definite reason, and it can represent only one number. You won't have to count through the entire list to figure out which number is represented by the object.

1

2

3

4

5

6

7

8

9

10

11

12

13

14

15

16

For No.1: Picture a magician's wand. A wand standing upright looks like the numeral 1.

For No. 2: Picture a swan. With a little stretch of the imagination, a swan looks like the figure 2.

For No. 3: I usually picture a three-leaf clover.

For No. 4: You can picture anything with four legs—a table, a chair or a four-legged animal.

For No. 5: Picture a five-pointed star.

For No. 6: Picture an elephant's trunk, curved to look like a 6.

For No. 7: A flag waves in the breeze.

For No. 8: Picture an hourglass.

For No. 9: A man's pipe standing on its stem.

For No.10: Picture a bat and ball. The bat represents the digit 1, and the ball represents the zero.

For No. 11: My original picture was of two strands of spaghetti. So, spaghetti will always represent No. 11 for me.

For No. 12: See a picture of a clock stopped at 12:00 o'clock.

For No. 13: You can picture either a black cat, or someone walking under a ladder.

For No. 14: Picture a bolt of lightning shaped like 14.

For No.15: I originally pictured myself stepping into an elevator and saying "fifteenth floor, please." So picture an elevator for this number.

For No.16: Picture a road sign that says, "Route 16."

With the little "memory aid" that I've given you for each object, you should have no trouble remembering them easily. Practice until you know them in and out of order. Here's the list once more.

1. wand		9.	pipe
2. swan		10.	bat and/or ball
3. clover		11.	spaghetti
4. table		12.	clock
5. star		13.	ladder (black cat)
6. elephant's trunk		14.	lightning
7. flag		15.	elevator
8. hourglass		16.	sign

Using the Memory Key

Now, if you have these in your mind, I'll show you how to use them. Don't try this until you're sure you know the sixteen "peg" words thoroughly. Let's say you want to do this as a stunt, to show off for your friends. Have someone call the numbers haphazardly, and give you any object for each number. He's to write them as he calls them, so that he'll remember them.

When all sixteen are filled in, you will be able to remember all the items in order, or he can call any number and you will tell him the item, or he can call the item and you will tell him its numerical position!

Here's all you have to do: When an object is called, simply associate it in a ridiculous manner to the "peg" that represents the number called. For example, if "window" is called for No. 9, see a pipe smashing a window, or a window smoking a pipe.

Try it now. I'll give you the sixteen items haphazardly, with a suggestion on how to associate each one. Make all the associations as ridiculous as you can; see them in your mind's eye, and you'll surprise yourself.

No.   9: Window—I've already helped you with this one.

No. 16: Wallet—see a large wallet instead of a road sign, or you open your wallet and a large sign falls out.

No.   3: Birdcage—see a clover instead of a bird locked in a birdcage.

No. 11: Ashtray—see yourself dropping ashes into your spaghetti

No. 7: Newspaper—you're waving a newspaper instead of a flag, or you're reading a flag.

No. 14: Radio—a large bolt of lightning demolishes your radio, or you turn on the radio and lightning shoots out of it.

No. 1: Hat—you're waving a hat instead of a wand, or you wave your wand at a hat and it disappears, or you're wearing a wand for a hat.

No. 12: Waste paper basket—see a basket on your mantel instead of a clock, or the basket is filled with many clocks.

No. 5: Bed—see a large star sleeping in a bed, or a bed hangs in the sky instead of a star.

No. 15: Light bulb—see yourself going up in a bulb instead of an elevator, or an elevator door opens and a million light bulbs roll out.

No. 6: Typewriter—see an elephant typing with his trunk, or an elephant has a typewriter in place of a trunk.

No. 13: Telephone—see a telephone climbing a ladder, or you're talking into a ladder instead of a phone, or a ladder is talking on the phone.

No. 4: Gun—see yourself using a large gun for a table, or a table is shooting a gun.

No. 10: House—see a house playing baseball, or you're wrecking a house with a baseball bat.

No. 2: Briefcase—see a briefcase floating on a lake like a swan, or you open your briefcase and a swan swims out.

No. 8: Picture—see an hourglass framed on your wall instead of a picture, or you keep turning your picture upside down to allow the sand to shift, as in an hourglass.

Now you should be able to call off all these items from 1 to 16. Think of your "peg" for No. 1. That's a magician's wand. You recall that you were wearing a wand instead of a hat. Therefore, No. 1 is hat. Your "peg" for No. 2 is swan. A briefcase was floating on a lake instead of a swan. No. 3's "peg" is clover—a three-leaf clover is in a birdcage. The "peg" for No. 4 is table—and a table was shooting a gun, and so on.

See if you can fill in all the blanks:

1._____   9._____
2._____ 10._____
3._____ 11._____
4._____ 12._____
5._____ 13._____
6._____ 14._____
7._____ 15._____
8._____ 16._____

Did you get most of them? If you missed one or two, your associations weren't strong enough. Strengthen them now. Of course, if an object is called, you can give the number immediately. Say "telephone" is called. Do you recall your picture of talking into a ladder instead of a phone? Ladder is the "peg" for No.13—therefore "telephone" must be No. 13.

Well, I hope I've shown you how a bit of organization and imagination can enable you to do something you've never been able to do before. I admit that this idea is limited, although you could make the list longer if you wanted to. However, the phonetic sound "peg" system taught in my other books and at my seminars can be brought into the thousands without any trouble at all.

Still, the system explained here can be used for a variety of purposes. If you have a list of errands and appointments to remember, simply tie them up with the "peg" list. You have to have your car washed—associate car with wand. Then you have a dental appointment—so associate dentist with swan. You have to buy an umbrella, associate umbrella with clover. You've got a bill to pay, associate bill with table, and so on with all your errands for the day.

Once you've compiled the list, simply go through it, one "peg" word at a time, to remember what you've got to do next. If you've got a sales talk to memorize, you can associate a different point with each "peg" word. I'm sure you'll find many ways of using the list.

Now that you see how your memory can be improved, you should be pleased to know that the following chapter will teach you how to remember names and faces.

Here's the answer to the "F" question asked at the end of the preceding chapter. There are six F's in the 4-line sentence. Ninety-nine percent of those who try it count three F's. Most eyes miss the F in—"of"—and there are three of those. Even if you came up with the correct answer (6), try it on friends; you'll be amazed at how many see only three F's. You can type the four lines onto an index card, exactly as shown, so that you can carry it with you.

CHAPTER SIXTEEN

How to Remember Names and faces

Memory, the daughter of attention, is the teeming mother of knowledge.
—Martin Tupper

At my lectures and performances I remember the names and faces of everybody in the audience! Perhaps you saw me do just that recently on the Jack Paar Show. (That's a giveaway, isn't it?! Since writing this, I've been on just about every national television show here and abroad—twenty-three times with Johnny Carson, at last count.) I've remembered as many as seven hundred people in one evening, after meeting them only once! I mention this, not to brag, but to try to prove to you that it can be done.

A universal complaint nowadays is: "I can't remember names". No problem with the faces, of course; it's always the name that creates the problem. I've never heard anyone say, "I remember your name, but I simply can't remember your face!"

Well, the reason for this is quite simple. We all tend to remember the things we see much better than the things we hear. We always see the face, but usually only hear the name—therein lies the problem.

There have been many systems devised to help people remember names. One man always asked people whose name he couldn't recall whether it was spelled with an "e" or an "i." This was fine, until he asked the question of a Mrs. Betch!

No, I'm afraid this won't do. The best, and as far as I'm concerned the only, way to remember names is to tie the name to the person's face. As long as you usually "place the face" anyway, why not take advantage of that, and let the face bring the name to mind for you? As a matter of fact, the system of association that I'm about to describe for you will work both ways. The face will bring the name to mind; and the name will help you to picture the face.

Remembering Names Without Faces

However, before going into the system itself, I think I can considerably improve your memory for names without it. Many people who complain that they forget names don't really forget them — they never remember them in the first place. As a matter of fact, sometimes they never even hear them.

Think of that for a moment! Many times, you never even hear the name, so how in the world can you remember or forget it? The first rule for remembering names is: be sure you hear the name when you're introduced to someone!

People are flattered if you show interest in their names, so you needn't be afraid to ask someone to repeat a name if you don't think you've heard it properly. The people who have reputations for prodigious memories for names won those reputations via the expedient of one little sentence: "I'm sorry, but I didn't get your name!"

Once you've made sure you've heard the name — if it's a familiar one, or if it's similar to that of a friend or relative, or if you've never heard it before — mention it. As I said, people will love you when you make a fuss over their names, and one or two remarks about it will help to drive it into your memory.

Now, if you simply make it a point to use the name occasionally during the conversation, you'll be amazed at how you'll improve your memory. I don't mean to keep repeating it like an idiot, but do use it occasionally, and particularly when you say, "Good night" or "Good-bye."

If you follow these simple rules, all you're really doing is concentrating on the name in a way you've never done before. This takes care of about 25 percent of the problem. If you're interested in solving the remaining 75 per cent, read on.

As I mentioned, the best way to remember names and faces is to associate the name to the face. The method is really easy. There are two steps involved. The first one is to make the name mean something. Let's discuss that for a moment. Actually, there are three categories that names fall into: (1) names that already mean something; (2) names that may have no meaning, but remind you of something tangible; and (3) names that have no meaning at all.

Of course, you have the least problem with names that already mean something, or that remind you of something. The problem is the meaningless names. Let me give you a few examples of each type, and then I'll show you what to do about the third category. Names like Brown, Stern, Taylor, Green, Coyne, Carpenter, Sommer, Byrd, Butler, Locke already have meaning.

Dempsey, Sullivan, McCarthy, Fitch, Arcaro and names of that type may have no particular meaning to you, but should remind you of something, bring a certain picture to mind. Sullivan and Dempsey should make you think of fighters. McCarthy might make you think of a ventriloquist's dummy (Charlie McCarthy). Fitch is the brand name of a shampoo; Arcaro should make you picture a jockey.

The list of names that have no meaning is a long one. You hear them every day. Names like Krakauer, Karowski, Cortell, Kolodny, Cohen, Platinger, Smolenski, Gordon, and so on ad infinitum.

The system I call "substitute words or thoughts" is what enables you to picture any name. All you have to do is make up a word or phrase that sounds as close as possible to the name you wish to remember, and that has some meaning to you.

Following is an example of the "substitute words or thoughts" system: the name Steinurtzel would probably confuse you ordinarily. But if you picture a beer stein that's covered with gold to make it worth selling — "stein worth sell" would help you think of Steinwurtzel!

There is no name — I repeat, no name — that cannot be broken down in some way in order to make it meaningful or tangible to you. I don't care how silly or ridiculous your substitute word or phrase is — as a matter of fact, usually, the sillier the better.

For a name like Krakauer, you could picture either a cracked clock — "crack hour?" — or a "cracked cow," which is close enough. For Platinger, picture a plate that's been injured — "plate injure" — Platinger. A small camera (lens) skiing, would bring to mind Smolenski.

For a name like Gordon, I always picture a garden. You see, after a bit of practice you'll start using certain pictures for certain names all the time. For instance, I always picture an ice cream cone for Cohen, or a blacksmith's hammer for Smith.

Remember: It isn't necessary to get the entire sound of the name into your substitute word or phrase. Remember the main element, and the incidentals will fall into place. This system is merely an aid to your true memory.

If the name you want to memorize is Belden, the picture of a bell would suffice; your true memory would take care of the rest of it. Of course, a bell in a den would make it definite.

The important thing is that in order to find a substitute word for a name you must hear it in the first place. Then you automatically become interested in the name, and interest is essential to memory.

Okay, I think by now you've got the idea—so long as you realize that any name can be made to mean something. As a sort of extreme example, I once had to remember the name Pukczyva. It is pronounced "Puck—shiv—va." I pictured a hockey puck shivering with cold. Recently I met a Mr. Bentavagnia. It is pronounced "benta—vay—nya." I pictured someone bending a weather vane.

Many names have similar endings, like "ly," "ton," "berg," etc. Make up a word for each of these and use it consistently. A lea is a meadow; a barbell, dumbbell or any weight can be used to represent ton; and berg means mountain in German, or visualize an iceberg. As far as prefixes are concerned—well, for any name beginning with "Mc" or "Mac," picture a Mack truck; for "Stein," a beer stein; and for "Berg," an iceberg or mountain. For Mr. Macatee, I'd picture a Mack truck running over a cup of tea: "Mack tea"—Macatee. For the name Steinberg, you might see a beer stein on top of an iceberg.

By the way, all this is a very individual thing. The first thought that comes to me upon hearing a name may differ from the one that comes to you. That's as it should be—but usually the first thing that comes to mind is the one to use.

Before going on to show you how to associate a name to a face, perhaps you'd like a bit of practice. Well, why don't you see what you can do with the following names? I'll give you my suggestions afterward, but first see what you can do on your own.

Stapleton	Zimmerman
Brady	Kolodny
Welling	Citron
Jordan	Zauber
Schwartzberg	Robinson
Fishter	McGarrity
Cortell	Kusek
Carruthers	

Here are my first thoughts on each of them:

Stapleton: See so many staples that they weigh a ton; or you're stapling a barbell (or whatever you're using to represent ton). "Staple ton" — Stapleton.

Brady: You can picture a girl's braid, or you're braiding the lines of a gigantic letter "E." "Braid E" — Brady.

Welling: See a well filled with ink instead of water. "Well ink" — Welling.

Jordan: Picture a river, the River Jordan. Or a jaw falling down. "Jaw down" — Jordan.

Schwartzberg: See an iceberg covered with warts. "Warts berg" — Schwartzberg.

Fishter: See yourself fishing and catching a toe or you're tearing a fish. "Fish toe," "fish tear" — Fishter.

Cortell: A length of cord is gossiping or telling. "Cord tell" — Cortell.

Zimmerman: Picture a man cooking or simmering in a large pot. "Simmer man" — Zimmerman.

Kolodny: See a knee that's all different colors. "Colored knee" — Kolodny.

Citron: Picture someone sitting and running at the same time. (A citrus fruit would do it too.) "Sit run" — Citron.

Zauber: See yourself sawing a bear in half, or sawing in the nude. "Saw bear," "Saw bare" — Zauber.

Robinson: See a robin and its son; or you're robbing your own son. "Robin son," "robbing son" — Robinson.

McGarrity : A Mack truck is carrying thousands of cups of tea. "Mack carry tea" — McGarrity.
Kusek :See a cue stick being sick. "Cue sick" — Kusek.

Carruthers : See a car with udders (like a cow). "Car udders"—Carruthers.

Putting the Right Name to The Right Face

Well, that's the first step—making the name meaningful. Now for step number two, which is tying the name, or the substitute word for it, to the face. All you have to do is look at the face and pick out one outstanding feature. This can be anything—high forehead, low forehead, large nose, big ears, lines, clefts, thick lips, thin lips, close-set eyes, dimples, large chin, receding chin—anything.

Again, this is an individual thing. Two people may look at the same face and pick two different features. But the one that's outstanding to you now is the one that will be outstanding when you see that face again. More important, while looking for that outstanding feature, you are getting a picture of the entire face in your mind, automatically.

When you've decided on the outstanding feature, associate the substitute word for the name to that feature in some ridiculous way. That's all there is to it!

Make your associations in the same manner that you learned to do with objects—make them ridiculous and "see" them in your mind's eye. If you meet a Mr. Markel who has great bushy eyebrows, you might see yourself marking those eyebrows with large letter "L's." "Mark L"— Markel. See that picture in your mind as you look at the person's face, and the odds are that when you see that face again, the eyebrows will make you think of the name.

Keep in mind, please, that all this is really a means to an end. Once a name is fixed indelibly in your memory, you can forget your associations. Also, what this system is really doing is forcing you to be interested in, listen to and concentrate on the name—and be interested in, look at and concentrate on the face.

If you could do this all the time without the system, you wouldn't need the system. The use of the system, however, makes it easier to do, since we're all basically lazy, and don't want to concentrate.

Before you know it, this system for remembering names and faces will become habit and you'll do it almost automatically—that is if you start using it now!

A Few More Examples:

Mr. Galloway has a deep cleft in his chin. Picture a girl or gal going away, or falling away, out of that cleft.

Mr. Sachs h a s a high forehead. See that forehead as a large sack; or thousands of sacks are flying out of his forehead.

Mr. Van Nuys has bulging eyes. See two large vans making lots of noise driving out of those eyes.

Mr. Smith has a large nose. See that nose as a blacksmith's hammer; or you're hammering on his nose with the hammer.

Of course, the best way to practice all this is to go ahead and do it. The next time you're introduced to a few people at a time, try the system—you'll be amazed, I assure you. Don't feel that it takes too long to do it, either. After a minimum of practice you'll have found a substitute word for the name (if necessary) and associated it to an outstanding feature of the face in about as much time as it takes to say, "Hello."

If you like, you can use a magazine or newspaper for practice. Cut out pictures of faces and use them as practice cards. Either make up names or use their real ones, and apply the system. Even though a picture is a one-dimensional thing, it will still prove the system's effectiveness.

Well, that about does it. There is much more I could teach you about memory, but I won't here. I just wanted to prove how organizing your mind, and a bit of imagination and concentration thrown in, could and must improve your memory.

CHAPTER SEVENTEEN

How to Make Anyone Like You:
The Secret of Personality

We possess by nature the factors out of which personality can be made, and to organize them into effective personal life is every man's primary responsibility.

—Harry Emerson Fosdick

The other day I was talking to a friend who mentioned that he'd watched a television star the night before. "He's just great!" was his opinion. I asked him if this star could dance? The answer was no. Could he sing? No. Was he a comedian? Not really. Well, why was he so wonderful? "Oh, he's such a nice guy!"

I guess this is of great importance to all of us: to possess the talent of making people like us more -- so in everyday life than in television, I'm sure. Macauley once said that "popularity is power," and to be popular among your own friends and acquaintances, it goes without saying that they must like you.

The way you look, the way you act and the way you talk are the three things that "set" your personality. The way you think is what controls your looks, actions and words. It is not an easy task for me to teach you how to obtain a good personality; I can only give you some general hints on how to make others like you.

You Must Like Others First

The best way, of course, is to be interested in other peoples' interests. There is no better way to gain their attention and their interest. I know of one man who makes his living interviewing celebrities for his newspaper. His specialty is in getting somewhere with people who usually don't like to talk to reporters His secret is a simple one. Before an interview, he makes it his business to take the time to find out what the interviewee is interested in.

He studies up on some of these things, so that he can show an intelligent curiosity and interest in them. It's surprising how those that ordinarily "clam up" will talk to him. And you can do worse than to utilize this idea when talking to anyone.

Everybody looks for and desires approval - to be liked and appreciated by others. And those who act as if they don't want, or don't care for, approval desire it most of all. They are, perhaps, too wrapped up in themselves - which, incidentally, makes a small package. It seems impossible to me that one can be interested only in one's self and be popular at the same time. Charles H. Parkhurst said it this way:

"The man who lives by himself and for himself is apt to be corrupted by the company he keeps."

I personally have started many lasting friendships by showing interest (even if it's feigned interest at first) in the projects, troubles, ambitions and general interests of others

You've got to learn to like people in order to make them like you. Try using the system of "similar attitudes." Most people will act toward you as you act toward them. It's easy enough to prove this statement. Frown at the next person you talk to, and the odds are he'll frown right back at you. Act as if you're looking into a mirror when you converse with friends or acquaintances. Keep that in mind, because your acquaintance's attitudes are usually reflections of your own actions.

I know a few cynics who think the world, or rather the people in it, are in bad shape. Nobody cares about these people, so they don't care about anyone. Of course, they're lonely people - they insist on building barricades around themselves, instead of bridges. You can build bridges by learning to smile instead of frown.

Remember: It has been said that it takes more muscles to frown than it does to smile. I don't know if that's true, but why not act as if it were. Make it easy on yourself- smile!

To Win Friends - Be One

If you're lonely, if you don't have enough friends - well, be a friend and you'll have friends. Go out of your way occasionally to help someone, as you would want a friend to help you. Remember these quotes by G. Bailey:

"It is one of the beautiful compensations of life that no man can sincerely try to help another, without helping himself"

"Those who bring sunshine to the lives of others cannot keep it from themselves." Remember them and live by them - you'll be a happier and better person for it.

Don't complain about people not being kind if you're not kind yourself. I believe that every kindness you show will come back to you someday, some way - if not from the people you showed it to, well then, from others. Sooner or later everything balances out. Bread cast upon the waters, you know.
Walter S. Landor and Dr. Grellet had this to say, respectively:

"Kindness in ourselves is the honey that blunts the sting of unkindness in another."
"I shall pass through this world but once. If, therefore, there is any kindness I can show, or any good thing I can do, let me do it now; let me not defer it or neglect it, for I shall not pass this way again."

Most people are trying to solve the same problems, the same war of nerves, the same hard fight that you are. Keep that in mind the next time you're about to be unkind to someone.
I don't hold with actions or attitudes that people display for which apologies are necessary but aren't always given. I refer to those people who excuse their unkindness or impoliteness with "I was very busy" or "I didn't feel well" or "I was in a bad mood."
I was in a hospital visiting a friend who had suffered a heart attack. He wanted to make an important phone call. He held his private telephone off the hook for about four or five minutes and got no response. Thinking that the switchboard operator couldn't hear the buzz, or that there might be something wrong with the phone itself, he clicked the receiver a few times.
Suddenly he heard the operator's sharp voice: "What the h___ are you clicking about? I'll give you a line when I'm good and ready!" The patient was stunned and complained bitterly. I went to a public booth to make the call for him. Some time later, the manager of the hospital came into the room and told my friend that the operator had been very busy at the time.
Well now, that's just what I'm talking about. It certainly would seem that a man who had just suffered a heart attack, and was in the hospital because of it, deserved a little more courtesy, even if the telephone

operator was three times as busy. And it would have taken less time to say something like "I'm awfully sorry, but I'll give you a line the moment one is free" than it did for her original discourteous remark. I can only assume that that operator is a terribly unhappy person.

There is always time for courtesy! Stop using your sickness, pains, worries and troubles as excuses for avoiding it. Remember the next time you snap at someone because you've got a stomachache that he may be dying, for all you know. Justice Felix Frankfurter said that, "Courtesy is the lubricant of society," and I couldn't agree more wholeheartedly.

Just as you like to be appreciated, show others your appreciation. The two most beautiful words we can utter are not used often enough nowadays. They are: "Thank you." Use them more often and you'll hear them more often.

So you may think the world's against you. You may want to change everything and everybody - but, believe me, you'll find that the best way, in many instances, to change your friends, acquaintances, husband or wife is to change yourself. And, according to Thomas a Kempis:

"Be not angry that you cannot make others as you wish them to be, since you cannot make yourself (entirely) as you wish to be."

We Are All Funnier Than We Think

I think that the most essential ingredient for a good personality is a sense of humor. Learn to laugh a little more at yourself and at life. Sooner or later, you're going to laugh at the petty annoyances and frustrations that face you now; why not laugh at them now, to begin with? And, incidentally, a sense of humor does not mean laughing at something happening to somebody else that would make you angry if it happened to you!

I don't know of a better antidote for nervousness or tenseness than a sense of humor. The problem, of course, is that those who do not possess this valuable attribute don't know it. According to Frank M. Colby "Men will confess to treason, murder, arson, false teeth, or a wig. How many of them will own up to a lack of humor?"

Well, I don't know that it's a question of "owning up" to it; it's rather a question of knowing that you suffer from a lack of humor.

Look into it; check yourself. Ask yourself if you're not taking yourself much too seriously. The heaviest burden you can carry is that proverbial chip on your shoulder. Shake it loose via a sense of humor. As with everything else discussed in this book, it's all in the mind. Try to think a little less about what's happening to you, and a bit more about what you cause to happen, and you'll see more clearly the humor in most things. Harry Emerson Fosdick said:

"Reduce to a minimum the things that mortify you. To be ugly, to lack desired ability, to be economically restricted - such things are limitations, but if they become humiliations it is because inwardly you make them so."

Limitations, you see, can be overcome or compensated for, but humiliations - well, they can set up insurmountable barriers. Your sense of humor will stop these barriers from becoming higher or wider. You've got to look at certain things with the proverbial grain of salt. Shrug, and carry on anyway. The limerick that follows, written by Anthony Euwer, and often quoted by President Woodrow Wilson, points out just the attitude I have in mind:

Do You Talk Too Much - or Too Little?

Now, the one thing all normal people possess is the ability to talk. And

As a beauty I'm not a great star.
Others are handsomer far;
But my face - I don't mind it
Because I'm behind it;
It's the folks out in front that I jar.

it's mainly by the way you talk that others judge your personality. I'm not referring to your diction, grammar, and tone, although these things are important. No; I mean, essentially, what you say. Robert Louis Stevenson wrote: "To talk is our chief business in this world; and talk is by far the most accessible of pleasures. It costs nothing in money; it is all profit; it completes our education, founds and fosters our friendships, and can be enjoyed at any age and in almost every state of health." This is all true, but there is another saying that goes: "The thing most frequently opened by mistake is the human mouth." I think most of us - except professional critics, of course - would be much better off if we followed this advice: if you can't say something complimentary or favorable, keep your mouth shut and say nothing!

Quite often criticism only manages to throw a bad light on the critic. It's also easier to criticize than to be right or to help - so most of us do it. You improve your personality immediately if you stop it.

Another method for improving your personality fast is to stop talking about your favorite subject - you - so much. Talk about the other person to that other person, and he or she will love you for it. Montaigne put it in a nutshell:

"When all is summed up, a man never speaks of himself without loss; his accusations of himself are always believed; his praises never."

Are you afraid to talk to people? Are you the type who looks at the floor, or over the other fellow's head, or at his right ear while you're conversing? The best place to look when talking to someone (unless you're on the phone) is squarely into his eyes. I know one man who practiced looking into his own eyes, in a mirror, for half and hour at a time. He was then able to look into the eyes of others while talking to them.

I don't mean that it's necessary to get so close that you breathe into peoples' faces. If you glare at them too hard, you will surely make your listeners uncomfortable.

Learn, also, to listen attentively (even if you've heard it before) again looking into the speaker's eyes. Listen well, and you'll be given credit for speaking well. And if you're a good listener, you will talk better.
Don't be afraid to talk. Erasmus said that by speaking men learn to speak. Just try to take a middle ground and give the other guy a chance, too. The worst thing you can ever do is to appear bored when someone is talking to you.

Remember: you're never really bored with others - or anything, for that matter - you are bored only with yourself.

Some other important points: Don't always insist on being so darn truthful. I'd prefer it if people thought more about being kind than being painfully truthful. William Blake put it this way:

"A truth that's told with bad intent, beats all the lies you can invent."

Malicious gossip, even if it's true, will not enhance your personality.
Use judgment and discretion; there are times when the exact truth is unnecessary. I once received a strange introduction at a lecture. The

speaker originally booked had been taken ill, and he asked me to fill in for him at the last minute. The program chairman said something to this effect: "Ladies and gentlemen, I'm sorry to have to tell you that Mr. _____ has been taken ill. So, unfortunately, instead of Mr. _____, may I present Mr. Harry Lorayne." (This occurred three decades ago; I don't "fill in" anymore!)

Of course, he didn't mean it the way it sounded (at least I hope not), but it would have been better if he had simply introduced me. There is no need to be utterly frank at such a time.

A perennial bore, of course, is the life-of-the-party type who just isn't the life-of-the-party type. Here again, it's important to learn to "know thyself." There are people who evoke screams of delight when they parade around with lampshades on their heads; others get yawns or looks of annoyance. Be sure you're not the latter type before you start cutting up.

It is the easiest thing in the world to advise another; the most difficult not to do it. Even when friends ask for your advice, they usually want you to tell them exactly what they've already made up their minds to do. If you feel you must give advice, tell people to do what they want to do, or don't give it. I guess advice is the only commodity that's more blessed to receive than to give.

And don't be afraid to say, "I don't know." I've never been able to understand people who give directions when they're not really sure themselves. For some reason, people are ashamed to admit that they don't know the way to Main Street or Broadway. Many is the time I've asked for directions and been sent on a wild goose chase. So, remember - if you don't know, say so.

Another reason why some folks are disliked is that they enjoy ordering people around. Preface your requests with phrases like, "I'd appreciate it if..." or "How do you think this should be done?" and you should have no trouble in this area. Of course, the best way to get anyone to do anything is to find a way to make him want to do it. Persuade him that you're working in his interests, and the task will get done.

Definite statements, unless you're absolutely sure of them, can get you into trouble, too. Again, an opening like "I believe," or "It's my opinion that," or "Don't you agree that..." can save much face later on. Even if you know you're right, soften your statement with one of these statements. I believe it was Samuel Butler who said, "There is no mistake so great as that of being always right."

You'll make people like you as never before if you cultivate the habit of approaching them with the attitude of "Oh, there you are" instead of "Look, here I am!" If you have to ask for information, they'll love you if you ask for some that (you know) they can give. People don't like to say,

"I don't know" (as mentioned a few paragraphs ago) and they won't be too happy if you force them into it.

What all this boils down to is attempting to make other peoples' interests your interests. If you realize that other people have the desire to win as strongly as you have, you'll never be a bad loser. I know people who get terribly upset over losing any petty game or competition. Well, bad losers are selfish people, and they show it in this way.

Be happy for the winner. What the heck, you'll have your day soon, and you'll want the loser to be glad for you. Nobody particularly likes a bad loser, or a constant complainer. Try to praise your competitor, and you'll be respected for it. Knock him, and you won't be believed anyway. Mark Twain said:

"Good breeding consists in concealing how much we think of ourselves and how little we think of the other person."

Being Well Informed Helps

Your over all personality is altered and shaped by your general knowledge, your awareness of the world around you.

— Are you practical-minded; can you figure things out logically?
— Do you read at least half as many nonfiction as fiction books?
— Do you make the time to listen to good music occasionally, or to worthwhile lectures?
— Do you know at least a little about art?

The answer to these questions should be "yes" if you want a well-rounded personality.

Of course, we all have our special abilities and particular fields of knowledge. However, you can't talk about these abilities or remain in the company of others who are familiar with the same fields of knowledge all the time. So try to enlarge your scope. There's no reason to be left out of any conversations because you know absolutely nothing about the subject being discussed.

Can you answer most of the following questions? Try.

1. Which baseball team won the World Series in 1989? 1988?
2. Who was the Soviet Premier before Gorbachev?
3. A woman goes into the butcher store. She sees a $.25 piece on the counter, and slips it into her purse. She then buys some meat which costs $.19. She gives the butcher his own quarter. He gives her $.06 change, and her meat.

When the woman is outside, she suffers a twinge of conscience and returns to undo her petty thievery. How much money does she return to the butcher?

4. Who starred in both Broadway shows, Two for the Seesaw and The Miracle Worker?
5. Is The Memory Book a work of nonfiction or fiction?
6. Who composed Rhapsody in Blue?
7. Can you name at least two states that border Kansas?
8. Is "Scrabble" the name of a food, a game, a car or a movie?
9. Assume that fleas in a jar double themselves every second. Start with 2 and you have 4 in one second, 8 in the next second,
   and 16 the following second, etc. The jar is exactly half full of fleas in 51 seconds. How many seconds before the jar is full?
10. It's possible to tell if a person is honest by the shape of his ear lobes. True or false?
11. Who ran for the presidency opposite Harry Truman the first time Truman was elected?
12. Once a trade name becomes famous or known, the company need not advertise any longer. True or false?
13. "Oregano" is an opera, a state, or an herb?
14. Which are usually more accurate, slow or fast workers?
15. What is the name given to the man who is seated on a horse and carries a lance at a bullfight? Matador, toreador, banderillo, picador?
16. Does iron have more of a tendency to crack than steel?
17. Can you think of the names of presidents of the United States beginning with the following letters: A, T, L, C, V, R, E?
18. Who painted 'The Blue Boy?"
19. Who wrote Crime and Punishment and The Brothers Karamazov?
20. Which is the better hand, a "straight flush" or a "full house"?
21. Which is the capital city of Maryland? Annapolis, Baltimore, Havre de Grace or Chevvy Chase?

Most of the questions are general knowledge, and a few are on logic, or what you might call practical-mindedness. How do you think you did? If you're not sure, here are the answers:

1. Oakland A's; L.A. Dodgers (in five).
2. Yuri Andropov.
3. Just what she stole - $.25.
4. Ann Bancroft.
5. Nonfiction.
6. George Gershwin.
7. Missouri, Oklahoma, Nebraska, Colorado.

8. A game.
9. One more second; 52 seconds all told.
10. False.
11. Thomas Dewey.
12. False.
13. An herb.
14. Fast workers.
15. Picador.
16. Yes.
17. Adams, Taft, Lincoln, Coolidge, Van Buren, Roosevelt, Eisenhower.
18. Gainsborough.
19. Fyodor Dostoyevsky.
20. A straight flush.
21. Annapolis.

If you have six or more wrong answers, I'd suggest you do a little more reading, or have more discussions on diversified subjects.

All in all, personality consists of getting along with people. I've often read that the majority of people who can't hold on to their jobs very long usually leave or are fired because they couldn't get along with the other personnel, not because they weren't capable of handling the technical part of their work.

I can only leave this subject with the following quote by Daniel Frohman:

"Half the secret of getting along with people is consideration of their views; the other half is tolerance in one's own views."

CHAPTER EIGHTEEN

How to Be an Effective Public Speaker Without Fear

The nervous speaker was introduced after dinner He approached the microphone and began haltingly: "My f-f-friends, when I arrived h-here this evening only God and I knew what I was going to say. Now - only God knows!"

It has been suggested that I include a little discussion on public speaking in this book. I suppose you would consider that an aspect of personality. So if you ever have to get up in front of a group to talk, you may find this chapter of some interest.

As far as nervousness is concerned; I can't really help you too much - except perhaps to remind you that you probably wouldn't have been asked to speak unless it was thought that you knew your subject. Just fix it in your mind that if anyone in your audience knew the subject better, he or she would be at the podium, and you'd be listening to him or her.

Of course, if you're ever in the position of having to talk about something you know very little about, I wouldn't blame you for being nervous. Don't allow yourself to be put in that position, and you'll have nothing to be anxious about.

At the risk of sounding repetitious, I must again bring out that if you aren't too interested in yourself - how you will sound, whether the audience will like you, and so on - you will rarely get nervous. Don't take yourself too seriously, and you'll do fine. In most cases, your talk will be listened to a few comments like "He's right" or "I disagree with him" will be made, and that will be the end of it. Too many of us insist on inflating the importance to others of things that just aren't that important to them.

How Long Should You Speak?

The most important thing in giving a talk is timing. The thing you should be nervous about is boring your audience, and the surest way to do that is to talk too long.

I've heard many speeches in my time - speeches at company affairs, testimonial dinners, rallies, charity drives and fundraisers - and 70 per cent of them were much too lengthy.

The biggest offenders, I think, are the people who introduce the speakers. Too often, the introduction is longer than the main speaker's talk. If the speaker is an important personality, and well known to everyone present, little introduction is needed. Just his or her name will do.

Perhaps one anecdote pertaining to the speaker may be apropos - if you've checked it with him in advance. If the speaker is not well known, state his qualifications quickly and succinctly, and leave the rest to him. Don't become hypnotized by the sound of your own voice!

The most difficult thing to do when giving a talk is to come to a period. You've got to learn to do that or you'll lose the audience. At many functions, speakers are given the amount of time they are not to exceed. They know this beforehand, and yet many of them go blithely over their time limit. They think that what they have to say is so important, and they say it so well, that it's okay for them to break the rule. If they think an audience that's collectively looking at its watches every few minutes is an attentive or happy one, they're mistaken.

Stand up - speak up - shut up!

There's the rule to follow. Get up, make your point as emphatically as you want to, then sit down. Perhaps we ought to use the system that an African tribe uses. They make their speakers stand on one leg throughout their talks.

Once the other leg touches the ground, the speaker must stop; in mid-sentence, if necessary (or spears are thrown!).

Will Rogers was once toastmaster at a dinner where each speaker was allotted ten minutes. One man droned on and on for over an hour. At the end of his marathon, he apologized to Will, saying that he'd left his watch at home. Mr. Rogers answered in a loud stage whisper, "There's a calendar right behind you."

Preparing and Delivering the Speech

As for the speech itself, I would suggest that you never try to memorize it word for word. If you do, and you forget one word, that's when the hemming and hawing starts. Even if you don't forget part of it, your speech will sound memorized, and that tends to alienate your listeners.

Another thing that can make the attention of the audience wander is reading your speech. You might just as well photocopy it and hand it out to them to read at their leisure. That would save a lot of time Also, if you're reading it, you may lose your place, and then you're really in trouble.

That seems to rule out everything but the completely extemporaneous speech, doesn't it? Well, not quite. Few speeches are ever completely extemporaneous, or "off the cuff." Every speaker has in mind certain points which he wants to get across to his audience. If he makes no preparation at all, many of these points may be forgotten.

I think that the best way to prepare your speech is to lay it out thought for thought. List the thoughts you wish to communicate on a piece of paper in sequence, and let these be your notes for the entire speech. In this way you're not memorizing word for word, yet you're not speaking extemporaneously either.

Remember: You know what you want to say about each idea or you wouldn't be introducing it in the first place. As you speak, all you have to do is glance down at your notes each time you've finished speaking on one point. Go to the next point and so on to the conclusion of the talk. One thing you should definitely prepare, or have clearly in mind, is the conclusion. — you must come to a period or you'll go on and on and on.

The ending of your speech is probably the most important part of it, the part most remembered by your audience simply because it's the last thing they will hear you say. If' you have a strong anecdote that slams home your final point, fine. If not, keep your strongest point for the end and deliver it with something of a flourish. Let them know you've ended.

It has always been my belief that a speech, whether it be formal or informal, should be entertaining. However, that does not mean that you need become a comedian. If you can't tell jokes or anecdotes well, don't tell them! But if you possibly can, get a little humor into your talk. Make the audience smile or laugh occasionally, and they'll be more interested in the serious parts of the speech.

How to Behave on Any Platform

Aside from the actual content of the talk, the most important consideration is you - the way you speak and the impression you make upon the audience. I can only advise you that the best thing to do is to be as natural as you can. Don't stand at the lectern stiffly. Move and gesture once in a while, so the audience can move their eyes.

Try not to speak in a monotone. Put emphasis on certain words. If you don't give the people in your audience a chance to shift their eyes, or to smile or laugh, or give them a different range of sound, they will make up for this by moving restlessly in their chairs, coughing or talking, and in general losing interest.

Don't be too concerned over the fact that you're nervous before your talk. Almost every good and experienced performer or speaker has this problem. There would be something amiss if you weren't a bit nervous and tense before facing an audience. Once you're on, that nervousness will disappear.

A trick used by many speakers is to catch the eye of one person at a time and imagine they're speaking to him or her only. That's a good idea, since it keeps you from staring over everybody's head, or gazing continuously at your notes. Incidentally, if you wish to eliminate notes altogether, I've shown you how to do that - how to memorize the thoughts you wish to speak about, in sequence - in the chapter on memory (Chapter 15).

1. keep your talk short and to the point
2. Try to get some humor into it.
3. Come to a definite ending.
4. Don't be monotonous.
5. Speak with some authority and look at your audience.
6. If you have to take a breath, take it.

There are some more points which may seem obvious, but it's amazing how many speakers overlook them. Don't use long, complicated words when simple, short ones will suffice. Be careful about the use of technical terms or phrases, unless you're speaking to people who are in the same business or profession and can understand the terms. If you must use them to a general audience, define them so that your listeners can follow you.

It's important to realize that the best way to get a point across is to call upon your audience's knowledge and experience rather than your own. To use an analogy pertaining only to your particular field of knowledge will leave the listeners confused. They'll still be thinking about it when they should be listening to your next point. This, incidentally, is also valid when you're having a conversation with only one or two people.

You can get up and talk in front of an audience - though you can probably think of many reasons why you can't, including: "I'm too shy," "I've never done it before," "I don't speak well," "I'm afraid I'll look like a fool," and so forth.

Well, remember this - if you wait until all objections are overcome, you'll never attempt anything. Thomas Bailey Aldrich said, "They fail, and they alone, who have not striven." Sure, you may fail as a public speaker, but you'll never know if you don't try it. The reason people don't try new things is the fear of failure, but you can't go through life without facing new things occasionally. Of course, if you never make an effort you'll never fail - but you'll stagnate; that's for sure.

So, if you have to make a speech, don't worry about it too much. Follow the suggestions in this chapter, and do the best you can. Your second speech will be better than your first, and your third will be better than the second. You can only improve as you keep trying.

As a pattern to follow in delivering most speeches, the following lines by the poet Dr. Leifchild, might be appropriate:

Begin low, speak slow; Take fire, rise higher; When most impressed, Be self-possessed; At the end wax warm; And sit down in a storm.

CHAPTER NINETEEN

Worry Control: The Secret of Peace of Mind

Build for yourself a strongbox, fashion each part with care; when it's strong as your hand can make it, put all your troubles there; hide there all thought of your failures, and each bitter cup that you quaff lock all your heartaches within it, then sit on the lid and laugh.

—Bertha Adams Backus

Wouldn't it be wonderful if we could all build ourselves such a strongbox -a place to pack away our worries, fears, failures, and disappointments? Then again, wouldn't that make all of us completely irresponsible? It may be all right to have a "light head," and not worry about anything, or be afraid of nothing - but that's going to the other extreme, don't you think?

The stress and strain of our current way of life makes it almost inevitable that we harbor some doubts, fears and worries. Dr. Theodore Van Dellen has written that, "The person who fears the modern tempo of living must choose between stress and stagnation."

I guess, as with everything else, we just have to learn to attain a happy medium. Worry has been described as the mental capacity for inaction. It is essentially a fear reaction over a future event which may never materialize. Of course, if you keep yourself occupied mentally and physically, there isn't much time to worry. However, since most of us do worry, I should devote a little space to the problem.

Paying Interest on Trouble Before It Comes Due

I know that telling you not to worry is about the same as advising you not to breathe. I can, however, try to show you why, in most instances, your worries are wasted effort. They do you absolutely no good, and can harm you.

Worry is a good example of squandered or noncreative imagination. Instead of using your imagination to help you create new ideas, or to improve yourself; you're using it to no apparent purpose. W.R. Inge said that worry is interest paid on trouble before it becomes due.

There is time enough to fret and wring your hands when the expected trouble actually appears - why worry about it now? Don't you realize that most of the things you worry about never happen anyway?

Prove it to yourself. Can you sit down right now and list all the things you were worried about, say, a year ago today? Try it - and I'm sure you won't remember too many, if any at all. While you have the pencil and paper out, list the things you're worried about right now. Put the list in a safe place, and check it a few months or a year from now. Again, you'll find that most of the things you dreaded never happened; or if they did, they weren't so bad as you thought they'd be.

If you make up your mind right now that most of the things you worry about won't occur anyway, and that the worry itself is more painful and agonizing than the event you're worried about, you're on your way to as close to a worry-free existence as is possible nowadays.

It may take a bit of intestinal fortitude to admit to yourself that it is impossible to go through life without some pain, failure, disappointment or frustration. But you might just as well admit it because you know that it's so. Schopenhauer wrote:

"A certain amount of care or pain or trouble is necessary for every man at all times. A ship without ballast is unstable and will not go straight."

The thing to do is to learn to accept annoyances of this type. They're inevitable anyway, so what have you got to lose? I know some people who welcome a certain amount of frustration or failure as a challenge - it gives them a "kick" to overcome it and head toward success.

Stop fretting over things that must be. Let's face it - there isn't much you can do about it when it's snowing - except wear boots. And there isn't much you can do about a tooth that must come out-except have it yanked.

I made up my mind years ago that I had no time for worrying. If I get a toothache, I don't worry about it until I can't bear the pain any longer, as I used to do. At the first twinge, I'm on my way to the dentist. No sense putting off the inevitable; you've got to go sooner or later - so I go sooner and avoid a lot of fear and anxiety.

Face the Worst - and You Can Meet Anything

Another trick I use to avoid worry is this: whenever something comes up that may cause trouble, I immediately think of the worst that can happen. As soon as I've visualized that, I prepare myself accordingly, then forget about it.

If I've made an investment which looks as if it may turn into a loss, I make up my mind that I'm going to lose the entire investment. Of course, I'll try my darndest to salvage what I can, but if it is a total loss - well, I expected it, and that's that. If it turns out well, or if the loss is not too bad (as is usually the case), then it's a pleasant surprise, and I haven't wasted time worrying about it.

So, instead of worrying without rhyme or reason, so to speak - regardless of what's worrying you, what's the very worst that can happen? If the worst is not death, or the end of the world, prepare for it in the best way you can - then forget it!

If it is death or the end of the world, you've really got nothing to worry about!

I know of one man who used to worry dreadfully about one thing. He traveled on business, and he had heard of several people getting attacks of appendicitis on such trips!

This bothered him terribly. He kept worrying about the business he'd lose if this happened to him. Also, since he wouldn't be near his own doctor, the thought of a strange doctor operating on him worried him something awful.

Well, the worst that could happen, he thought, would be to be away from home at a very busy time and get an appendicitis attack. So during a slow period in his business, he went to his own doctor and had his appendix removed! He doesn't worry about that anymore!

This, as I'm sure you realize, is going to somewhat of an extreme. However, I think it brings out my thought about facing the worst, and then preparing for it.

There's got to be some frustration, "lest," as Shakespeare said, "too light winning make the prize light." When the frustration presents itself; realize that it is a necessary part of life, and it won't bother you half so much as it does now. William G. Milnes, Jr. was quoted in the Saturday Evening Post as saying, "You're on the road to success when you realize that failure is merely a detour."

I use this quote to stress again, as I have elsewhere in the book, that too many of us too often worry about failure, and in so doing never really try for success. Worrying about failure is the most asinine thing I can think of; if it keeps you from trying. If it motivates you to try to avoid the failure, fine. But, again, don't waste too much time worrying about it. Go ahead and start - once you do, you'll handle automatically any little failures that appear.

Sidney Smith said:

"A great deal of talent is lost in the world for want of a little courage. Every day sends to their graves obscure men whom timidity prevented from making a first effort; who, if they could have been induced to begin, would in all probability have gone great lengths."

I think that says it better than I could. "I can't" or "I'm afraid I'll fail" will never get you off the ground. "I'll try" can put you into orbit! Have I made my point? Worrying over possible failure won't avoid the failure. If you must worry about it, let your worry be the starting point for action. Whatever you're afraid may happen, prepare or plan for it, and you'll not have to worry about it any more.

I am a great believer in planning for the unexpected. I know that a little extra effort on my part can sometimes avert months of needless worry. No sense being a pessimist; but being a "cockeyed optimist" can be just as bad. The thing to do is to have a realistic attitude, and make up your mind that things do not always go as planned. (Just when you've made your plans, life happens!)

Handling Those Everyday Worries

Many of us who haven't any really big problems will spend countless hours worrying about little things. So plan for those minor dilemmas and stop worrying about them.

If you're leaving for an appointment, start earlier - why worry about being late?

If you're driving into a strange area, get a map or good instructions - why worry about getting lost?

If one of your tires is nearly bald, get a new one now (you'll have to soon anyway) - why worry about getting a flat?

If you're not sure your teeth are in good condition, get them checked - why worry about getting a toothache?

Preparing for the unexpected (without going to extremes) can be quite useful for eliminating minor (and sometimes major) worries. Many years ago I used two specially built blackboards and two easels for my lectures. They were kept in specially built cases, in the trunk of my car. I used to worry about what would happen if I ever lost them; if the car was stolen or if the blackboards or easels broke. I got rid of this worry very easily. I had another set of boards and easels made, which I kept at home. I haven't had to use them yet - but I don't worry about them any more either! (I haven't carried blackboards for over a quarter of a century. My talk - and demonstrations - are in my mind and in my attaché case.)

So you see, you may not be able to avert minor worries from time to time, but you can put a stop to their habit of lingering and growing and festering.

When it comes to major worries - family difficulties, financial troubles, things of that nature - many of the rules expressed here still apply. Of course, if the worry is over something that can't possibly be eradicated or cured, I can only suggest you stop running full tilt and head on into stone walls. Make up your mind that the situation is inevitable and go on the best way you can. There's an old Chinese proverb that goes: "You cannot prevent the birds of sorrow from flying over your head, but you can prevent them from building nests in your hair."

On the other hand, if you're very worried about something that has a possible solution, the best advice I can give you is that given by Dr. George Stevenson in a wonderful little pamphlet called How to Deal with Your Tensions. He said, in part:

"When something worries you, talk it out. Don't bottle it up. Confide your worry to some levelheaded person you can trust; your husband or wife, father or mother, a good friend, your clergyman, your family doctor, a teacher, school counselor, or dean. Talking things out helps to relieve your strain, helps you to see your worry in a clearer light, and often helps you to see what you can do about it."

But If You Must Worry, Get It Off Your Chest

It's difficult to add much to that; except perhaps to stress the value of talking your worry out, not only to get it off your chest, but to someone who knows more than you, who may be of some help. I'm sure you've heard or read about people who ruined their lives because of things that could easily have been straightened out had they only talked to someone who understood their particular worries or problems.

Don't take advice, of course, from people who know only as much as, or less than, you do about a certain problem. I'm reminded of an acquaintance who was suffering from an annoying and painful skin irritation. A well-meaning friend told him to cover the afflicted area with iodine. This did not improve the condition, and it gave him a third-degree burn to boot. The wiser thing would have been to visit a doctor.

Now - to go from the extreme to the ridiculous - are you the kind of person who drags through life always worrying about things like:

- Did I set the alarm clock? Did I put out the tights?
- Did I turn off the oven? Did I unplug the iron?
- Did I put out the garbage? Did I lock the door?

Of course, the best way to help you to avoid these minor worries is to tell you to learn to remember. Learn to remember to do these things, and you won't have to worry about them. At the risk of sounding commercial, I can only advise you to pick up a copy of one of my books on the subject. Absentmindedness is really a memory problem, and I've gone into detail on this in a few of my books. Or read the chapter in this book on habits. Get into the habit of doing things in their proper order and proper time, and you won't have to worry about them.

To adhere strictly to the subject of worry - just stop worrying about these things, will you? If you forget to lock your door, and the house is burgled, I assure you you'll never leave it open again. If you are late to work once because you didn't set your alarm, the odds are you won't make that mistake again.

Remember: the best attitude for you to cultivate if you're really plagued with this type of worry is -"So what!" If you're wrong once or twice, you'll know better or do better next time. Again, what's the worst that could happen? If the worst, in your opinion, is really bad, then take the time to check on the thing you're worried about.

If you've been worrying about whether you put the lights out, in your home or car - well, the worst is that you'll need a battery charge for the car, or your electric bill will be a few cents more. It's up to you to decide whether that's worth worrying about. If a few cents more on your electric bill doesn't matter too much, why worry.

The Last Thing to Worry About

Well, okay - what else do you worry about? Getting old? Oh, yes, that's something many of us worry about. Benjamin Franklin said:

"All would live long, but none would be old."

How true! Why worry about getting older (older, not old) - think of the alternative! Anyway, how do you know that old age is not the finest and most rewarding part of life? In this case, it would be wise to look forward to the inevitable. I don't mean to sit and wait for old age, but neither do I mean to worry about it. Prepare for it? Sure. Work out a retirement or pension fund; get interested in hobbies, in which you can participate when you're older, if you like. But, for heaven's sake, don't worry about it! According to Dr. Theodore R. Van Dellen, "Growing old is not so much of a problem as the fear of being old."

And Harry Golden, in his best seller, Only In America, had a good thought on the subject. He suggested that you start each day with the thought in mind that you will live forever. "Start a major alteration on your house at the age of seventy, and at seventy-five enter upon a whole new course of study or learn a new language. Just keep going as though it will never end. And when it does come, you'll hardly notice it."

What else? Are you worried about sickness? Go to your doctor - let him worry about it!

Worried about going insane? Good! People who worry about going crazy rarely do!

And don't worry too much about going to hell - you've been there!

CHAPTER TWENTY

How to Conquer Fear and Overcome Inevitable Troubles

I have no other foe to fear save fear.

—Frederick Lawrence knowles

There is not much to differentiate worry and fear. Actually, it's a case of the boil (worry) coming to its painful head (fear). Again, I can't advise you merely to cut out fear completely. Not only is that impossible, but it isn't wise.

Erich Fromm once wrote: "Rational anxiety due to the awareness of realistic dangers operates in the service of self-preservation; it is an indispensable and healthy part of our psychic organization. The absence of fear is a sign of either lack of imagination and intelligence, or a lack in one's will to live." (The italics are mine.)

Rational anxiety or fear of realistic dangers, of course, is an essential part of living. Fear, like pain, can be a warning of, a protection against, imminent danger. If you had no fear of fire, sooner or later you'd probably be badly burned. I could give you a thousand examples, but I'm sure it isn't necessary.

Knowledge brings awareness, and being aware must in some cases incite fear. So, I guess the more you know, the more there is to be afraid of. This is no reason to look askance at knowledge, because no matter how you look at it, ignorance is not bliss.

Many fears, of course, are instilled in us during childhood; and a good thing, too. The burned child fears the fire; although naturally that fear is instilled through the pain of an accident, not by someone inflicting a burn.

Fear can also be a good creative force. It was the fear of ignorance that created schools; the fear of food poisoning that caused safer and healthier methods of preparing and packaging; the fear of accidents that caused safety measures to be applied to buildings, factories and automobiles.

How often have you passed a bad accident on the road, and driven slower and more carefully for at least the next twenty miles? Or heard of someone getting a dread disease, and run to your doctor for the checkup you had put off for such a long time?

In these instances, your fears did you no harm. On the contrary, they may have done some good. It's the abnormal and unreasonable fears that we must get rid of.

The most universal fear of all is the fear of death - fear of the death of oneself or of loved ones. This fear must touch all of us at one time or another. The only way I can think of easing this fear a little is to remind you that it seems silly to fear or anticipate the inevitable. Shakespeare, as usual, said it beautifully, in the tragedy of Julius Caesar:

"Cowards die many times before their deaths; the valiant never taste of death but once. Of all the wonders that I yet have heard, it seems to me most strange that men should fear; seeing that death, a necessary end, will come when it will come."

Know Your Fears - and Make Them Your Tools

Nobody is without fear - no normal person, that is. The greatest and bravest heroes will tell you honestly that when they did their heroic deeds they were as frightened as you or I might have been. The difference is that they were able to overcome that fear they resisted the urge to give in to it.

You may have to face many things or situations that frighten you. Don't be ashamed of your fear, but practice resisting it, overcoming it. As a matter of fact, one adage for eliminating fear is: "Do the thing you fear."

Many things that you fear now can, believe me, be faced squarely, and even eventually enjoyed. You may be terrified of getting onto a pair of ice skates, but if you face that terror, and learn to skate, you may find you've been missing something pleasurable all these years.

Don't hide your fears from yourself. Harry Emerson Fosdick said:

"To get our fear out into the open and frankly face it is of primary importance."

You'll never be able to do anything at all about a fear that is not brought out so you can look it squarely in the eye.

Fear of failure? Well, I've discussed that in the preceding chapter. I can only repeat that people who are terrified of failure are the ones who usually are failures, since they're afraid of trying. Make up your mind that the real sign of success is not a straight unmarked line to achievement, but the manner in which you overcome failures!

As far as I'm concerned, if your thoughts lean too heavily to the side of "I might not succeed," you'll never start at all - and that's the worst crime of all. Start - and aim high. As Joel Hawes once said:

"Aim at the sun, and you may not reach it, but your arrow will fly far higher than if aimed at an object on a level with yourself."

Make your fears work for you whenever you can. If you fear failure, you should plan ahead so that you can't fail. Prepare an alternative in case you do fail at first. In this way your fear is helping you, not keeping you from beginning.

I was afraid of people when I was very young. I was terribly shy. I decided to face that fear and do something about it. I started to talk to people whenever I could. I had always felt that I had nothing to contribute, so I tried to entertain them. I tried to make them laugh or show them things they had never seen before. I'm certainly not terrified of people any longer; and I put that original fear to work for me.

Sometimes you've got to pretend or act as if many of your fears didn't exist. Theodore Roosevelt once wrote:

"There were all kinds of things of which I was afraid at first, but by acting as if I was not afraid I gradually ceased to be afraid. Most men can have the same experience if they choose."

You can have the same experience of overcoming certain fears. Force yourself to act unafraid, and before you know it, it will be true. This has worked for me for years; there's no reason why it shouldn't help you.

I don't believe that most of us are very frightened of the present. It's usually those imaginary future events that fill us with fear. Here, of course, we're getting back into the "worry" problem. It is very often true that if you take care of the present the future will take care of itself. "How much pain have cost us the evils which have never happened" is as valid today as it was when Jefferson said it many years ago.

Don't you realize that the more you dread tomorrow, the less time and inclination you'll have to face and enjoy today? Stop being afraid of life and you'll enjoy life. After all, we pass this way but once!

Remember: You just can't avoid some trouble in life. There's a cliche that says, "Into each life some rain must fall" - but why open your umbrella while the sun is shining?

Keep Two Days a Week Free From Fear

If you're afraid of something, don't let it eat away at you. Bring it out into the open so that you can do something about it. Face it, and in most cases you'll realize the fear was childish in the first place.

Nowadays, fear of fatal diseases - cancer, heart trouble and so on - causes more anxiety than anything else, I suppose. If that fear makes you get a physical checkup occasionally, that's all to the good. But don't harbor unreasonable dreads.

There's a story about a man who went to see his doctor because he thought he had cancer. The doctor asked him if he had any pain. "No," said the frightened patient. "Well, have you been losing weight consistently?" asked the doctor. The patient replied that he hadn't; as a matter of fact, he'd put on a pound or two. "Then what makes you think you have cancer?"

"I read somewhere that cancer can start with no symptoms at all, and that's exactly what I have!"

I think that more sickness may be caused by the dread of incurable disease than by the disease itself. Sure, it pays to be careful, and to have regular check-ups, but if you are and you do, you're doing all you can, so forget about it. Don't spend so much time avoiding trouble that you have no time for anything else.

Do you suffer from kainophobia - the fear of new things? People do, you know, or it wouldn't have been necessary to coin the word. My wife wouldn't get on an airplane for years. She had never flown and she would just as soon leave it at that. Finally, we were offered a deal which would have been sheer folly to refuse. But to accept it, it was necessary that we fly across the country. Well, my wife clenched her fists and prayed silently throughout the trip. To make a long story short, she now virtually refuses to travel any other way; arguing that it's faster than any other mode of travel, more comfortable, and certainly safer than the tremendous amount of mileage we drove through all kinds of hazardous weather.

Stop denying yourself pleasures by being frightened of new things, or of things you've never done before. Try it once, anyway, to find out whether you should be afraid. As I wrote in the chapter on learning, don't be a spectator all the time - participate once in a while, and you'll find out that what you were afraid of can really be enjoyed.

Many books are available on the subject of worry and fear, and I know that a psychiatrist can do wonders, if you'll let him, about unreasonable fears. But perhaps the best way to look at them is the way Robert J. Burdette did. He wrote:

"There are two days in the week about which and upon which I never worry. Two carefree days kept sacredly free from fear and apprehension. One of these days is Yesterday - and the other - is Tomorrow."

CHAPTER TWENTY ONE
Replace Positive Thinking with Positive Doing

Son: Mom, I don't think I can pass that test I'm taking in school tomorrow.
Mom: Now, now, son! Remember - positive thinking!
Son: Okay; I'm sure l can't pass it!

In doing research for this book, I have of necessity read quite a bit about "positive thinking." It seems that positive thinking is the thing nowadays. Many people I've spoken to consider it almost a panacea, a cure-all for just about anything. (Bear in mind that I wrote this almost thirty years ago.)

Well, don't misunderstand me: positive thinking is alright - except that in all the books I went through on the subject I didn't read too much about positive doing. It is hard to believe that sitting in your room all day and thinking positively is going to do you much good. As a matter of fact, I'm sure that you'll agree that spending all your time considering isn't going to leave much time for accomplishing.

As mentioned earlier, thinking in the present tense is problem solving. If you're thinking in the past tense, you're remembering -and that's awfully close to reminiscing. Thinking of the future is anticipating - and while anticipating problems can be useful at times; why not concentrate on the ones that need solving now?

So, you've got a few problems that are bothering you right now. Then go ahead and do something about them. Sitting around thinking about what you will do may put you in the position of never finding out what you can do about them. Certainly I'm not advocating that we should do things without giving them some advance thought, but it seems plausible that if we got rid of some of our negative thinking, the positive thinking would take care of itself.

Thoughts Must Become Actions to Work

It's not so easy as it sounds, I know. Many people, I suppose, do need psychiatric help to rid themselves of their negative thoughts. In many cases, however, I can't help feeling that common sense plus a little will power would do it. According to Dr. Karen Homey, "Fortunately analysis is not the only way to resolve inner conflicts. Life itself still remains a very effective therapist." I am, of course, not referring to the severe neurotic, for whom competent help is the best, and perhaps the only, solution.

To the normal person with normal anxieties and tensions, the "normal neurotics" (Dr. George Stevenson maintains that anxiety and tension are essential functions of living, just as hunger and thirst are), I say get off that negative kick. Voltaire would have told you that:

"The longer you dwell on your misfortunes, the greater is their power to hurt you."

If you have something to do, don't let indecision plague you. Do it the best way you know how at that moment. Why worry about whether you make a mistake or not? Sure, you may make a mistake - then again you may not. And can you think of a better way to learn than from your own mistakes? In most cases, you'll feel better after the thing is done, whether you goofed or not. And keep in mind Dr. William J. Reilly's thought: "The only person who makes no mistakes is the person who does nothing - and that's the greatest mistake of all!"

A happy medium between negative and positive thinking is most desirable. Each can be overdone. For example: don't cultivate the completely pessimistic and self-centered attitude of the person who gets caught in a downpour and thinks, "Why do these things happen only to me?"

At the other extreme is the fellow who falls from the twentieth story of a skyscraper, and as he falls past the ninth story, thinks "So far, so good!" How optimistic can you get?

Don't waste time completely in negative thinking, and don't waste too much time in positive thinking. A study at Michigan State University proved that you use more brainpower and energy in preparing to solve a problem than in the actual solving.

Please don't just agree with me, shaking your head affirmatively, then go right back to doing as you usually do. Make the effort necessary to try out these ideas.

If I hadn't believed in them, this book might never have been written. Sure, all the ideas and thoughts were already in my mind, but so were thoughts like: "I don't think I could put them into words! I don't think I could write well enough; I don't know whether people will be interested; I don't know where to start." (Again, I wrote this thirty years ago!)

Well, I solved the last problem very easily. I just started! How true that all progress comes from daring to begin. I would still be fighting those negative thoughts if I hadn't simply begun. "He has half the deed done who has made a beginning."

I am a great believer in "learning by doing." Picturing or seeing my ideas as successful books, is always a pleasant thought, but without the doing there just wouldn't be any books. I guess the thing to do is to make the thinking and doing work hand in hand. You've got much more going for you that way.

Those Obstacles Are There for a Purpose

To get back to positive doing: Are there many things you would like to do, but are afraid to try for fear of failure? You're afraid that there are too many difficulties involved? Well, here's a place where positive thinking can be of help. Just remember and believe that the surmounting or equalizing of difficulties is part of learning something new or different.

If you can make yourself believe this truth emphatically, you'll not worry about difficulties for the rest of your life. And a little analyzing on your part will show you that it's so. Just try to think of anything you have ever accomplished - anything, no matter how trivial or how important. Now try to recall the annoyances or difficulties that you had to overcome in doing it. Honestly now, didn't you learn something from nearly every one of them? Just think about it for a while and you'll surely agree. W. M. Punshon put it this way:

"There are difficulties in your path. Be thankful for them. They will test your capabilities or resistance; you will be impelled to persevere from the very energy of the opposition. But what of him that fails? What does he gain? Strength for life. The real merit is not in the success but in the endeavor; and win or lose, he will be honored and crowned."

But suppose you feel that it's senseless to try a thing because you know it's beyond you - you could never learn to do it well.

Why worry about doing it well? The first thing to do is to learn it, even if not well. Learning to do something at all is the springboard to learning it well. Secondly, how do you know you can't do it? "I can't" is not a fact, but an idea. A good illustration of this is the old chestnut about the young man who was asked if he could play the piano. His answer was, "I don't know if I can play or not, I've never tried." Now there was a well-adjusted young man.

One entire book I read on how to be happy and/or successful could have been trimmed down to a single concise paragraph. It told me to simply see in my mind's eye whatever I desired to happen. If you desire to be a millionaire, see yourself doing the things a millionaire would do. See yourself living, working, acting like a millionaire. In other words, see yourself as a millionaire.

Of course, that's just another way of saying, "Think positively." I'm sure what the author meant was that this seeing would lead to doing. However, you can "think thin" with all your might, but if you keep overeating, you're bound to stay fat, or grow fatter.

On this particular subject Shakespeare wrote:

"Our doubts are traitors and make us lose the good we often might win by fearing to attempt."

You see what I mean, don't you? Why think that you can't do something before you've tried it? In most cases, you'll surprise yourself once you try. And certainly there is no shame involved in doing something the best you know how, even if you fail. At least you'll know you've tried; then you can turn your thoughts and energies to other things. Your victories will outweigh your failures, I assure you.

Too many good things have been lost to the world because of people fearing to put their ideas into practical action. It shouldn't be necessary for me to remind you of all the great thinkers and inventors who were ridiculed at first, but who persevered over fantastic odds to achieve success. It's a human failing to deride new ideas or efforts. The thing you must do is laugh at the scoffers and go right ahead and do what you feel is right.

Don't get me wrong, I'm not urging you to turn into a nonconformist; that's up to you. I'm just advising you that it might be better to stop worrying about what others think and find out, and concentrate on, what you think.

Turning Duties into Exciting Challenges

Some seemingly unpleasant duties that you must perform can be made easier to accomplish if you look at them as challenges. This idea has been, and is, a great help to me. I've used it since childhood, and it certainly works for me. There's no reason why it shouldn't work for you as well.

Try making a mental wager with yourself that you can do this thing, or that you can handle a particular situation with good sense. In my own work, lecturing and entertaining for audiences with my memory demonstration, anything can happen. Through experience, of course, I have learned to handle most eventualities. Occasionally, however, I will find myself performing for a completely unfriendly audience.

Years ago, when I saw an audience that was, let us say, a bit under the weather, my first impulse was to leave. My stomach would start churning; I'd break out into a cold sweat; in other words, I was scared. My thinking ran something like this: "Why should I have to put up with this? After all, I'm a well-paid performer, I don't need this. Why put up with their rudeness for the hour I'm on stage? If they don't want to listen to me, it's their loss, not mine. Why do they bother hiring entertainment if they don't intend to pay attention to it?" (This, of course, is no longer ever a problem for me. I'm a keynote or after-dinner speaker at high-level corporate gatherings.)

I finally realized that this was not only egotistical thinking, but completely useless. It did nobody - mainly me - any good whatsoever. The fact remained that I had to go on. There was more involved than the audience - there were agents, managers, committee chairmen, and so on. I had no choice but to go through with my performance.

The trouble was that I had worked myself up to such a point that I went on stage mad, hating the audience, and of course I lost them completely.

Fortunately, these audiences were, and are, few and far between. But those were the ones I remembered. They stuck in my mind and made me feel awful.

Well, I finally got smart. My present thinking prior to a show for people I think comprise a bad audience is: "Well, most of the audiences I appear for consist of friendly people. It's a pleasure to work for them. This audience will make me appreciate them all the more. But I can handle them! After all, I'm a seasoned performer; this is a test of my mettle; it's a challenge. I won't shirk the challenge. I know I can quiet them down. They're all decent, friendly people basically and I know I can sober them up.

What a world of difference! What I realized was that it never had been the audience that beat me; I had defeated myself! I was doing a bad show before I stepped in front of the microphone. (I also realize as I read this that I paid my dues!)

Looking at the whole thing as a challenge not only made the job easier, but gave me a greater feeling of accomplishment when I came through with a good performance.

Remember: Positive thinking is fine when it goes hand in hand with positive doing; and that when you have something that must be done, but you think it's an unpleasant duty, make a challenge out of it. In that way, some unpleasant duties can actually give you a finer sense of accomplishment than pleasant or ordinary chores.

Why not make things easier for yourself if you can? Don't let things bother you too much; just do the best you can under the circumstances. One thing though - don't use "the best I can" as an excuse for bad work or poor showings. Too many of us brush things off with "It's the best I can do" and leave things practically undone. So when I say, do the best you can under the circumstances, I mean the best you can, not second best. Then you'll never have to look back at it and feel sorry about it.

CHAPTER TWENTY TWO

What Kind of Success Do You Want?

Success is a prize to be won. Action is the road to it. Chance is what may lurk in the shadows at the roadside.

—O. Henry

There is one sure way for a person to become a millionaire almost overnight and that is to come up with a guaranteed formula for success. How I wish I could come up with a set of instructions that could assure success to its reader or user.

Unfortunately, there is not, and never could be, any such thing. One reason is that there are many schools of thought as to what constitutes success. Does the word "success" mean to be rich, to be famous, to be happy? I don't know myself. I do know that it is quite possible to be rich and/or famous, yet not happy. Then again, there are many fortunate people who are neither rich nor famous, but are happy.

Success is strictly a personal concept. There are those who feel they could not be happy unless they became famous or wealthy, or both. Those who can attain happiness without fame or wealth are indeed fortunate and are to be envied. It's all in the mind. It is possible to be happy under almost any circumstances, if your mind allows it. And who's to say that being happy is not being successful?

Don't Measure Success Backward

I've always been a little concerned (and amused) over the fact that we too often measure success backward. We set up examples of what we consider successful people, and then try to imitate them. It's mass syllogistic thinking again. Let me give you an example:

Mr. Z was a full-time chicken plucker at the age of eight. Mr. Z is now a very wealthy and/or famous man. Therefore, if you want to become wealthy and famous, it is a good idea to be a full-time chicken plucker at the age of eight.

This sounds pretty funny; but sometimes the laugh's on us. I know many people who think like that, knowingly, and still others who do so subconsciously. We do it with regard to almost any kind of achievement. Not long ago I read a newspaper story about a man who was 105 years old. When asked to what he attributed his longevity, he answered that he never drank or smoked. Being a somewhat heavy smoker, I started to cut down immediately!

I even stopped smoking altogether for a while, until I read about another man who was 110-years old! In his interview, he bragged about the fact that he'd been smoking since he was fifteen years of age. Well, I've been smoking again since then.

I'm not trying to advise anyone as to whether to smoke or not, you understand - I'm just trying to demonstrate how success of any kind is usually measured backward.

Professor Einstein failed a mathematics entrance exam when he was sixteen; Abe Lincoln split logs when he was a young man; Glenn Cunningham, the great runner, was burned so badly when he was a child he was told he'd never walk again.

These people are all to be admired, but I don't think we can use their lives as examples. There must be thousands of scientists or mathematicians who did not fail entrance exams; not every man who became president had to live in a log cabin when he was a boy; and I'm sure that there are many female movie stars who did not have to be "nice" to producers to get where they are! That a man has never smoked is not necessarily the reason he's lived to be 105. What about all the people who never smoked and who died young?

Please don't think that at any age you can purchase paints, brushes and canvas and, because Grandma Moses never took an art lesson and became a famous painter late in life, you can too! There may indeed be another Grandma Moses out there, but for most of us lessons and long study are necessary before we can paint anything worthwhile.

Some people seem to think that the one way to be successful is to imitate another successful person at his present state of success. That may work occasionally, but usually it won't, and what's more, the imitators are usually considered just that - imitators.

Yes, you should learn from others, but imitating them seldom leads to success. Too often, nowadays, success is measured not by what we give to society, but rather by what we can take from it. It's the same story - keep others in mind, think of what you can contribute to society, and your chances of being successful will be greatly increased.

You Are More Successful Than You Realize

If you feel you're not getting anywhere in life, stop complaining about your bad luck. It has always been my strong belief that ability (or talent) seeks its own level.

If you have the ability you must, eventually, rise to the level of society where that ability belongs. If you don't have it, you'll never reach that level until you've acquired the necessary ability. I, personally, have always agreed with James M. Barrie's philosophy:

"Not in doing what you like, but in liking what you do is the secret of happiness."

This can be paraphrased to show one difference between success and happiness: "Success is getting what you want. Happiness is wanting what you get." However, it would seem to me that there is no reason not to mix a bit of each. If you can attain some measure of what you want, and be happy with it after you've attained it - well, friend, you've got it made!

So now your complaint is that if you could just attain a little success, you'd be happy with it - isn't it? Well, I don't believe you! I don't think you are being truthful with yourself. I'm willing to bet that you have already attained some measure of success. Stop to think about it for a moment. I'm right, am I not? In some way or other, you have attained some sort of success!

Being alive and thinking is success! I once heard a lecture on metaphysics in which the lecturer said, "The age of miracles is certainly not gone - you are a miracle!" Now then, if you agree that you have attained some measure of success, are you happy with what you've already accomplished?

If you aren't, don't fret! It's quite normal. To be completely and wholly satisfied is to start dying. There just wouldn't be anything else to look forward to. Everybody has some feelings of insecurity. That, too, is normal. It was Dwight D. Eisenhower who said:

"The best example of perfect security is a man who is serving a life sentence in prison."

If a man is serving a life sentence, and knows definitely that there is no hope for parole, and if he has no family outside to think and worry about, he's got complete security - and is also a good example of living death.

So stop worrying about reaching complete security, or complete success

- there is no such thing. Even if there were, we wouldn't really want to attain it. Why should we, when the real enjoyment and thrill of living comes from working toward some goal? Spanish writer Cervantes said it very simply many years ago:

"The road is always better than the inn."

I'm sure that many times you've striven for some particular goal, finally attained it, and then lost interest - immediately substituting another goal.

If you always seem to be harboring a slight feeling of insecurity, that's nothing serious. As a matter of fact, you're better off than if you did not have any feeling of insecurity. It's that very feeling that forces you to seek out success, to set your goals higher each time, and that gives you the incentive. William Feather said that, "Insecurity is the chief propulsive power in the world."

You understand, of course, that when I write of success, I'm referring to individual success in your own chosen field.

Having Trouble Meeting the "Right" People?

Too often, I hear people complain that they have no particular or outstanding ability; or that they don't know the right people; or that they've tried and tried and keep failing; or that they have no luck - so they might as well give up. In answer to the first instance, I can only repeat what H. J. Heinz replied when asked the secret of his success:

"To do a common thing uncommonly well brings success."

So you see, no matter what you do, if you learn to do it uncommonly well, you'll have an outstanding ability.

If you feel that you are being held back because you don't know the right people, you're merely setting up a good excuse for yourself.

Remember: "Ability seeks its own level." If you have the ability, the "right" people will seek you out. You may have to make it your business to be in the right place at the right time to help them find you - but they'll find you sooner or later.

But be prepared for a possible disappointment when you do meet the "right" people. They may be searching for someone to help them! In most cases, you're better off if you help yourself than if you wait for others to give you a push. Justice Brandeis was so right when he wrote:

"No one can really pull you up very high - you lose your grip on the rope. But on your own two feet you can climb mountains."

Yes! You can climb mountains! If you've tried and failed repeatedly, either try something else or try to find out what you're doing wrong. In any case, try again. I think you'll find it's true that most successes are achieved by 99 percent perspiration and 1 percent inspiration.

Here, positive thinking comes in handy. Try to see your goal, whatever it may be. Picture that little success you're aiming toward, and you'll find it easier to overcome each obstacle that gets in your way. Get a definite picture in your mind of what you're trying to achieve, and you'll have something to work toward.

Instead of grumbling over difficulties and obstacles, make each task or duty an adventure, a challenge. when you finally reach your goal, those obstacles will seem quite trivial to you. Harold Helfer put it this way: "Success is a bright sun that obscures and makes ridiculously unimportant all the little shadowy flecks of failure.

Too many of us are ready to quit too soon and too easily. Nothing worthwhile is ever achieved without a bit of hard work and a few failures. There are many things that cannot possibly be accomplished without failures. Keep in mind that little failures multiplied bring success, and you'll feel better about them. Think of trying to open a jar whose cap is stuck. You can force and pry ten times without results; the eleventh try may get that cap off easily. But without those first ten failures, you'd never make it.

If you drive a car, or type, or speak a foreign language - if you are the master of any ability that took time and effort and practice to develop - you've probably forgotten the mistakes and discouragements that were part of the learning process. It is difficult perhaps for you to picture the time when you couldn't drive, type or speak that foreign language. And yet, if you think back, you'll realize that it was a series of mistakes, and minor failures that led to the final accomplishment.

So don't waste time looking for people to help you. I think you'll agree, sooner or later, that the best place to look for a helping hand is usually at the end of your arm. Don't waste more time by continually worrying about whether you're doing the right thing, or whether you ought to do it at all. According to Emerson: "Don't waste life in doubts and fears;

spend yourself on the work before you, well assured that the right performance of this hour's duties will be the best preparation for the hours or ages that follow it."

Don't Depend on the Predictions of Others - Make Your Own

What else can I tell you about achieving success? Well, let's see. Although someone once said; "Striving for perfection in all things is an open invitation to failure" - and I agree with him - I also think that you must know your business. Work at it! Many of us think we know something well when we hardly know it at all. Sophocles said that:

"One must learn by doing the thing; for though you think you know it, you have no certainty until you try."

Without work there can never be success. Unfortunately, the very thing that can help people who are failures, or who suffer from boredom, laziness, loneliness and what have you, is often the only thing they won't try - work!

So pick a starting point, if you haven't already done so, and work from there. You've got to start someplace. James Watt watched a kettle boiling - that was his starting point. The end result was the steam engine! Isaac Newton saw an apple fall...

Starting is not always easy, I know. As a matter of fact, it's the hardest part of achieving success. You'll need all your energy just for the starting; after that you may be able to coast for a while. Only a small percentage of a motor's power is necessary to run your car, but all its power may be necessary to start it!

I believe that this is so with any task. Did you ever have to clean out a drawer or closet that was full of many years' accumulation of junk? Usually you keep putting the job off time and time again, as the drawer or closet gets worse and worse. You know from your own experience that once you actually get started the job isn't anywhere so bad as you thought it would be. It's the getting started on any project that's the most difficult part of the project.

Glenn Cunningham was once told that he could never walk again, and he became a famous and successful runner. Similarly, many people have been discouraged because of the results of intelligence and capability tests, and still attained success. The results of these tests are not always correct. And even if you don't think you've got the ability, you may have it anyway.

It's like the performer who was telling his psychiatrist:

Performer: "Doc, I can't sing or dance or tell jokes - what should I do?"
Doctor: "Quit show business."
Patient: "But I can't - I'm a star!"

People can take an exam under bad conditions - perhaps they're ill or have something on their minds - and spend the rest of their lives living according to the findings of the unrealistic results. I don't intend to knock I.Q. or aptitude tests, but - let's face it -they aren't always 100 percent reliable.

This reminds me of a sign hanging on the wall of a General Motors plant:

"According to the theory of aerodynamics and as may be readily demonstrated through wind tunnel experiments, the bumblebee is unable to fly. This is because the size, weight and shape of his body in relation to the total wingspread make flying impossible. But the bumblebee, being ignorant of these scientific truths, goes ahead and flies anyway - and makes a little honey every day."

I mention all this for the benefit of those whose confidence may have been shattered because of the negative results of a test at one time or another. Take the test again - you may be surprised. I've met people who for years have exclaimed that they couldn't tolerate, say, roast beef. I then found out that when they had originally tried it years before, the beef had been either bad or improperly prepared. If they had tried it again, under favorable conditions, they might have loved the stuff. Don't let the results of one instance change your life. You may miss out on something good.

If you do have skill, and your confidence in it has been shattered, that skill is wasted. There's a saying that goes "Skill and confidence are two soldiers who can conquer armies.

There are a few more thoughts on the subject of success in the next chapter. Right now, let me leave you with this notion over which to ponder:

"A poor man can be happy, but no happy man is poor!"

CHAPTER TWENTY THREE

How to Make Your Own Good Luck

> People of mediocre ability often achieve success because they don't know enough to quit.
>
> —Bernard Baruch

I've tried to tell you a little bit about how I feel about the subject of success. I hope my thoughts will help you, at least by giving you something to think about. I realize that the most difficult thing in the world is to change someone's outlook, one's way of life, one's ideas.

Let's face it - most will read this book and go on doing and thinking just as they always have. Well, that's as it should be, perhaps. Who am I to say you'd be better off if you changed? However, if you've been discontented - if you've been, or are, unhappy with your lot - some of the ideas in this book may be of some assistance.

Of course, the only way in which they can be of any help is if they're used. Even if they're exactly opposite to what you've usually done or thought, try them! If they don't help, forget them - but give them a chance first. If you find they do help, they will become habit in no time at all.

The way you think is the way you live. Your mind is the ruler of your life - so why not train it to the best of your ability? Your way of thinking, your outlook on life, can overcome any obstacle that possibly presents itself. And never mind telling me that ignorance is bliss - if it was, there would be more ecstatic people in this world!

Are Other People Holding You Back?

Do you feel that people are holding you back, that you have enemies who are keeping you from success? Well, perhaps that's so - although this kind of thinking is usually just an excuse for failure. But, assuming you really do, why not accept the fact that just about everyone has some enemies.

It's unfortunate, certainly, but it's unlikely that anyone could go through life without making at least one foe. If you're in business, or just starting a business, you might as well be prepared for, not necessarily enemies, but certainly competition. Be happy for it! Without competition it wouldn't be much fun trying to reach success.

It's difficult to start at the top in any job or business - unless that job is digging a hole(!), or unless you're fortunate enough to marry the boss's daughter after a really short engagement. So stop blaming your enemies. As a matter of fact, they usually help you! Edmund Burke wrote:

"He that wrestles with us strengthens our nerves and sharpens our skill. Our antagonist is our helper."

It's true, you know. Healthy competition and even out-and-out enemies should only make you work better and harder.

Success, it seems, is nothing more than a state of mind. It's all in the way you look at it. Avoid measuring success backward, or measuring it with a warped ruler. It's like the publicity given each year to the "ten best-dressed women" in the world. It has always bothered me a bit because the women chosen are always wealthy ones. I can't see why they should receive any special acclaim since it's certainly no hardship for them to be well dressed. If the ten women chosen as a "best dressed" were all of moderate means, that would make more sense. Not having the wealth with which to purchase any clothes they desire; making do with what they have; not being able to afford the advice of top designers and still being well dressed - that's more impressive; that's more like achievement and success.

To get back to basics - back to you - has it ever occurred to you that many people have become successful simply by making themselves available? What I mean is, if you think the "big break" is going to seek you out, forget it! You've got to be there when it arrives. Of course, this holds true for any kind of break or opportunity, not only the big break.

If you're selling a product, you must see your clients over and over again. Remember that the little failures build up to success. You can see a client perhaps twenty times and not sell him a thing - the twenty- first time you see him may be the time you get the big order that makes all the other visits worthwhile and it probably was the twenty "unsuccessful" visits that eventually caused the breakthrough.

How to Contact People on a Higher Level

Of course, learning to deal with people is an important factor toward making the road to success easier to travel. There've been many hints and suggestions on this subject scattered throughout this book. There is one other little idea or trick that has helped me tremendously through the years. This is for you if you find it difficult to speak to those you think are on a higher social or economic level than you are.

If you find yourself staring in awe and unable to speak intelligently, or perhaps stammering and stuttering, when you are confronted by the big man who may perhaps open some doors for you - if you are the type who always berates himself afterward for acting the fool in front of important people - this idea should be of more than a little help.

Usually, the more important the person is, the easier it is to speak to him or her. But if knowing or believing this doesn't help, here's the little trick. The problem is to manage to get such a person down to what you believe is your level. Once this is done, you can speak to him as you would to a friend. Well, when you walk into a large office and are confronted by an awe-inspiring executive, the first thing to do even as you say "hello," is to picture that person in some basic human position!

That's all there is to it. You might picture the person in his or her underwear, for example. I won't go into intimate detail, for obvious reasons! However, I'm sure you have the idea. If you can really picture or visualize the person in this basic human position, you'll have no trouble being yourself, and speaking to that person as you'd like. It's awfully difficult to be awe-inspiring in your underwear!

It took only one paragraph to explain this to you, but don't sell the idea short. It was a great help to me years ago, and there's no reason why it shouldn't help you, too. It puts you on an equal level with anyone. It's like being in a nudist colony. There is no way to tell the executive from the laborer when all outer garments and embellishments are removed.

Just try it; see for yourself. The only problem for me, now, is that when I meet people who've read this and find them staring at me, I'll wonder how the devil they're picturing me!

Remember: If you want others to have confidence in you, you must earn that confidence. The little things that are overlooked can be most important when it comes to earning this confidence and trust.

If you've told someone that you'll call at a certain time or on a specific day, do so. If you've told him that you'll mail something that day or be somewhere at a definite time, mail it or be there. Of course, there are always extenuating circumstances, but you can't use them as excuses too often and expect people to have confidence in you, depend on you, or want to do business with you.

Sure there may be (and are) some famous and successful people who can not be depended upon. You may know of them because they can't be depended on. Don't measure success backward! Those are the exceptions. They didn't become popular because they weren't dependable; they became popular in spite of it. That's the hard way.

Making Your Own Luck

Acquire a reputation for being dependable, and opportunity will keep knocking. Be there to open the door, and you're in! If your argument is that you have no luck, opportunity never knocks for you - cut it out! You're making excuses again.

Most successful people will tell you that you must make your own luck. When asked if he believed in luck, Jean Cocteau replied, "Certainly. How else do you explain the success of those you don't like?"

The trouble is that, too often, we apply this excuse even to people we do like. Everyone else's success is due to luck - our failures are all due to bad luck. Well, I doubt it. If you were to find it possible to spend every minute of a few days with someone whose success you ascribe to luck, you would realize that he or she works much harder than you do. If you insist on envying these people, at least envy them for their ability to look opportunities squarely in the face without mistaking them for obstacles or difficulties!

Luck is being ready. Or, according to an old Chinese proverb: "The more you know, the more luck you will have." So, instead of wasting precious time bemoaning your unlucky fate, prepare yourself for luck! That's right - prepare yourself so that when an opportunity does come along, it won't be dissipated because you aren't ready, or don't know enough to take advantage of it.

If you feel you are ready and do know enough, then go out and look for opportunity - and be sure you can recognize it when you see it. H.L. Mencken said that, "People seldom recognize opportunity because it comes disguised as hard work." There is really no substitute for work, you know, so accept the inevitable! Think of how you'll feel after you've worked hard for years, achieved some measure of success, and hear people say, "Aw, he's lucky, that's all!"

I've already talked about how being backed into a corner can sometimes be the best thing that can happen to you. Henry J. Kaiser said almost the same thing: "Trouble is nothing more than opportunity in work clothes."

Nat Cole was a piano player, working in small clubs whenever he could get the bookings. One of the occupational hazards in this type of work is drunks! One evening an occupational hazard kept insisting that Cole sing a song. Nat had never sung in public before, but he was in a spot. The drunk kept insisting noisily; Cole thought he'd better humor him or else cause a free-for-all, which could cost him his job. So he sang! This bit of trouble started Nat "King" Cole along the road to one of the most successful singing careers in modern show business!

Years ago, Mary Martin had a nickname on Broadway. She was known as "Audition Mary." Perhaps she had read that Disreali said, "The secret of success is constancy to purpose," and believed it! She sure kept on trying, and learning, even in the face of rebuffs and failures. She could have called it bad luck and given up, and never been heard from again. It took work, time and plenty of intestinal fortitude - tenacity - but she finally got "lucky"! If you still think she was lucky, well you may be able to get lucky too - and probably will - if you work as hard as Mary Martin did, and have the talent, to boot.

Opportunity Never Stops Knocking

Some are of the opinion that they had their chance, perhaps years ago, to become successful. They feel that once an opportunity has been overlooked or wasted, there is no second chance. Nonsense!

There is no allotted number of chances being sparsely handed out, one to a customer. It's only the hordes of failures, who have stopped seeking opportunity after their first chance at it, who have promoted the idea that it knocks only once!

Walter Malone wrote a little poem called Opportunity, which it might not hurt you to memorize, or at least read, concentrate on and believe.

They do me wrong who say I come no more
When once I knock and fail to find you in;
For every day I stand outside your door
And bid you wake and rise to fight and win.

Wail not for precious chances passed away!
Weep not for golden ages on the wane!
Each night I burn the records of the day -
At sunrise every soul is born again.

Are you a martyr type? Are you really happy when you're in trouble because you like the idea of having people feel sorry for you? Doug

Jerrold said, "Some people are so fond of ill luck that they run halfway to meet it." I know people like that who don't realize it themselves. Look into it. I know that this seems silly on first reading - the thought of people actually looking for bad luck - but there are people like that. Make sure you're not one of them!

Instead of complaining about your bad luck, go out and look for good luck by doing something about it. You'll be surprised at how lucky you may get after working hard toward what you wish to attain or accomplish. All the talent, knowledge or skill in the world won't help you any if you don't use them. Go out and act - do something - don't just sit there!
There are chapters throughout this book that I hope will help you to observe better, understand more, think more clearly, use your imagination and learn from facts - but none of these things can, or will, do you much good if you don't go out and do something with them.

You can improve yourself if you really want to, if you're not afraid of a little work. At the beginning of this chapter I said that the most difficult thing for one person to do is to change another person's way of thinking and living. It's true, unfortunately. "Unfortunately" because I know so many people who need not be failures, or at least could be more successful than they are, if they would allow their thinking and living patterns to be altered.

The Harvard Business Review once reprinted the letterhead used by a large corporation. It read as follows:

To look is one thing.
To see what you look at is another.
To understand what you see is a third.
To learn from what you understand is still something else.
But to act on what you learn is all that really matters.

Well, I've touched on some ideas in this book that I sincerely hope will be acted upon by some, that I sincerely hope will be beneficial to those who do try them and apply them.

Remember that just agreeing with me doesn't help you any. At the risk of seeming repetitious, I must warn you that nodding agreement and doing nothing about it is just as bad as, or worse than, actively disagreeing. And if you're thinking that you will try some of these ideas "someday" - forget it! You'll never get around to it if you don't do it now.

I leave you with this thought of William James:

"No matter how full a reservoir of maxims one may possess and no matter how good one's sentiments may be, if one has not taken advantage of every concrete opportunity to act, one's character may remain unaffected for the better. With mere good intentions, hell is proverbially paved."

CHAPTER TWENTY FOUR

When to Begin

A violin virtuoso living in America truly believed that he could play so well that he could actually charm a savage beast. Despite the warnings and pleas of his friends, he decided he would go to the jungles of Africa, unarmed, with only his violin to protect him. He stood in a clearing in the dense jungle and began to play. An elephant picked up his scent, and came charging toward him; but when he came within hearing distance, he sat down to listen to the beautiful music.

A hungry cat sprang from a tree with fangs bared but it, too, succumbed to the music. Soon a lion appeared to join the others. Before long, many wild beasts were seated near the virtuoso. He played on, unharmed.

Just then a leopard leaped from a nearby tree onto the violinist, and devoured him! As he stood licking his chops, the other animals approached, and asked, "Why did you do that? The man was playing such lovely music!"

The leopard, cupping his ear, said, "Eh, what'd you say?"

One of the things that I've often repeated throughout this book is the fact that if you don't use, or at least try, the ideas and suggestions, they can't possible do you any good.

The anecdote at the head of this chapter points it out beautifully. Unfortunately, good music means absolutely nothing if it can't be heard. Similarly, the greatest aids and ideas are wasted if they are not used.

As I emphasized in the section on learning, having the wish to do, try or learn anything is not enough. You've got to really want to utilize these ideas and suggestions.

Abraham Lincoln said:

"Your own resolution to succeed is more important than any other one thing."

If you resolve to use the ideas contained herein, they cannot help but aid you in your business, social life and everyday living.

Of course, it's much simpler to fall back into old comfortable habits whenever some sort of obstacle appears. But remember that there wouldn't be much gratification if there were never any obstacles in your path.

According to John Neal, "Kites rise against, not with the wind. No man ever worked his passage anywhere in a dead calm."

If you keep in mind that the obstacles more often than not become stepping stones to success, they won't deter you any longer. On the other hand, you must learn to distinguish between insurmountable obstacles and the "stepping stone" variety.

Don't waste time with the insurmountable ones. Try various ways to avoid them. Learn to accept the inevitable and you'll save yourself many frustrations and heartaches. You can't have everything, and philosopher Bertrand Russell was so right when he said:

"To be without some of the things you want is an indispensable part of happiness."

Let me stress again that most problems can be satisfactorily solved, and most goals reached, if you will simply do something about them. Don't always wait until you can "see your way clear" - a little action can do wonders for the eyesight. Your activity will create activity - or, to put it succinctly, action brings action.

Sitting around waiting for her is the wrong way to court Lady Luck. You must go out and find her. How? Well, humorist Stephen Leacock said, "I am a great believer in luck, and I find the harder I work, the more I have of it!"

I've tried to instill confidence, which is not to suggest that you become a braggart or a nonconformist. A great portion of one's personal attractiveness lies in his confidence, but don't go overboard. Remember, work toward a happy medium in most things. If you want to be different, fine; but don't act superior about it.

An important ingredient for success is the ability to make others like you. The chapter on personality will help toward that end. I've stressed it before, but it bears repetition: be kind to others and they will be kind to you. I can't put it much better than Edgar Albert Guest did:

Let me be a little kinder
Let me be a little blinder
To the faults of those around me,
Let me praise a little more.

Will You Have the Same Excuse Ten Years from Now?

I know there have been many gags about, "Do it now." Such as the one about the employer who hung a sign counseling this in his office, and the next day his accountant absconded with all the company funds, a clerk ran off with the employer's wife and a trusted and essential employee went to work for a competitor. Well, extremes aside, "Do it now" is a pretty good idea.

If you want to learn a new skill, start now! If you want to start some sort of savings - bonds, funds or insurance - start now! I know that the usual excuse for not starting now is "Oh, it will take years for me to learn that" or "It will be years before that fund would be worth any real money."

Well, here's a way to avoid that trap - just think of what your excuse will be ten years from now! The same thing, probably! Don't you see? A new skill may take five years to learn, but it will still take five years to learn five years from today. Waiting will not make the learning time any shorter, and waiting won't help your savings any either.

Do it now, start now, or you will be quoting John Greenleaf Whittier's:

For of all sad words of tongue or pen, the saddest are these: "It might have been!"

Well, I'm sure that by now you must agree that your mind controls your life. Try the ideas in this book - use them - and you'll be a happier person for it.

If I have taught you only that it is the training and organization of the mind which alone can lead you toward a happy and successful life, I have more than accomplished my purpose. I have to agree with Shakespeare':

"There is nothing either good or bad, but thinking makes it so."

NOTES

....
....
....
....
....
....
....
....
....
....
....
....
....
....
....
....
....
....